T0248013

ANOTHER LITERARY TOUR OF ITALY

TIM PARKS

ALMA BOOKS

ALMA BOOKS LTD
Thornton House
Thornton Road
Wimbledon
London SW19 4NG
United Kingdom
www.almabooks.com

This collection of essays first published by Alma Books Limited in 2024
Copyright © Tim Parks, 2024

Tim Parks asserts his moral right to be identified as the author of this work
in accordance with the Copyright, Designs and Patents Act 1988

Unless otherwise specified, the translations are by the author.

Printed and bound by CPI Group (UK) Ltd, Croydon, CR0 4YY

ISBN: 978-1-84688-472-6

Contents

Introduction

A book makes sense, or not, in relation to the context we bring to it. My experience of the *Divina commedia*, for example, was much enriched by Marco Santagata's extraordinary account of Dante's life and times. As again my understanding of Machiavelli was transformed by Alexander Lee's meticulous reconstruction of his political career. It is no longer fashionable to speak of national literatures these days, or indeed of anything national. One is invited to move in a global world where texts circulate freely in the English lingua franca. Certainly Dante and Machiavelli are two writers who long flew the nest of their Italian origins. Yet a local reality indisputably remains, a certain cultural humus, composed of shared reference points, shared debates, struggles and disagreements, boasts and humiliations. To know Dante better, or Leopardi, or Manzoni, or Verga, is to appreciate how much later writers were influenced by them or reacted against them. And if it's true that Italian writers have often looked for inspiration from abroad (Manzoni himself from Walter Scott, Verga from Zola), it is always the case that they did so with their own cultural world in mind, to bring fresh material to ongoing discussions with their compatriots. What they took, they made Italian. To see how Pavese used what he learnt from the American novels he translated when he wrote *The House on the Hill* is to appreciate the profound difference between the Italian and American milieux.

All this by way of excusing a second collection of essays that seeks to put Italian authors in relation to each other and to the Italian world that nurtured them. It is a collection where some of the "greats" – Bassani, Morante – are given a second, I hope deeper, look, while the absolute cornerstone, for better or worse, of the modern Italian novel, Alessandro Manzoni's *The Betrothed*, is discussed for the first time. If the range is wide – Lorenzino, the sixteenth-century Medici prince and murderer; Casanova, the eighteenth-century adventurer – this is simply to suggest the richness and scope of territory and the constant intertwining of political and literary issues. It's extraordinary, for example, running my eye down the book's index, how many of these writers, from Dante to Pavese, Machiavelli to Morante, were at some point in their lives exiled or excluded from the national debate, while others – D'Annunzio, Pirandello – aligned themselves all too openly with the status quo. Two of my favourite pieces are that on the seventeenth-century Giambattista Basile's exhilarating Neapolitan fables, which, courtier and public official though Basile was, he was unable to publish in his lifetime, and the essay on Pasolini's first novel, *Boys Alive*, which faced a trial for obscenity immediately on publication. Centuries apart, both writers struggled to bring scabrous street life and earthy dialect into mainstream public life. Then, when it comes to understanding the political polarization in Italy's post-war cultural life, nothing could be more instructive than the careers of Gianni Rodari, with his determinedly left-wing children's stories, written initially for the Communist paper *L'Unità*, and Dario Fo, who possessed an apparently boundless ability to provoke anyone in a position of authority. Neither of these authors really come to life without an awareness of the context they were working in.

Unlike the first collection of essays, this one includes a number of contemporary, or near-contemporary, authors, notably Umberto Eco, who owed his success as a novelist very much to an international readership in love with a playful postmodern approach to fiction, as a result of which he had rather different profiles outside Italy and within, where he was known as a powerful professorial figure and cultural commentator. Roberto Saviano has also combined an international reputation with a ferocious local battle against the Neapolitan *camorra*. Edoardo Albinati's great book,

The Catholic School, simply could not be more Italian in its conception and tone, its constant mix of metaphysics, eroticism, violent crime and politics. And if some readers will be disappointed that no essay is dedicated to the mysterious figure of Elena Ferrante, they would do well to look at the closing paragraphs of the essay on Domenico Starnone, to my mind the most monstrously accomplished novelist working in Italy today.

A final word. One still hears the old adage that Italy is more a heterogeneous collection of warring regions than a united country. Looking at the authors gathered in this collection, almost all are strongly associated with a particular region or city: Pirandello and Camilleri with Sicily, Magris with Friuli, Albinati with Rome, Saviano with Naples. But Italy's regions live in fertile collaborative competition with each other, defining themselves in proud contrast to their near neighbours, and indeed each writer in this collection seeks to affirm the local identity, culturally and linguistically, in the national mix. They cannot be thought of separately from each other. Isn't this, in the end, very much what storytelling is about – establishing a complex web of relations so that we can find our own position within it? Hopefully, English readers of this book will have a better sense of their Italian affinities after they have enjoyed voices and regions as different as Morante's and Pavese's, Bassani's and Fo's. Taking sides is very much what Italian life is about.

Another Literary
Tour of Italy

DANTE
(1265–1321)

Between the Guelfs
and the Ghibellines

Put real people in a work of narrative these days and you immediately face libel and privacy issues. The publishers will demand a legal report; every correspondence between your story and reality will be scrutinized. Nor will it be enough simply to change names or avoid unpleasant aspersions; the mere idea that someone might recognize themselves and feel aggrieved will set alarm bells ringing and have editors requesting revisions. How would Dante's *Divine Comedy* have fared in an environment like this? Large numbers of the poet's fellow citizens are named and shamed. It's true most of them were dead, but by no means all. Two living characters are pronounced so evil that the Devil has carried off their souls to hell leaving demons in their bodies to perpetuate a zombie life up above. Others are declared by the damned to be "expected shortly".

Add to this that Dante places the prophet Muhammad in hell, launches violent insults against various cities and political and religious groupings, doing so for evident motives of personal resentment and self-interest, and it's hard to imagine his great masterpiece would be an easy book to publish today. Reading Marco Santagata's fascinating new biography (*Dante: The Story of His Life*, translated by Richard Dixon), the reader is soon forced to acknowledge that one of the cornerstones of Western literature, a poem considered sublime and universal beyond all dispute, is largely the product of a vicious factionalism and packed with local scandal, much of it deployed in the hope of accruing benefits to the author.

Aside from his published writings, eleven surviving letters, a scattering of official records and one or two brief personal testimonies, we have so little information about the life of Dante Alighieri that Santagata is obliged to proceed deductively and speculatively, counterpointing the history of Florence and Italy in the poet's lifetime (1265–1320) with references and allusions to the same in the *Divina commedia* and Dante's other works. What we know about Dante we know largely because he was embroiled in public life and because his writing always took a position on the political situation of the moment. What makes the going hard is how complicated the politics were, how much they depended on an intricate network of family relationships, and how ambiguous and mobile Dante's loyalties were within the general mayhem. The payoff for keeping track of all this comes when we finally set aside the biography and reread the *Commedia*: at once it seems more urgent, more scandalous and more beautiful than we remembered.

Santagata tells us about Guelfs and Ghibellines, about Church and empire and their competing claims to the allegiance of Italy's numerous feudal lords and city-states in the thirteenth and fourteenth centuries. The Guelfs, the Church party, dominated where people felt they had more to fear from the German-based emperor than the Roman pope. It was also the party of the nouveau riche, the bankers and traders, those who had an interest in the formation of a looser, less rigidly controlled society. The Ghibellines, siding with the empire, were largely made up of those who had an investment in the old hierarchical structures of feudalism, or simply found themselves uncomfortably close to a papal state bent on territorial expansion.

But this is reductive. Any party or grouping was as much tribal as ideological. Families, corporations, even whole cities tended to show their allegiance collectively. If a large city was Guelf, very likely the smaller cities around it would be Ghibelline, with an implicit appeal for protection from afar. And vice versa, of course. Nor did either party have a stable hold on people's identity.

Divisions over commercial, religious and family issues were always on the cards. Thus, after decades of fighting between Guelfs and Ghibellines within Florence, when the matter was finally settled in 1289 (Dante being twenty-four) with the defeat and mass expulsion of the Ghibellines, the victorious Guelfs, now in complete control of one of Europe's most populous and wealthy cities, lost little time in dividing themselves into Black Guelfs and White Guelfs, who would then fight each other with the same intensity and ferocity as they had previously fought the Ghibellines. Santagata's account of how this schism came about and how the terms Black and White (with no more content or significance, as it turns out, than the letters a or b, x or y) were borrowed from a similar schism in Pistoia – a town that, precisely to overcome the impasse caused by internal division, had taken the drastic course of handing over control of its affairs to Florence – requires maximum attention on the part of the reader. But again it's worth the effort. Factionalism spread like a virus, and Dante wasn't immune.

These conflicts were unspeakably cruel. Enemies were imprisoned and tortured. If exiled, their property was confiscated, their houses, even in the centre of town, razed to the ground. Tongues were cut out and hands amputated. People were left in dungeons to starve, or disembowelled and dragged through the streets, or burnt at the stake before jeering crowds. Imaginative though Dante's infernal punishments may be, the spirit behind them was all too familiar.

What was Dante's position in all this? Third child of a mother who died when he was very young, he belonged to neither the old landed elite nor the successful new commercial community. Of the two, although his father had been a small-time money-lender, he tended to prefer the former. Always innovative and forward-looking when it came to writing and art, convinced that language and culture must necessarily be on the move, he was generally conservative on questions of society and govern-ment: only an antique social stability, he thought, would allow artists to flourish.

The Alighieri family was Guelf by tradition, but obscure enough
to have avoided exile with other Guelfs when the Ghibellines were
in the ascendant shortly before Dante's birth. Of his education we
know only that his family wasn't rich enough to provide him with
a private tutor. Dante's father died when his son was ten, leaving
him, as Leonardo Bruni would put it, "not greatly rich... but with
moderate and sufficient wealth to live honourably". The problem,
as Santagata construes it, was that Dante's notions of honourable
living were not Bruni's. He was ambitious, had the highest possible
opinion of himself and aspired to the life of a noble – or at least
to a noble life, a life dedicated to writing. Which brings us to one
of the core themes of this biography: Dante's self-image, the way
it dominated his writings and conditioned every move he made
within the treacherous cut and thrust of Florentine factionalism.

Giovanni Villani, almost the only person to write about Dante
who had actually known him, thought him a "great poet and
philosopher" but "presumptuous, contemptuous and disdainful"
as a person. A generation later, Boccaccio, whose biography of
the poet is based on conversations with people who had known
him, describes Dante as "proud and disdainful" and prone to
losing his temper. Around these meagre testimonies, Santagata
gathers a quantity of detail, largely drawn from Dante's writing, to suggest a man intent on constructing a myth of himself
as both nobly born and destined to greatness. All three of his
major works – the *Vita nova*, the *Convivio* and the *Commedia*
– were, for their time, remarkably autobiographical. "Dante
seems incapable of imagining a book in which his person, or at
least a person bearing his name, doesn't play a significant role,"
Santagata writes. However, the Dante on the page is subtly transformed from the Dante seeking to overcome the limitations of a
modest background.

There's no hint of criticism here. Santagata isn't arguing that
Dante is a lesser poet than we thought, or in any way disreputable.
But he's not in the business of hagiography. His consideration of

the Beatrice narrative is typical. Dante first presents the story in elaborate form in his late twenties in the *Vita nova*, which gathers together his poems of the previous years, linking them with an autobiographical prose narrative. The ideas of the so-called *dolce stil novo*, the "sweet new style" of writing that had recently introduced elements of religious reflection into courtly love poetry, were thus tied to the poet's personal development. This in itself was a remarkable innovation. Dante describes an early encounter with Beatrice at nine years old; he falls in love and remains faithful and devoted to her until the next meeting at eighteen, when she acknowledges his presence, though no word passes between them. The fact, well known to his Florentine readers, that Dante had addressed love poems to other women is explained as a deliberate attempt to draw attention away from Beatrice, who, higher born than himself, had married in her early teens. Dante had married at eighteen. After the second meeting, his love intensifies, but without further exchanges between the two; finally, Beatrice's early death in 1290, at twenty-four, triggers a shift in the poet's interests from sentimental to divine love.

That the story is idealized and in a tradition of idealization is evident. Any real relationship between the two, Santagata suggests, could only have occurred in the late 1280s, long after the two meetings described. But the way Dante hangs on to the story throughout his career, making it "one of the classic features of his intellectual and literary biography" and seeking "to give credibility to a story that had been largely invented by sprinkling it with references to real life", is unusual. The effect, Santagata insists, is always to make the real Dante appear "someone exceptional" to whom exceptional things happen. In one poem, he speaks of having suffered a seizure at the age of nine months, on a day and hour corresponding to Beatrice's birth and foreshadowing their love. In general, the seizures he experiences on meeting his beloved go far beyond conventional accounts of romantic fainting, and, along with similar episodes elsewhere in his work, could suggest epilepsy. But rather than considering these fits a mark of the Devil, the standard interpretation at the time, Dante takes them as a sign of "a predestination decreed by a supreme power". He had been chosen.

Various details in the *Vita nova* contribute to a false impression of the poet's social status. "Dante refers several times," Santagata writes, "to a 'room' of his own where he could go alone to think, to weep, and also to sleep". Since the Alighieri house was small and the family hardly of the aristocratic kind where a member might enjoy such a private space, this can only be "one of the many signs of distinction by which he was seeking to hide his lowly origins". Another, years later, would be the reconstruction in the *Paradiso*, through an imagined meeting with his great-great-grandfather Cacciaguida, of a supposedly noble lineage for the Alighieri family.

Santagata's point is that this self-aggrandizing blend of biography and fiction can't be seen separately from Dante's attempts to improve his position in Florentine society. The unusual quality and content of his writing, the decision to use the vernacular rather than Latin so that his work would be available to the greatest number of local readers (though not to the wider community of foreign scholars) would draw attention to him in Florence as somebody who could play an important part in public life. Literary ambition and social status were linked. Dante's closest friend in his twenties, Guido Cavalcanti, was both a fine poet and heir to one of the city's largest fortunes. Dante could only aspire to a relationship on equal terms "by virtue of his personality and his genius". Equality, however, wasn't enough for Dante: in the *Vita nova*, he suggests that Cavalcanti is his John the Baptist, which of course makes Dante "the Messiah".

By his mid-twenties he already had a reputation as a poet. There are indications that he had been to Bologna to use its libraries and to read philosophy; he knew Latin and had most likely studied with Brunetto Latini, an eminent rhetorician forty and more years his senior; people were beginning to invite him to write poems and letters for them. But if it was now possible to surpass Cavalcanti in verse, it was more difficult to appear the aristocrat and live the aristocratic life without a substantial income. Dante had married, or been married, upmarket, into the Donati family, but precisely because his family was relatively poor his wife, Gemma, brought only a modest dowry. The two children the couple produced had to be provided for. In 1289 Dante fought as a light horseman at the battle of Campaldino in which the Guelfs defeated the Ghibellines. This meant he had invested a great deal of money on a horse and arms in order to be among the city's elite. In later years, some of the few official notices we have of Dante are papers associated with the substantial loans he and his half-brother were obliged to take out. In a letter to a friend Dante "emphasized his own bravery" at the battle, "yet his name," Santagata points out, "does not appear among those who were compensated for having put themselves at particular risk during the action."

In 1295 or thereabouts, probably in order to become eligible to hold government office, Dante joined the Guild of Doctors and Apothecaries, and his political career began. Five years later, in the summer of 1300, he would have the supreme honour – and, as it turned out, the great misfortune – of being elected as one of the city's nine governing priors at the height of tensions between the Black and White Guelf factions. He was not a neutral figure. The Cerchis, a family of bankers at the head of the White faction, had gained the upper hand over the more aristocratic Donati family, who led the Black faction, which, however, had the support of the pope. Dante's election for the two-month stint of office suggests that he, like Cavalcanti, was in with the Cerchis, despite being married to a Donati. There was strife. Appeals from the pope on behalf of the Black Guelfs were rejected. Attempting to be or seem even-handed, the priors exiled and interned prominent members of both families. But shortly after Dante's term of office was over, the Cerchi exiles, who included Cavalcanti, were pardoned, while the Donati exiles were not. As Cavalcanti's close friend, Dante was suspected of having instigated this unwise decision. In 1301, after the Blacks, with papal assistance, regained control of the city, Dante was among 559 Whites sentenced to death. However, like most of those condemned, he was already well out of the city, which he would never see again, though he would continue to write about it until his death twenty years later.

What is true nobility, and what kind of community best fosters it? This is the question that runs obsessively throughout Dante's work. In the *Vita nova* and the poems of his twenties, nobility is emphatically not an attribute of family or wealth but a matter of education and disposition. In the *Convivio*, written in his first years of exile, the nobility is assessed more positively as a class that, despite being infiltrated and corrupted by merchants and moneymen, has the duty of providing the community with a peaceful, civilized existence under the auspices of the empire. This shift in position, which now recognizes the value of noble birth or, more subtly, acknowledges that God in His wisdom has contrived to concentrate noble attributes among the aristocracy, was perhaps not unconnected with the decision by the newly exiled White Guelfs, Dante included, to ally with the long-exiled and aristocratic Ghibellines in the hope of recapturing Florence from the Black Guelfs. "One of the typical features of Dante's personality," Santagata comments,

which qualifies him as an "intellectual" in the modern sense of the word, is his endless reflection on what he is doing, both as an author and as a man. The main motivations for his writing come from what he himself has seen, experienced and said; and so he relies on the hic et nunc... Another characteristic is that of arranging the details of an experience into a theoretical or conceptual framework that explains them, and thus of rising to higher levels of generalization.

In short, there is an urgent back and forth between Dante's personal predicament as an impoverished exile and his reflections on the nature of human society, with an inevitable tension between what it might be convenient to say and the conclusions he has genuinely reached, not to mention his feelings of resentment towards those in Florence who had destroyed his life, and of gratitude towards the growing list of those, many of them Ghibellines, on whose charity he now depended. It was out of this troubled state of mind, Santagata sets out to show, that the *Divine Comedy* was created.

Convivio means "banquet". Written in the vernacular, it was an invitation to all who could read to feast together on Dante's knowledge of philosophy, itself the result of the poet's need for consolation after Beatrice's death. In the process, Dante would demonstrate his innocence and justify a request to return to Florence. Precisely this personal element made it important that the largest possible number of Florentines be able to read what he was saying. Boldly pronouncing the vernacular equal to Latin for refinement of expression, the *Convivio* encouraged his fellow citizens to leave behind any inferiority they might have felt about not being familiar with Latin. It should have been a popular move, but the poem was never finished. Dante had planned fourteen books, but stopped at the fourth. Santagata suggests that quickly moving political circumstances were largely responsible. The alliance between the White Guelfs and the Ghibellines had been defeated. A letter sent to the Florentine priors requesting pardon and admitting his error in allying himself with the Ghibellines had been promptly circulated among the Ghibellines and done nothing but win Dante their contempt, restricting even further the places where he could find safe haven. In a gloomy poem written in the last months of 1306, Dante imagines all the virtues as banished from human society, while he, sharing their destiny, now decides that "the exile given me brings me honour". It was in this spirit, oscillating between humiliating requests for pardon and defiant claims of innocence and moral superiority, that he abandoned the decorous *Convivio* and embarked on the fiercely visceral, hugely ambitious *Inferno*, where Dante the poet is now special beyond the wildest imagining, a unique human being selected by divine intervention for a passage through the realm of the dead and thus empowered to pronounce with authority on the sins and virtues of the living. As a rule of thumb, the more abject Dante's circumstances, the more exceptional he appears in his poetry.

Santagata's method from here on is to map the poet's movements around Italy in relation to the characters who appear in the *Divine Comedy*, inviting us to imagine Dante sharing his work in progress with his various, often poorly educated protectors, each of whom would be pleased to see their enemies, or enemies' ancestors, appearing in hell or themselves praised as instruments of divine predestination. More generally, though, it is the biography's evocation of the factional world of the time and the values sustaining it that throws light on the great poem and helps us to read it with fresh awareness. Embarking on *Inferno* around 1306, Dante dated the action in 1301, just before his exile, thus allowing the dead to foresee all that will occur in the intervening years and creating an impression of prophetic powers. The decision also has the effect of suggesting that the moment when, in the middle of life's path, the poet loses his way, is not unrelated to his loss of his home, of Florence. So hell presents itself first and foremost as a place of exile. To an extraordinary degree death is annulled, in the sense that the dead are to be considered dead only insofar as they are not among the living. Otherwise, however awful their punishments, they are hardly changed. All are recognizable, in possession of their wits, perfectly able to speak. And what they want to speak about is home, which for most means Florence.

Dante meantime is distinguishable from the dead above all insofar as he hopes to return to the world of living, to Florence. The power he boasts, as he meets each of the damned and asks them to tell him their stories, is his ability, as a poet, to affect their reputations among their Florentine peers, a gift of greater value to them than any theological considerations underpinning divine justice. It is this that gives so many of the conversations in the *Commedia* their dreamlike quality. Always condemning the destructive consequences of factionalism when such matters are discussed, the poem as a whole upholds the values of a society where inclusion is the supreme good, and exclusion hell.

No sooner is Dante through the infernal gates than he is met by the crowds of those who failed to take sides in life, a group epitomized by the angels who refused to support either God or Lucifer in the quarrel that split the heavenly powers. Neither heaven nor hell wants these pusillanimous souls, while they envy both the blessed and the damned. Worst of all, "The world does not permit report of them." They are excluded and forgotten. In short, it is established that whatever mistakes Dante may have made, being an active member of a faction isn't one of them. Shortly after this meeting, he's introduced to the great poets of the classical world – Homer, Horace, Ovid, Lucan – who do him the extraordinary honour of inviting him to join their "noble school" so that he becomes "the sixth among those high intelligences", the fifth being Virgil, the poet's guide through the underworld. Again, everything is understood in terms of inclusion and exclusion. At the other end of hell, at the bottom of the ninth circle, will be those who betrayed the trust of the groups that included them, and here, in Bocca degli Abati, who betrayed his Guelf companions in battle, we encounter someone who, unusually, doesn't want to be recognized or have his story told. Treachery is more or less the only sin that is unspeakable.

Again and again Dante opens his cantos with extended analogies likening the landscape of hell with sights and features of Italy, many of them discovered in the course of his exile and associated with it. Hell is always more extreme and terrible than anything it's compared to, but the effect is to suggest that the place of punishment isn't so different from the world we know. Similarly, if people on earth are thought of as members of competing groups, the damned are all grouped in categories according to their sins; the poem thus becomes a huge effort of sorting, or rather re-sorting, where Guelfs and Ghibellines, Whites and Blacks suddenly find themselves forced together or torn apart depending on their individual vices.

One of the most curious allocations is that of Dante's old teacher, Brunetto Latini, condemned to the seventh circle among the sodomites. Doomed to continual movement to keep his feet from burning, his face charred by the hot cinders that drift in the air, Brunetto nevertheless greets Dante with evident pleasure, calling him "my son" and prophesying that if he follows his star he can't fail "to reach a glorious port". Analysing Dante's ongoing negotiations for a possible return to Florence around the time the text was written, Santagata remarks: "Describing himself as Brunetto's son means declaring himself as his heir – it means pointing to himself, though a banished citizen, as the true interpreter of the city's traditional Guelf values."

The implications are many and curious: did Dante put Brunetto in hell simply because it was important to claim his political blessing as soon as possible – he couldn't wait long enough to put the man in the *Paradiso* – and did he then choose the sin of sodomy because it wasn't something that would damage Brunetto's reputation to the extent of making his recommendation useless? There is after all no record elsewhere of Brunetto's being homosexual. The bizarre quality of the scene reaches its height when Dante acknowledges that it was Brunetto who "taught me how man makes himself immortal", where immortality presumably refers to writerly fame rather than the miserable immortality of Brunetto's eternal punishment. In line with this, all the condemned man seems to care about as the two part company is that Dante remind people back in Florence of his writing, which Dante says he will do, granting Brunetto a last homage with the words

> After he turned back he seemed like one
> who races for the green cloth on the plain
> beyond Verona. And he looked more the winner
> than the one who trails the field.

The tension between divine justice and the mutual regard could hardly be greater. Damned, Brunetto still seems a winner. It's as if God's punishment were an unfortunate irrelevance to be born as best one can, with the result that Brunetto's stoicism in dealing with his torment actually increases his nobility in the eyes of the reader. This is hardly conventional Christianity, though Dante always insisted on his own orthodoxy. From the background Santagata provides, our impression is that the extraordinary poetry that emerges from this blending of theological debate, contemplation of suffering and anxious self-regard is the largely unplanned consequence of special circumstances meeting remarkable genius.

One of the reasons, Santagata suggests, why Dante says nothing about the events leading up to his exile, and is careful in the *Inferno* not to attribute blame to specific faction leaders in Florence at the time, is that he was still hoping that the ruling Guelfs could be persuaded to change their position in his favour. But by the time he was writing *Purgatorio* those hopes were dead, and once again the emperor and the old nobility are held up for our admiration. Extraordinarily, as if to gratify Dante's wishes, in 1310 the new emperor, Henry of Luxembourg, launched a military campaign in Italy to put an end to factionalism and reclaim a hegemony in the peninsula that had been lost generations before. Dante took time out from the *Purgatorio* to write *Monarchia*, his most didactic work, which contrives to be both a profound reflection on the relation between temporal and spiritual powers and a possibly self-serving text that would sanction the end of his state of exile. He also visited Henry's court and addressed letters to the Florentine priors and all the political powers of Italy prophesying terrible consequences if they did not accept the emperor's civilizing and divinely appointed power. Henry's campaign was already faltering, however, when, in 1313, he fell ill and died.

Dante took refuge at the Ghibelline court of Cangrande della Scala in Verona, praising the feudal lord and his family extravagantly in the *Paradiso*, only to drop all further mention of them

after being invited in 1319 to enjoy the protection of the more con-
genial and artistically inclined court of Guido Novello da Polenta
in Ravenna. Guido was himself a poet, and Dante's relationship
with him such, Santagata writes, that he was spared engaging in
"the shameless courtly praises lavished on Cangrande". It was just
as well, since Dante would soon be embarking on the last cantos
of the *Paradiso*, and it was important finally to turn his attention
away from "the threshing floor that makes us so fierce". That did
not mean, however, that he had given up all hope of swaying minds
in Florence. The simple quality of the writing might be enough on
its own. This is from Canto XV:

> If it ever happens that the sacred poem
> to which Heaven and earth have set their hand,
> making me thin for many years,
> wins over the cruelty that locks me out
> of the fair fold where I slept as a lamb,
> foe to the wolves that make war against it,
> with other voice then, with other fleece
> will I return…

In 1321, with the poem now completed, Dante paid for his host's
hospitality by accepting a diplomatic mission to Venice, returning
from which he fell ill and died. Guido Novello promised he would
build a noble tomb for him, but almost at once the deceased Dante
fell victim to the kind of conflict that had dogged him throughout his life. Guido briefly left the city, handing over control to
his brother. The brother was assassinated by a cousin who exiled
Guido in perpetuity. The noble tomb was never built.

Elegantly and accurately translated by Richard Dixon, Santagata's
biography avoids the quarrels among critics that often dominate
Dante studies, relegating its references and accounts of diverging
opinions to a hundred pages of useful notes. Yet an account like this
obliges us to reflect on the vast distance between the meaning of a

work to its author, to the readers of the time and to us now. One irony is still very present to me more than a month after reading the book: excluded from his home culture in his lifetime, Dante is absolutely at the centre of it seven hundred years on. Pathetically wrong when he supposed his own self-important interventions might swing the course of history, he was triumphantly right when he prophesied that the vernacular would prevail over Latin and that he would be numbered among the great poets of all time. In the early nineteenth century, Giacomo Leopardi would remark that the factional fragmentation of Italian society was such that no Italian past or present was ever entirely honoured or dishonoured, "since there can be no honour without a shared sense of society". Dante is the exception that proves the rule: more honoured, it seems to me, than any other Italian in history perhaps because his great work so completely captures and in its way celebrates the endless divisiveness that unites Italy's present with its past.

NICCOLÒ MACHIAVELLI
(1469–1527)

Whatever It Takes

"Is Machiavelli good, then, or is he evil?" asks the French scholar Patrick Boucheron discussing *The Prince*, a book "whose whole programme is to uncouple political action from conventional morality" (*Machiavelli: The Art of Teaching People What to Fear*, translated by Willard Wood). Is he, that is, advising political leaders to be treacherous, violent and dishonest (as Diderot believed), or revealing to common mortals the mechanisms behind their leaders' dishonesty, violence and treachery (as Rousseau believed)? "We would like to have an answer," Boucheron says, but the matter is better "set aside". Machiavelli, after all, was simply saying "the truth about things". Still, the question hangs in the air, if only because it is his anxiety over the deteriorating morality of politics today that has Boucheron turning to the Italian for guidance.

Machiavelli has a way of prompting his commentators to assert their moral concerns. They do not want to be tarred with the villain's brush. The British historian Alexander Lee closes his biography of the man (*Machiavelli: His Life and Times*) on a resolutely pious note: on his deathbed Machiavelli "knew how greatly he had sinned. Over the past fifty-eight years, there had been no crime he had not committed, no vice he had not indulged... At every turn, he had thought only of himself, his ambitions and desires... One can hear him inwardly shrieking with terror at the pains of Hell." It's a harsh conclusion after the mostly sympathetic picture painted over the 570 preceding pages.

Niccolò di Bernardo dei Machiavelli was born in Florence in 1469, the same year Lorenzo de' Medici, il Magnifico, came to power in the town. "Let's acknowledge that he often exaggerates," writes Boucheron, reacting to Machiavelli's claim that he was "born

poor and learnt to work before having fun". Boucheron's short
book is based on a series of radio talks and retains a spoken voice
that constantly seeks complicity and dramatic effect. Lee explores
Machiavelli's background soberly, at length. The family, once well
respected, had fallen on hard times, partly because relatives on both
the father's and mother's side had conspired against the Medici,
partly because Bernardo, Niccolò's bookish father, had inherited
debts, was unable to pay his taxes, and hence excluded from holding public office or practising law, the profession for which he had
studied. Rumours that he was an illegitimate child compounded
the problem, since such a person was, again, excluded from public
office. The family had a house in Florence and a farm some six
miles to the south. On occasion Bernardo was obliged to sell his
clothes to make ends meet. Such transactions were recorded in
his "memory book", typical instrument of domestic economy in
a Florentine household. "Coldly, methodically, he recorded the
minute facts of family life," Boucheron elaborates, something that
"reminds us that all power starts at home". Lee details Bernardo's
twenty-year debt-repayment plan and his despair when not properly compensated for a consignment of brushwood. He shows
him compiling a topographical index to Livy's *Ab urbe condita* in
return for a copy of the book. Power is conspicuous for its absence.
Machiavelli was poor in relation to the peer group he aspired to.
He never accumulated any wealth.

The family ambition was that Niccolò should overcome the
stigma that had obstructed Bernardo and participate in public life.
He was sent to school, then educated with private tutors, one of
them a priest who sexually abused him. It was not unusual, nor
was Niccolò's eventual bisexuality. Boucheron does not believe
he went to university – Lee gives evidence he did. Meantime,
Florence's political life moved on. Niccolò was eight when the
Pazzi conspiracy against the Medici failed and the conspirators'
corpses were hung from the windows of the government palace.
Exploiting the drama, il Magnifico had the constitution rewritten

to give even more power to himself. He was twenty-three when Piero de' Medici, Lorenzo's son, was chased out of Florence following his inept handling of a French invasion and the priest Girolamo Savonarola became the main force in the city. Again the constitution was rewritten, this time along republican lines. But the economically vital subject city of Pisa had seized the chance to break away from Florentine control. A disaster. Niccolò was twenty-seven, still unemployed, still on the margins, when Savonarola ordered the first "bonfire of the vanities" in Piazza della Signoria, a sixty-foot pile of fashionable clothes, books, paintings, dice, playing cards and musical instruments. A year later, after fierce factional tensions, Savonarola himself was burnt in the same place.

To add to the precariousness of politics and finance, in 1479 there had been a bout of the plague. Seriously ill, Niccolò's father passed urine samples through the window of his house to have the smell examined. Niccolò and his brother and sister were sent off to the country. The world was a dangerous place where one struggled in vain for some measure of control and safety. Nevertheless, Machiavelli at last profited from one upheaval. After Savonarola was executed and his supporters purged, he was elected both second chancellor and secretary of the Ten of War, two important government posts that had fallen vacant. "He was the ideal candidate," Lee writes, "relatively obscure – able, but not outstandingly brilliant – and, crucially, untainted by success in any quarter."

Machiavelli was completely unprepared. He had attended the lectures of Marcello Adriani, who suggested one should "harness the wisdom of the ancients to rise above factional conflict". He had read Lucretius and made notes on his understanding of the balance between determinism and free will and the chances of controlling fate by understanding "the cause of things". But he had no experience of administration or diplomacy. From striving to find a place for himself in Florence, he was suddenly faced with the problem of finding a place for Florence in the chaotic world of Italian and European politics.

Lee's fine book describes in dogged detail Machiavelli's involvement in a long series of wars and diplomatic negotiations: first Florence's hapless campaigns to recapture Pisa, then its struggle not to fall victim to the expansionary ambitions of Cesare Borgia in Romagna, the pope, the Venetian Republic, the Duchy of Milan, the Spanish house of Aragon that came to possess Naples and Sicily, the French king and the Holy Roman Emperor. Other players in the game were Switzerland, which had a powerful army, the Duchies of Modena and Ferrara, then Bologna, Imola, Lucca, Genoa and Siena. The feudal system whereby pope and Holy Roman Emperor had afforded their protection to smaller city-states in return for tax incomes was now clearly obsolete. The concept of the nation state, gaining ground in Spain, France and England, was still far from producing the notion of a people's right to self-determination. In the absence of generally agreed principles, everything was up for grabs. The French king wished to possess Milan. But so did the emperor. Both the Spanish and the French believed they had a right to Naples. The Venetians, the pope and the emperor all believed they had a right to the towns of the Veneto and Emilia Romagna. Each sought alliances with the others in a rapidly shifting pattern of opportunism and treachery. Meantime, the exiled Medici family offered support to any of Florence's enemies that might return them to power. Again and again towns were besieged, their outlying territories laid waste, their merchandise seized, men slaughtered, women raped.

To complicate matters further, most states did not keep a standing army for fear that its commanders would seize power. Instead they employed *condottieri*, mercenary military commanders with private armies who waged war on their behalf. With no commitment to a campaign beyond their own wealth and prestige, the *condottieri* were perfectly capable of halting manoeuvres at a crucial moment to ask for better terms – or sacking a defeated town and keeping the booty. Asked to collaborate, they invariably plotted against each other.

Machiavelli found himself being sent as Florentine envoy to negotiate with friends and enemies. In the summer of 1499 he was in Forlì trying and failing to hammer out an agreement with Caterina Sforza. In 1500 he spent five frustrating months following Louis XII round France, begging his protection for Florence at a price that could never be agreed. In 1502 he was seeking to mollify Cesare Borgia while the tyrant moved from town to town settling old scores, on one occasion inviting two *condottieri* to negotiations and having them strangled, then waking Machiavelli in the early hours to dictate terms to Florence.

These were not easy journeys, travelling on horseback, days at a time, in all weathers, across mountain and swamp. Accommodation and couriers were expensive and often had to be paid from his salary. Negotiations dragged on. Machiavelli was forced to borrow. Louis XII made him wait days for an audience. Courtiers and envoys from other states gave conflicting news and advice, or spread false information about his intentions. When proposals were made, messages had to be sent to Florence for a response. Couriers could not always get through. Their dispatch bags were stolen or confiscated. A letter hidden in a shoe might prove unreadable on arrival. Since republican Florence was run by a series of committees, decision-making was slow and confused, especially when responding to demands for money. The Florentines wanted security, but were averse to taxes. The military situation could change rapidly. The words "alarmed", "temporize" and, above all, "too late" turn up again and again in Lee's account.

In 1503 Machiavelli was in Rome for a papal conclave which coincided with a recurrence of the plague. "Everywhere he looked there were dead bodies." In January 1504 he was back in France. In 1505 in Perugia, then Mantua, then Siena. "All these intrigues were making his head spin," writes Lee. In 1506 he was trying to deal with Pope Julius as he marched north to reconquer the towns of Romagna and Emilia. In the winter of 1507 he set off on a six-month journey to negotiate with Holy Roman Emperor

Maximilian, following his army as it tried and failed to invade northern Italy from the Tyrol. In 1510 and 1511 there were increasingly desperate missions to France.

All the time Machiavelli was away, he had to worry about his position at home. Was his mission perceived as a failure? Were his colleagues conspiring against him? Friends wrote advising him to hurry back. His bosses ordered him to stay. And he was married now. Children were born in 1502, 1503 and 1504. There were illnesses and anxieties. Not that this prevented him pursuing affairs and visiting brothels, male and female. "Machiavelli is definitely an unsavoury character," Boucheron observes, commenting on a letter where Niccolò describes "his 'desperate rut' with an old and atrociously ugly prostitute" in Verona. Lee gives the full story: tricked by low light and a bawd's wiles, the Florentine envoy did not actually see the woman until, after sex, he lit a lamp and "nearly dropped dead on the spot".

Overall, though, what emerges from Lee's careful chronicling of these missions is Machiavelli's diligence, his patience with his dithering superiors, his financial honesty and commitment to the Florentine cause. After every trip he wrote reports that went far beyond the terms of his brief. He was fascinated by the leaders he met and the way they dealt with the ups and downs of fortune: the systematic ruthlessness of Borgia, the stubborn self-belief of Julius, the hauteur of Louis XII, the ineffectual pleasantness of Maximilian. But he was equally fascinated by the domestic politics and traditions that largely determined these leaders' successes and failures: Borgia seeking to impose himself on lands that had sunk into anarchy, Louis benefiting from France's unity, stability, efficiency, Maximilian hampered by the loose affiliation of peoples that made up his empire.

Piece by piece, Lee shows Machiavelli collecting the material he would use in *The Prince*, the *Discourses on Livy* and *The Art of War*. He also details his growing involvement in the war against Pisa. A siege in 1499 led to Florence's *condottiere* Paolo

Vitelli being beheaded for treason when he broke off engagement exactly as victory seemed assured. In 1504 an expensive project to divert the Arno to dry out Pisa's port, thus depriving the town of supplies from the sea, turned into fiasco. Eventually, Machiavelli became convinced that mercenary armies were part of the problem, not the solution. Having persuaded the Florentines to experiment with a citizens' army, he raised it, trained it and largely led it himself. Only a powerful sense of belonging to a community, he thought, would steel soldiers to face death. In 1509 Pisa was retaken.

Three years later, following a shift in alliances, Florence succumbed to a Spanish army supported by the pope and the Venetians. With the Spanish came the Medici and regime change. Machiavelli tried to show his willingness to work with the family, writing letters of advice suggesting how best they might govern the town ("he would betray everything and say anything," Lee comments). To no avail. He was dismissed, then implicated, erroneously, in a conspiracy against the Medici. He was imprisoned and tortured. From his prison cell, aware that the chief conspirators had been executed, he wrote a surprisingly ironic, delicate poem to Giuliano de' Medici, son of il Magnifico, whom he had known years before. Again to no avail. Then Pope Julius died and Giovanni de' Medici, another son of the Magnifico, was elected pope. Medici power in Florence was suddenly assured. An amnesty was announced. Machiavelli retreated to his farm, where after a period of depression he began to write.

Short summaries of Machiavelli's works are almost always misleading. "Machiavelli tried to find princes to admire," writes Boucheron, "but when he found none he was forced to invent a prince on paper." This is not the case. *The Prince* sets out to establish how power is wielded in a principality and what qualities are required in its leader. It concludes that different circumstances will require different qualities. Lee feels the book is marred by being too obviously an attempt to curry favour with the Medici by purporting to "reveal how princes could learn to master Fortune". Again this is reductive. Analysing the very different careers and qualities of Borgia and Pope Julius, Machiavelli observes:

> If someone is behaving cautiously and patiently and the times and circumstances are such that the approach works, he'll be successful. But if times and circumstances change, everything goes wrong for him, because he hasn't changed his approach to match. You won't find anyone shrewd enough to adapt his character like this, in part because you can't alter your natural bias and in part because, if a person has always been successful with a particular approach, he won't easily be persuaded to drop it. So when the time comes for the cautious man to act impulsively, he can't, and he comes unstuck.

The relation between character and circumstance is also crucial in the debate that made *The Prince* notorious. Opening Chapter 15, Machiavelli remarks:

> If you always want to play the good man in a world where most people are not good, you'll end up badly. Hence, if a ruler wants to survive, he'll have to learn to stop being good, at least when the occasion demands.

"When the occasion demands..." Earlier, in a less celebrated passage, Machiavelli had observed that in

> hereditary monarchies where people have long been used to the ruler's family... all a monarch need do is avoid upsetting the order established by his predecessors, trim policies to circumstances when there is trouble, and, assuming he is of average ability, he will keep his kingdom for life.

Here occasion doesn't demand; no bad behaviour is required. But in early-sixteenth-century Italy power, as Lee's biography remorselessly confirms, was a rollercoaster of internal factional intrigue and external predators. One could not ride it on a prayer. So a hierarchy of values had to be established: for Machiavelli the well-being of the polis was the supreme value, and the political survival of the prince was intimately tied up with that, since instability only breeds more instability. "When the occasion demands", what is normally considered bad behaviour can be the best course.

With the determination of the man who has had to struggle to join the elite and resents its complacencies, Machiavelli goes out of his way to rub in this idea, pursuing his line of reasoning far beyond what was expedient to win the approval of the Medici. Borgia was ruthless, but in "forcing people to respect authority" he fostered political unity and economic prosperity. Tackling this "ends justifying means" debate as it emerged some years later in the *Discourses*, where Machiavelli insists that Romulus had to kill his brother Remus if he was to establish a lasting state in Rome, Boucheron is relieved to conclude that Machiavelli allows us to "recognize the legitimacy of what [Romulus] has founded" while leaving us free to "condemn the founder's violence". This is cavilling. Machiavelli doesn't condemn the founder's violence, and would be dismissive of our niceties. He does not afford absolute value to individual moral goodness: it is always trumped by the long-term well-being of the community.

Lee prefers the *Discourses* to *The Prince*, in part because they focus on republics rather than principalities, and in part because they were written with a particular group in mind: the circle of intellectual, mostly republican friends who revolved around Cosimo Rucellai and were instrumental in helping Machiavelli come to terms with his fall from power. But again, although Machiavelli insists that a people flourishes best when it enjoys freedom, he is not an ideologue. One chapter of the *Discourses* is entitled: "If some unexpected event should free a people used to living under a prince, it is unlikely that they will be able to preserve this free-dom". Because they are not used to freedom – it is not part of their political tradition. Hence they will soon end up "under a yoke that is often heavier than the one they had shaken off".

Perhaps the text that best captures the complexity of both Machiavelli's position and manner of exposition is his *Life of Castruccio Castracani*. Lee offers an engaging account of Machiavelli's years in the political wilderness, his surprisingly sentimental love affairs, his friendships with historian and statesman Francesco Guicciardini and diplomat Francesco Vettori, his success as a writer of darkly comic plays, where foolish husbands and sighing lovers show the same passion for subterfuge that Niccolò had observed in international politics. Then in 1520, perhaps partly in response to the much-praised *Art of War*, the Medici at last began to bring Machiavelli in from the cold. He was sent to Lucca to sort out a commercial dispute, and, while the negotiations dragged on, wrote a brief life of the fourteenth-century *condottiere* and Duke of Lucca, Castruccio Castracani.

Lee is at a loss to understand why Machiavelli alters so many details of Castracani's life, especially since his readers would be aware of the facts: "Whereas Castruccio had, in reality, been born into one of Lucca's most illustrious noble families, Niccolò concocted a cock-and-bull story about him being abandoned by his mother while still an infant and found under some vines in the garden of a priest called Antonio Castracani." Lee supposes Machiavelli is crafting "a version of Castruccio's life which... could... inspire his readers to emulate the ideals of military and political leadership he had expounded in... the *Arte della guerra* and *Il principe*."

It seems more likely that Machiavelli is exploiting his readers' knowledge of the facts to give sense to the fable he is creating. All the changes he makes point in the same direction. His Castracani is illegitimate, hence outside society, excluded. He is brought up by a priest, but proves immune to the religious nurturing imposed on him. His qualities, that is, are innate, severed from any tradition. A local *condottiere* and aristocrat takes him under his wing. Castracani wins prestige, but also envy and enemies. In his special situation the only way to survive is to crush them, exploiting factional conflict to become duke of Lucca. Then he has to see off his helpers, who are now jealous. From here on he simply reacts brilliantly, efficiently, ruthlessly to more and more extreme circumstances. He crushes enemies in the surrounding towns, but in doing so creates a highly unstable situation that only his personal brilliance can keep under control. Finally, after a magnificent victory over the Florentines, in the prime of life, he succumbs to a chill and dies.

So much for governing Fortune. On his deathbed Castracani addresses the son of the *condottiere* who initially helped him. Having never married, never become part of society, he can offer no secure succession. The state he decides to leave to this young man is large, he says, but "weak and unstable". "Your own city of Lucca will never be content to live under your reign." The people of Pisa "will always scorn the rule of a lord from Lucca". Likewise the people of Pistoia. The Florentines are hostile and offended. Et cetera. To suppose that "in Niccolò's eyes, Castruccio was the perfect prince" is surely to miss the point. Lee acknowledges that Machiavelli is perhaps warning the Medici not to pursue "further territorial expansion". More deeply, he is inviting them to consider their relation to the town they are governing and its republican traditions. It is pointless having outstanding personal qualities if everything one builds is quickly destroyed, because it is not part of an ongoing collective project.

Machiavelli followed up his life of Castracani with a detailed account of Lucca's complex constitution, focusing on its failure, as he saw it, to balance the competing claims of common people and *grandi* (the rich and noble). Months later he was being invited to draw up proposals for a new constitution in Florence. Someone had been paying attention.

This brings us to the core of Machiavelli's vision and vocation. In the *Discourses* he had argued that Rome achieved success not despite internal conflict, but by harnessing such conflict, which is natural and inevitable, in institutions that allowed each area of society to control and complement the others. The idea was controversial. Nevertheless, Machiavelli set about devising a constitution for Florence that would appease all classes, balancing Medici power with republican aspirations. It was rejected.

This concern with inclusion, coloured no doubt by Machiavelli's growing up in a family that felt excluded, is intimately connected to his insistence that the polis constitutes the supreme value. Religion itself should be at the service of the community, a valuable resource to be nurtured and respected regardless of whether it was true. And Machiavelli did respect it, to the point of writing an *Exhortation to Penitence* for the confraternity to which he belonged. He liked to be part of things. Equally, language, at least the vernacular, was the expression of a specific community, at the community's service, not something that an individual could manipulate, as Dante had claimed to have manipulated Florentine, to make it the language of all Italy. Dante, Machiavelli felt, was speaking from the bitterness of exile, exclusion. Lee feels this attitude is "parochial". But the implication was that a language of all Italy would come naturally if ever Italy was united – something, as Machiavelli explained in the *Discourses*, that the Church made extremely unlikely, since the pope occupied the territories at its centre and prevented any leader from conquering the entire peninsula while being unable to conquer it himself.

"I have always been most loyal," he wrote to Vettori in 1513 in relation to his willingness to serve the Medici regime. "My poverty stands witness to my loyalty and goodness." And he means loyalty to Florence. He is a civil servant, serving regardless of regime; the Medici were hardly worse than many others. They were part of Florence's tradition. When Machiavelli travels, it is with Florence in mind; when he considers Rome's past, it is to apply it to the

Florentine present. In 1521 he was offered a lucrative job as chancellor of the city of Dubrovnik. He refused. He wasn't a mercenary. He never conspired against any Florentine government. What mattered were family, friends, particularly circles of friends, lovers, the polis. Lee's magnificently detailed biography shows throughout what a convivial fellow he was, how important to him were such qualities as solidarity, cheerfulness, willingness to advise, practical joking, and how easily he could move from gambling in a village inn to debating in the government palace.

"When a storm is threatening" and our institutions are in crisis, Boucheron concludes his book, Machiavelli can "teach us to think in heavy weather". He names Brexit and Trump as examples of our present crisis. Machiavelli no doubt would have been fascinated by Trump, but even more so by the circumstances and society that allowed his particular approach to be successful. And whatever he might have thought of Brexit or the American president, the slogan "Florence First" would have made sense to him.

LORENZINO DE' MEDICI
(1514–48)

The *Apology*

What do you do if you come into the world bearing the same name as various ancestors, of whom some were considered good and others even great? Born in 1514, christened Lorenzo de' Medici, a young boy discovers that not only was his grandfather called Lorenzo, but likewise his great-great-grandfather, a man who is still revered as the good and generous brother to the even more revered Cosimo the Elder, who set up the Medici dynasty. Worst of all, there is the oppressive memory of Cosimo's grandson Lorenzo the Magnificent, whose posthumous fame is still growing despite the fact that he actually embezzled much of the wealth of your side of the family.

Well, one thing you can do is to call yourself something different. In general, Italian has two ways of altering a word or name. There is the affectionate diminutive produced by the suffix *-ino*, and the insulting pejorative created by the suffix *-accio*. Hence we have *ragazzo*, a boy, *ragazzino*, a nice little boy, and *ragazzaccio*, a young hooligan. Curiously, Lorenzo came to be known both as Lorenzino, perhaps because he was short, perhaps because it was understood that he was bound to be less important than his ancestor namesakes, and Lorenzaccio, "Lorenzo the Scoundrel". Quite probably he got this second name because of the way he reacted to the implications of the first.

Orphaned young, Lorenzino went down to Rome to live under the guardianship of Pope Clement VII, illegitimate son of Lorenzo the Magnificent's brother, and hence a man on the other, embezzling side of the family. This was now very much the heyday of the Renaissance after a century bent on rediscovering the noble gestures, artworks and writings of the ancient world, largely at the expense of the medieval Christian values of humility, poverty and chastity.

The constant search for role models in ancient Rome and Greece, and in particular the tendency to judge political leaders by comparing them with famous figures of antiquity, had a variety of consequences, both positive and negative. Certainly there was an enhanced sense of human nobility, of a greatness and beauty that could be achieved and contemplated aside from Christian metaphysics. But there was also the danger of falling into parody, or cynicism, of feeling that every action was merely the tired repetition – and, what's more, out of context – of something done centuries before. On a wild night in 1530, the adolescent Lorenzino went out and vandalized the bas-reliefs on the Emperor Constantine's triumphal arch in Rome, plus various fine statues from the age of Hadrian. Was this destructive act a rejection of the encumbering past, or was Lorenzino mimicking Alcibiades, who had supposedly mutilated various busts of Hermes almost two thousand years before? In any event, the young Medici was obliged to abandon Rome on pain of death. Fleeing to Florence, he wrote a play, the *Aridosio*, which begins with the complaint that it is impossible to find anything new to write about because the ancients have already done it all.

Florence at the time was itself enjoying a collective déjà vu. After a period of republicanism, the pope and the Holy Roman Emperor had got together to impose, once again, a Medici leadership on the city. Alessandro de' Medici, bastard son, so it seemed, of Pope Clement, was declared duke. Poor but resourceful, Lorenzino befriended his distant cousin – Alessandro was only two years his senior – and became his companion in debauchery, an able procurer of women, an adviser, a buffoon, a heavy drinker. Then at a certain point he decided to kill him. "My beautiful aunt," he told Alessandro one night in 1537, "is at last ready to grant you her favours. You can wait for her in my bedroom." Alessandro rose to the bait. He lay down on his cousin's bed and shut his eyes. Together with a hired assassin, Lorenzino, now decidedly Lorenzaccio, stabbed him to death and fled before the body was discovered.

Why did he do it? There appears to have been no plan and certainly no proper preparation for replacing the duke either with himself or with the prominent republicans whom Alessandro had exiled. In the *Apologia* Lorenzino offers an explanation, of a kind. The things to look out for as you read the piece are the passion and elegance of its arguments, the ease with which internal contradiction is ignored, the insistent sincerity of its false consciousness, and the fact that at the end of the day nothing at all is really explained.

Life is only worth living if man is free, Lorenzino begins, therefore tyrannicide is a duty. The ancients always said as much. The Florentines know it in their republican blood. Alessandro was worse than Nero and Caligula put together. It's amazing it took so long for someone to find the courage to be rid of him. The implication is that the author himself is a modern Brutus.

Up to this point the piece is no more than a vehement repetition of the principles of Roman republicanism, an exercise in finding parallels in the ancient past. But then Lorenzino enters into a fine discussion of the whole question of the legitimacy of political power. Surprisingly, now, he doesn't take a doctrinaire republican position. He is flexible. Traditionally, Florence has belonged to its people, not to a hereditary duke. But even if it were conceded that the Holy Roman Emperor had the right to impose a leader on Florence, Alessandro would have forfeited any hypothetical legitimacy with his appallingly cruel and licentious behaviour. For what really gives a government the right to rule is its performance.

All this seems admirably pragmatic. There is a discussion of Lorenzino's obligations to a member of his extended family with whom he was in a close relationship. Here he oscillates wonderfully between his supposed commitment to republicanism, which would oblige him to kill a tyrant even if it were his own brother, and a sense of social superiority in being the true legitimate son of a Medici and not merely a bastard fathered on a serving maid by God knows who. But in any event, since the end justifies the means (Lorenzino was clearly familiar with Machiavelli's *The Prince*, published twenty years before), then his treacherous exploitation of his special relationship with Alessandro is more than excusable: the important thing was to kill the pig.

This discussion of ends and means leads us to the core of the *Apology* and its underlying irony. For the goal of the whole project, Lorenzino claims, was to return Florence to its republican constitution. This end failed, he complains, because the people who should have risen up on the announcement of the duke's death were so pusillanimous. The question now arises: is the means justified if the end is not achieved? And we see that Machiavelli's famous precept introduces an element of technical expertise into morality: only a correct calculation of the consequences of any action will allow us to understand whether it is morally justified. Lorenzino got it wrong. He killed Alessandro, but this only led to the installation of another Medici, Cosimo I, as duke. That was definitely not the plan. All the same, the murderer claims the justification of his *intended end*, which only he could really know and which, as we have said, he does not seem to have planned or provided for in any serious way.

What then are the intentions behind the *Apology* itself? At first glance the text seems to be a genuine political treatise and an attempt to win support for a possible return to Florence. But Lorenzino could not have been so foolish as to have imagined that the ruling Medici would ever forgive him. He knew there were paid assassins forever on his track as he moved nervously from town to town. So what was the purpose of this eloquent piece of writing? Like the destruction of the statues in Rome, the writing of his play, the assassination of the duke, it can best be seen as just another attempt to achieve fame. This was Lorenzino's real goal, the only explanation. He wanted to be noticed.

At this point the relevance of the *Apology* to our own times becomes evident. Renaissance humanism, with its combination of eclecticism and stress on the noble individual, offered a gallery of gestures, usually bereft of context, that would lead to fame. After centuries of a Christianity that allowed for nothing outside itself, the door was opened on the supermarket of ideas and role models we live in today. From now on, modern man could invest in this or that role to achieve notoriety not because he believed in it, but because he believed he was capable of distinguishing himself in this way. At which point everybody begins to insist on their sincerity precisely because we sense its absence. Immoral and aristocratic, Lorenzino de' Medici becomes famous writing a work of great morality and enthusiastic republicanism. The nineteenth-century poet Giacomo Leopardi would refer to the *Apology* as the best prose writing of its time. It's high praise. The fact that we are reading Lorenzino today is an indication of his triumph.

Then in 1548 the hired killers caught up with him in Venice. To read, immediately after the *Apology*, Cecchino da Bibbona's colourful account of how he and an accomplice dispatched Lorenzino is to find oneself at the opposite pole of literary achievement, far away from classical reference, eloquence, propaganda or spin. Here is that recognizable figure who, for a large sum of money, carries out the brutal command without asking any questions, then tells and sells his story. Lorenzino deserved no better. The two men and their writings call to each other: deep down they are accomplices in a pathological pursuit of notoriety, the notion that saving oneself from the oblivion of anonymity is sufficient justification for any atrocity.

GIAMBATTISTA BASILE
(b. 1566 or 1583, d. 1632)

The Rabelais of Naples

It kicks off with an act of indecent exposure. An old woman, mistreated and insulted outside the king's palace, lifts her dress to reveal "a woodsy scene". A series of events is set in motion that ultimately induce the king to call together the best storytellers of the realm to tell ten stories a day for five consecutive days to keep his pregnant wife happy. So we have the so-called "pentameron", a backward nod to Boccaccio's *Decameron*. Written by Giambattista Basile and published posthumously in 1634 under the title *Lo cunto de li cunti* (*The Tale of Tales*), and with the subtitle *Entertainment for Little Ones*, it is the first authored collection of literary fairy tales in Western Europe.

But "entertainment for little ones" it is most certainly not. I first came across Basile's work in Matteo Garrone's film *The Tale of Tales* (2015), and was struck by the focus on questions of family and belonging, still so central to Italian life. Garrone intertwines three stories, all centred on kings, queens, princes and princesses – emblematic families. Panoramic shots of the Italian landscape show walled towns topped by moated castles perched on lonely hilltops. None of the drama involves conflict or commerce *between* these distant, spectacularly segregated communities, or even *within* them – rather we have the drama of the passage from inside to out, or outside to in: leaving home to become a stranger, a wife perhaps, or inviting a daughter-in-law or son-in-law into one's own small world. The self-sufficient family is the ideal: but to perpetuate themselves families must produce children, and that means looking outside to find a partner who is not one of the family, hence potentially dangerous.

On the battlements of his castle keep the handsome king hears a beautiful female voice from the houses of the poor below. She sings so sweetly the king knows he must have this woman. But the door where the singing came from is bolted against him. Inside are two ancient and unspeakably ugly sisters. However, the king can't know that. What would he know about people outside his castle?

Fired up by the seductive voice, he declares his love. After eight days, one of the women pokes a finger through a keyhole for him to caress, a finger she has spent hours sucking and smoothing. The king is ecstatic. In her tiniest voice, one of the hags says she will come to his bed if he will agree to have her in complete darkness. He agrees. When, in the middle of the night, he discovers the truth, he calls his men and has her thrown out of his high bedroom window down into the wild woods beneath the castle.

The story is far from over. In the woods there are fairies. Amused to find an old hag hanging by her hair from a tree, they cast a spell, transforming her into the most beautiful woman there ever was. Out hunting, the king sees her and immediately falls in love: this is the sort of creature he was after. "Don't bar the door of pity against me," he begs. "Don't raise the drawbridge of mercy against me." Now it is him praying to be admitted to the stronghold of her graces. Amazed, she lets him in and he takes her back into his castle. The two marry.

Still the story is not done. You can marry into a different world and leave your loved ones behind, but you cannot altogether forget them. Hadn't our enchanted beauty spent her whole life with her poor sister? It's the only company she has ever known. So she invites her to the wedding. Once the old crone recognizes her sister, she is overwhelmed with envy. She refuses to go back to her hovel. She is *family*, she deserves a place in the castle. But of course the king would never put up with such a loathsome in-law. "How did you do it?" the ancient sister demands. "I skinned myself," the queen lies. She had been beautiful *underneath*.

Eager to be part of this new and glamorous family, the old hag goes to a barber and asks him to skin her. In Garrone's adaptation these are not easy scenes to watch. When it comes to it, we are shown no more than the barber sharpening his knives and the first incision, but it is the *idea* that is so upsetting. The old woman cannot accept that her sister is worthy of the king's bed, while she has been abandoned. It is not enough that the queen promises to help her secretly. She demands respect and recognition. What she gets is unspeakable pain.

Another of Garrone's selections presents a king so self-obsessed he spends his time breeding his own body fleas, entirely ignoring the needs of his gorgeous daughter who wants to get out of the family and start a life. Eventually, he breeds a flea as big as a pig, only to be afflicted by grief when it dies. Pestered by his daughter, he has the dead flea skinned, hangs up the pelt and organizes a competition. The man who recognizes what animal it was can marry the daughter. Needless to say, all the nice young men the daughter yearns for have no idea. But a huge and horrible ogre is all too familiar with the smell of common fleas and royal self-obsession. He gets the girl and carries her off to his lonely cave. If the king is the centre of the world we know, the ogre condenses everything alien and threateningly erotic.

Garrone's third story again uses the magical to focus on some spectacular family dysfunctions. A king is so depressed over his failure to have a child with his now ageing queen he isolates himself in his castle, ashamed of his sterility: there will be no further dealings with the wider world. But a bearded sage seeks out the king and offers a solution: capture a sea dragon, have a virgin cook its heart, then give it to the queen to eat. All is done as prescribed, and both the virgin, a common serving girl, and the queen immediately swell up and give birth to identical boys. This uncanny similarity and the ensuing close friendship between two children of such unequal status becomes a problem for the queen. She needs her boy to be unique and the families kept separate. Her attempt to murder the other boy forces him to leave home and set off into the wider world, where of course he immediately falls prey to an evil ogre.

Gloomily gripping, Garrone's film is charged with emotions central to so much Italian fiction: fear of abandonment, an obsession with worthy and unworthy family members, children forced into exile and intruders breaking into families to bring discord. Intrigued, I decided to read Basile. But despite my nearly forty years in Italy this proved impossible, at least in the original. *Lo cunto de li cunti* is written in Neapolitan dialect, a language in its own right. The great Italian critic Benedetto Croce translated the tales into Italian in the 1920s, and the scholar Michele Rak offered his own parallel Neapolitan/ Italian text in 1985. In English a much adulterated selection appeared in 1848, while Richard Burton offered an error-strewn version, perhaps more imitation than translation, in 1893. However, in 2007 the American scholar Nancy Canepa translated the whole text into English working directly from Basile's original. To open the pages of any of these translations is to enter a world utterly different from that of Garrone's film.

The reader familiar with Perrault or Grimm or Italo Calvino's collection of Italian fables expects a certain dispatch in this kind of writing, an economy that allows the shape of the story to stand out before everything else. Basile is not like that. Instead we have the exuberance, outlandishness and hilarity of an Italian Rabelais, or "a deformed Neapolitan Shakespeare", as Calvino called him. Lists abound, proverbs proliferate, metaphors come in multitudes, insults are tirades, praise panegyric. The text teems with a good-tempered, baroque liveliness and endless allusions to Neapolitan customs of every kind. It is a unique reading experience.

Take the frame story that encloses the fifty others. The king of Hairy Valley's daughter will not laugh, and the "miserable father whose sole life breath was his only daughter" calls on "hoop jumpers, acrobats, Master Ruggiero, jugglers, strongmen, a dancing dog, Vracone the jumping monkey, the ass that drinks from a glass" and even "bitchy Lucia" to cheer her up. A footnote tells us that "bitchy Lucia" refers to an ecstatic whirling dance performed by "a man in blackface dressed as an Oriental woman", at whom the Neapolitan crowd yelled "bitch".

The daughter doesn't laugh. The king orders a fountain of oil to be set up outside her palace window causing passers-by to "hop about like crickets, jump like goats and run like hares, slipping and bumping into each other". The princess is unimpressed. But when an old woman filling her jar with the precious oil has it broken by a stone thrower (one of many references to the Neapolitan passion for throwing stones), she insults him thus:

> Ah, you worthless thing, you dope, shithead, bed pisser, leaping goat, diaper ass, hangman's noose, bastard mule!... May you suffer a thousand ills and then some with winds in your sails! May your seed be lost! Scoundrel, beggar, son of a taxed woman, rogue!

A footnote explains that Neapolitan prostitutes were taxed "two carlins per month". The stone thrower gives back as good as he gets: "Baby drowner, rag shitter, fart gatherer." Furious, the old woman exposes herself. Up at her window, the princess bursts out laughing. Humiliated, the old woman curses her: she will never marry, unless to the prince of Round Field, who can only be wakened from his enchanted sleep by a girl who in just three days can fill the pitcher over his open tomb with her tears.

So the princess leaves her doting father to venture into the wide world. With fairy help she almost fills the pitcher, then falls asleep exhausted, allowing a "cricket-legged slave girl" to sneak in and cry a last tear or two to break the spell and marry the handsome prince. Basile's is not a politically correct text: a footnote explains that "cricket-legged" was a standard Neapolitan insult for people of Middle Eastern or North African origin.

Many of the stories pose this situation where a young person is duped into choosing the wrong partner or cheated of the partner they should have married, circumstances that will require a lot of guile, magic and narrative manipulation to sort out. In this case fairies help the increasingly astute princess to engineer a situation where the deceitful slave-girl wife, now pregnant, feels an irresistible craving to hear stories. Four hundred pages later it will be her undoing.

To tell the stories of his *Decameron* Boccaccio chose seven beautiful, witty, well-educated women and three fine young gentlemen. Basile has "lame Zeza, twisted Cecca, goitred Meneca, big-nosed Tolla, hunchback Popa, drooling Antonella, snout-faced Ciulla, cross-eyed Paola, mangy Ciommetella and shitty Iacova". A footnote tells us these are all ironic distortions of "noble names" common in Naples. The thrust of the project is now clear: Basile had spent his life as a courtier and government servant in various parts of Italy, putting together a respectable oeuvre of mainly conventional poems, plays and stories written in the Tuscan Italian that was the country's literary language and often with the intention of flattering a duke or king to further his career. His use of the pseudonym Abbattutis – meaning Downtrodden or Depressed – suggests how frustrating he found it all. But now, in middle age, he would take time out from the social climbing and nascent individualism of the modern court to evoke the earthy energy of an older, tight-knit Neapolitan community. The use of dialect is a declaration of belonging, as it still is in modern Italy: only a native speaks dialect. And the tales he collected are to be packed full of references to the world of local people, so that the reader (or more likely listener, for the stories were probably intended to be read out loud) would feel exactly that secure sense of shared community so precious to the people who populate these stories.

One example must do for all: having injured the king's son in a stone-throwing fight, a young man is forced to leave Naples in haste, but turns back to gaze at the city with heavy heart:

Here I go, my beautiful Naples, I'm leaving you! Who knows if I'll ever be able to see you again, bricks of sugar and walls of sweet pastry, where the stones are manna in your stomach, the rafters are sugarcane, the doors and windows puff pastry?

There follows a long, heavily footnoted list of the various parts of town and their different activities, ending with this tribute to local cooking:

Farewell, carrots and chard; farewell, fritters and cakes; farewell, broccoli and pickled tuna; farewell, tripe and giblets; farewell, stews and casseroles! Farewell, flower of cities, glory of Italy, painted egg of Europe, mirror of the world!... I leave you to become a widower of your vegetable soups; driven out of this dear village, O my cabbage stalks, I must leave you behind!

The problems for a translator are evident. The modern English reader is not a native of Naples and will not feel the powerful emotions roused by the dialect nor pick up the allusions to local mores or recognize the proverbs Basile so frequently quotes but also slyly distorts and subverts. On the other hand, to eliminate all this or, worse still, to bowdlerize it would rob the work of much of its energy and purpose. Canepa steers a middle route, delivering a highly readable prose that mixes modern vulgarity with a vaguely proverbial aplomb ("every piece of shit has its own smell"), often refashioning old Neapolitan sayings into something credibly contemporary ("they were given pizza for pasty"), and never failing to use footnotes to offer the curious reader a sense of the rich life beneath the surface of the story. So you can learn that in court a bankrupt would have to bare his buttocks and touch them against a stone column, that tight socks were fashionable for the upper classes, that dice were made from bones and ink a popular remedy for burns, that parents might ask for their unruly child to be briefly incarcerated in the public dungeon, and so on. Explanations of children's games, gambling habits and dances are also generously provided. In short, always acknowledging her debt to Croce, Rak and others, Canepa gives us a whole world, and gives it in the liveliest possible way.

Basile structures his encyclopedic ebullience in a fairly rigid framework: each storyteller opens with a barrage of proverbs which her tale is supposed to exemplify, then bows out in the same manner once the action is over. Since the proverbs are comically inadequate to describe the complexity of the action, and since the stories often end in unpredictable fashion, critics observe that Basile doesn't offer the moral schematism or didacticism discernible in later fable collections. His Cinderella, for example, far from being a sweet, obedient girl, murders a first stepmother only to find herself saddled with a worse one. No doubt this apparent waywardness and the work's ease with obscenity explains why it was never a favourite with the Catholic conformism that still plays such a large part in shaping Italian culture. You are not, for example, going to find Basile on the national school syllabus.

Yet, though virtues and vices may not always line up with happy and unhappy endings, there is never any doubt as to what is proper behaviour in these stories. As Basile runs the gamut of family situations – brothers who want to marry sisters so as not to have to look outside the family, promiscuous daughters and daughters determined to remain for ever virgins, brilliant children and dumb children – it's evident that blood relationships must be respected: a brother must go to the end of the earth to help a sister and vice versa, a father must not obstruct his daughter's future, a son must help his parents to find the money to marry off his sisters, and so on.

There is little that is Christian here. The only people to offer assistance to those who are not family are fairies, or in some way magical. For ordinary folk altruism is not on the agenda. Somebody outside the family who has behaved badly can be mercilessly punished without the slightest compunction. So the deceitful slave girl in the frame story will be "buried alive, with only her head above ground, so that her death would be more tortured". No one objects. Amid all the rich detail of Neapolitan life, the word "church" does not appear once; neither Jesus nor the Madonna is mentioned. In contrast to the *Decameron*'s satire of everything ecclesiastical, priests get only the most oblique of mentions in the dumplings known as *strangolaprievete*, "priest stranglers". Nor is there so much as a hint of the kind of spirituality that was the constant concern of the painters of the time; nobody prays, nobody agonizes.

Why Basile would exclude such a large part of the Neapolitan life he was otherwise meticulously cataloguing is not clear. It's true that Naples was the only major Italian city to have kicked out the Church's inquisitors in the mid-sixteenth century, and that Basile was writing at a time of fierce religious polarization, when an anti-clerical stance might have got him into trouble. Or perhaps it was precisely because the modern world of the court, the advances of science and technology and the debate between rationalism and Catholicism were making such inroads into popular culture that Basile set out to record and celebrate that culture in all its pre-modern, pagan vitality.

So, while Christianity is conspicuous for its absence, references to the sun, the moon, the stars and the night abound. Every dawn and dusk is recorded with some elaborate metaphor. "When with both hands the Sun brandished its broadsword of light in the middle of the stars, shouting, 'Out of my way, scoundrels!'", or "And as the Sun, like an unsuccessful whore, began to change quarters", or "Before the Sun unpacks the merchandise of its rays at the customs house of the East", and so on. Below every human activity lies the deep determinism of the natural world and the inexorable passage of time, hence the need to accept the seasons and the different prerogatives of youth and age. "Those who oppose the stars are crazy," ends one story – which does not mean one cannot try to improve one's lot with a little guile.

Certainly Basile was constantly looking for ways to improve his own life, and was frequently disappointed. In her introduction, Canepa argues convincingly for the presence of autobiographical elements in the tales. "Hapless is he who is condemned to live in that hell that goes by the name of court," we hear in one story, "where flattery is sold by the basket… deceit and betrayal weighed by the bushel!" Between each of the five days of ten stories, Basile inserts an eclogue, where two courtiers discuss such things as a crucible which can reveal the dark reality behind the bright appearance, or a dye used to mask the deeper motivations of the apparently virtuous, or again a "hook" that becomes a metaphor for all the grasping ways people seek wealth at others' expense. Effortlessly cataloguing depravities of all kinds, the eclogues are less attractive than the tales, but give us a better sense of Basile's position in relation to them. Fortunately, he himself was rescued from a languishing court career by his sister, Adriana, just as so many of his fairy-tale heroes are saved by their siblings. Having achieved fame for herself as a singer, she drew attention to her brother, first in Naples and again at the famous Gonzaga court in Mantua – and it was she who published *The Tale of Tales* after her brother's death. Even at court, family was all.

Since Basile's stories spring from an oral tradition, it's appropriate that Canepa's translation is available as an audiobook. To establish the contrast between court and commonality, a plummy, male BBC voice reads the introductions to each day while ten women with strong American accents of various kinds perform Basile's gutsy storytellers. Crude as this may seem, it works. After some initial disorientation, the vitality of Basile's writing takes over, and however much might be lost in translation the meshing of the folk content and baroque verbosity plays out wonderfully. As when experiencing any masterpiece from the past, the listener is bound to reflect that there is no progress in the arts – only milestones of excellence pointing up deserts of bad behaviour. Basile's fellow Neapolitan and writer Domenico Rea remarked of these stories in 1984, "There is no pleasure and no brutality that is not contemplated there."

GIACOMO CASANOVA
(1725–98)

The Venetian

In an angry footnote to his *Discourse on the Customs of the Italians*, written in 1824, the philosopher-poet Giacomo Leopardi complains:

> No matter how remarkable a man may be, no matter how independent, how forthright, how stubborn in his behaviour and opinions and judgements of whatever kind – yet, if he live in society, his thoughts and actions are truly his own only to the smallest degree. In almost every way he is determined and modified by others, even those for whom he has little or no respect.

Isn't this infuriating? No one could have been more stubbornly independent than Giacomo Casanova, more remarkable and resourceful, but *The Duel* is the story of how his apparently free spirit is fatally hijacked by the opinions of a resentful ballerina, the crass insults of a drunken Polish officer and the absurdity of a society that demands that in certain circumstances a man behave in a manner at once suicidal and punishable by death.

I first came to Casanova's writing through W.G. Sebald, who in his novel *Vertigo* refers at length to the Venetian writer's *History of my Flight from the Prison of the Republic of Venice*. Sebald's evident enthusiasm persuaded me to buy the book. It begins in Kafkaesque fashion. For no apparent reason, Casanova is arrested at dawn and imprisoned in a stifling, rat-infested cell beneath the roof of the Doge's Palace. Languishing here for months, he has no way of knowing whether he is to be released next week, next month or ever. He is afraid he will go mad. After a year of frustration and false starts, he dreams up the most daring and complicated of escapes – few works of fiction can compete – and as the book closes, he is escaping north through the Alps to Austria and Munich.

How strange then, to open *The Duel* and find Casanova picking up his story with the regret that he ever bothered to leave his cell. It seems he was shortly to be released. He could have returned to his familiar life in Venice. For if a man is inevitably conditioned by those around him, better, Casanova feels, as do most Italians, if those people are his own people. Now he is an outlaw, liable to immediate arrest on return. Throughout the book, the author refers to himself in third person as "the Venetian", as if, being exiled, he had somehow been estranged from himself, yet is still most determined by the city and culture that gave him birth.

Casanova may regret escape and exile, but the reader does not. *The Duel* proceeds with a splendidly cheeky account of the adventurer's travels through the capitals of Northern Europe. Never have so many courts and kings been so quickly caricatured and dismissed. Expelled from his own society, the Venetian is free to see every other for what it is: absurd. Again and again the long, sonorous sentences – the product, it would seem, of a lofty civilization – end in a lash of corrosive wit. Again and again the object of ridicule is a figure of authority, a king, even the pope. These are only the 1760s, but the Revolution is already in the air. How ridiculous that a queen who casually remarks that chicken fricassee is the best dish in the world starts a whole country eating chicken fricassee and swearing blind that it is indeed the best dish in the world. Just because she is the queen! How crazy that people respect me because I wear a fancy medal awarded to me for no other reason than that I once kissed the holy pontiff's sacred feet. Aren't people stupid? Convinced of his superiority, our Venetian toes society's line, eating up court freebies beside princes and ladies, perfectly aware that the emperor has no clothes, but with no intention at all of "undeceiving the deceived". Absurdity is fun.

Then, in Warsaw, an Italian ballerina comes to town. Casanova admires her, but he admires another just as much. Actually, and rather out of character, he isn't paying a great deal of attention. Is this something to do with "a certain medicine" he is taking? The dancer, no doubt aware of his reputation, is angry. Meantime, one of her more attentive admirers is General Braniscki, a man whom Casanova mocks as having "learnt to shed his enemies' blood without hatred, to take revenge without anger, to kill without discourtesy, to prefer honour, which is an imaginary thing, to life, which is the only real asset a man has".

Fatal words. Fatal pride. All too soon, it will be the insulted Venetian who will be risking his life as he challenges this pompous Pole to a duel for the sake of honour.

The remarkable thing about Giacomo Casanova is that not only did he have a bewilderingly eventful life, not only was he a thinker of wide reading and great shrewdness, but he also knew how to tell a tale as well as the cleverest of novelists – knew, above all, how to wring out the maximum tension and irony from a fairly squalid adventure. Both the Venetian and the reader have been beautifully set up in the opening pages of this book. We thought we had seen through all society's self-regarding theatre. We thought we were immune. Then, in the space of a few lines, here we are enthralled by one of the most grotesque and artificial rituals ever devised: two men back to back in the snow, loaded pistols in their hands, everything at stake, all because of a woman who is now entirely forgotten and indeed never again mentioned throughout the book.

Public opinion may be a matter of no substance, observed Schopenhauer, yet if everybody else foolishly pays attention to it, then you will have to do likewise. For it conditions your whole existence. Especially if you depend on your charm and social graces to scrounge a living through the courts of Europe. Such, more or less, is the Venetian's reasoning when he decides to challenge the man who has insulted him. A loss of reputation would be a loss of earning power. Yet, as the two combatants warm to their madness, as they become extravagantly deferential to each other in a delirium of mutual admiration – what crazy courage we are showing! – one can't help feeling that there is more to the ritual of the duel than our hero supposes.

More than a hundred years after Casanova's death, discussing *Varieties of Religious Experience*, the psychologist William James suggested that risking one's life could give you a sense of sacred transport. He quotes a certain General Skobelev: "A meeting of man to man, a duel, a danger into which I can throw myself head-foremost, attracts me, moves me, intoxicates me. I am crazy for it, I love it, I adore it. I run after danger as one runs after women…"

Well, who ran after women more than Giacomo Casanova? Here is the key. The Venetian may merely be responding to society's absurd notions of honour when he challenges his opponent. He hadn't planned to do this. It is a loss of independence. But once he engages, the absurd duel gives this jaded, disillusioned man a sense of meaning that even young ballerinas are no longer capable of providing. Curiously, it also forges a new and very intimate society: between the Venetian and his opponent, and between this eighteenth-century adventurer and ourselves. We all share the disturbing awareness that, precisely because it is our most precious asset, there comes a time when life must be risked.

ALESSANDRO MANZONI
(1785–1873)

I've 71 Sheets to Wash

"Suppose there are five or six of us, Milanese, at home," Alessandro Manzoni wrote in his essay 'On the Italian Language', "talking together in Milanese, about this and that. Along comes someone with a friend from Piedmont, or Venice, or Bologna, or Naples, or Genoa, and, as good manners demand, we stop speaking Milanese and switch to Italian. You tell me if the talk will flow as it did before... if we will have the same readiness and confidence in the words we use that we had only moments ago."

In the early nineteenth century, Italy was divided linguistically as well as territorially. People from different regions managed to talk to each other, Manzoni observed, by falling back "on the generic or approximate". But for writing that wouldn't do: what was needed was maximum capacity of expression. It's true that there was an Italian literary language which had served the country well enough for centuries, a sort of distillation of the Florentine of Dante, Boccaccio and Petrarch, but this was hardly an idiom for modern times – not the sort of thing you could put in people's mouths in a novel. And it had suddenly become very important that Italian writers produce novels.

"High literature is for the few," the poet Ugo Foscolo observed in 1809, but there were now large numbers of literate people with nothing to read but the "ignorant malignancy" of newspapers, "the extravagance" of old tales, "the twaddle" of rhymesters. France, he thought, had shown how the novel could be used as an educational tool. Giacomo Leopardi made a more obviously political argument: Italy could only make progress towards national unity when "she has books suitable for the times, read and understood by common readers from one end of the country to the other".

However, the literary elite still looked down on the novel. When, in 1821, Manzoni let it be known that he was writing one, "the mere announcement," the literary journal *Biblioteca Italiana* later observed, "ennobled the profession and encouraged other fine minds to try their hand."

Manzoni was born in 1785, only fruit of an arranged marriage between Giulia Beccaria, daughter of the Milanese intellectual Cesare Beccaria, author of the hugely influential *On Crimes and Punishments* (1764), and Pietro Manzoni, a minor nobleman who divided his time between Milan and Lecco, some thirty miles to the north of the city, in the company of his seven spinster sisters. Pietro was twenty-six years older than his spouse. She was bored by his company, and it is widely believed that Alessandro was not his child. Sent away to a wet nurse in the country, the boy spent most of his infancy and adolescence in Catholic boarding schools, where classical literature proved a major consolation. In 1792 his mother obtained a separation, and in 1795 went to live with a lover in Paris, where Alessandro joined her ten years later. Henceforth the two were inseparable, albeit with the addition, in 1808, of Enrichetta, Manzoni's wife, who would bear him nine children. Domestic stability brought with it an outpouring of poetry, which, after his conversion in 1810 from agnosticism to the severe doctrine of Jansenism, took a decidedly religious turn. For years the author followed a long list of rules prepared by his spiritual adviser, Father Luigi Tosi, which included the injunction "Your work is to be considered part of the general penitence that God has imposed on the sons of Adam." In 1815 he published the *Sacred Hymns*, and in 1819 the book *Observations on Catholic Morality*. A first tragedy, *The Count of Carmagnola*, was published in 1820, and a second, *Adelchi*, in 1822. But when in the autumn of 1821 Manzoni told Tosi that he planned to work on a novel, the priest was not happy, and would keep a censorious eye on the pages the author sent him as he wrote.

Manzoni was now thirty-six. Throughout the summer of 1822 his friend Tommaso Grossi was a guest at his house, reading aloud every evening from the novel he was writing, *The Lombards in the First Crusade*. Both men had just read Walter Scott's *Ivanhoe* in its French translation. Historical novels, they believed, encouraged national consciousness, while offering an opportunity for veiled political statements. In nineteenth-century Lombardy, you could be jailed for criticizing Austrian rule. Manzoni chose to write about the seventeenth century, when the region was ruled by the Spanish. After extensive research he had settled on a plot, which perhaps not surprisingly, given his background, had to do with the aspiration to form a family based on love: the night before a young peasant couple are to be married, the wedding is cancelled because a local Spanish lord has decided he wants the woman for himself. The years from 1628 to 1630 offered the dramatic backdrop of a famine, a military invasion and a devastating outbreak of the plague. "The material is rich," Manzoni wrote to his friend, the French historian Claude Fauriel. "There's plenty of the sort of stuff that puts mankind to shame."

But there was still the problem of which language to use, of never being sure how a word might be understood in other parts of Italy. Manzoni wrote a first draft in the idiom he knew best ("writing badly", as he described it), then rewrote the book substituting Tuscan words for Lombard, since Tuscan was by far the most widely known of the country's many dialects. No sooner was *The Betrothed* published, however, in three volumes between 1824 and 1827, than Manzoni, dissatisfied despite its immediate popularity, took his family to Florence for a month to work on a definitive revision. "I've 71 sheets to wash," he wrote to Fauriel, meaning the printed sheets from which the book's seven hundred pages were folded, "the waters of the Arno and two laundrymen, Cioni and Niccolini." Gaetano Cioni was a Florentine philologist, Giovanni Battista Niccolini a Pisan playwright. But even after the two experts had been through the text, Manzoni wasn't convinced.

He wanted to recreate the spoken Tuscan of the cultured classes, which he felt combined propriety with comprehensibility. For ten years he set the project aside, unsure as how to proceed, then eventually invited the twenty-three-year-old Emilia Luti, Florentine governess to the family of a friend in Milan, to check that his use of idiom and diction was up to date. There was no attempt in fact to use the language of the seventeenth century, since any authentic reproduction of how his characters might have spoken would have meant using language Manzoni feared would be incomprehensible and unattractive. Even as the 71 sheets finally went to press in 1840, he was still infuriating the printer with numerous last-minute corrections. But it was worth it: twenty years before political unity was achieved, the new edition offered a persuasive model of what a future national language might look like. In the 1850s the novel was already being taught as exemplary in many schools, and by the time of Manzoni's death in 1873 it had assumed the status of a national institution. In 1923, the Fascist reform of the education system made it compulsory reading for Italian children for generations to come.

Given the author's obsession with readability, it makes sense that the new English translation of *The Betrothed* is by Michael Moore, an American who for many years was an interpreter at the United Nations, hence accustomed to focusing on the spoken word and the need for comprehensibility. The most recent previous translation, by Bruce Penman in 1972, published by Penguin, was already more than readable, but Moore goes further in reformulating Manzoni's elaborate syntax and giving the narrative voice a strong spoken feel. That said, no translation of *The Betrothed* can aspire to the cultural significance the novel enjoys in Italy – so what of its quality as narrative? It is curious, for example, that there has been no new French translation since 1877.

The opening pages offer comedy and drama with great dispatch: Don Abbondio, the priest in a village south of Lake Como, encounters two thugs, or "*bravi*", who have clearly been waiting for him.

"*Non potendo schivare il pericolo,*" we're told, "*vi corse incontro, perché i momenti di quell'incertezza erano allora così penosi per lui che non desiderava altro che d'abbreviarli.*" Moore translates: "Unable to avoid the danger, he rushed into it, since the uncertainty was so painful that all he wanted was to get it over with." Penman has: "Not being able to avoid the danger, he hurried to meet it, for he found the moments of uncertainty so distressing that his main wish was to shorten them as much as possible."

When the thugs demand to know whether the priest is planning to celebrate the marriage of Renzo and Lucia, the betrothed couple, Don Abbondio replies, apologetically, in the affirmative. This prompts the threat that sets the plot rolling, and which every Italian schoolchild must learn by heart: "'*Or bene,' gli disse il bravo, all'orecchio, ma in tono solenne di comando, 'questo matrimonio non s'ha da fare, né domani, né mai.*'" Moore: "'Well, then,' the *bravo* said in his ear, but in the solemn tone of a command, 'this marriage ain't gonna happen. Not tomorrow, not never.'" Penman: "'Very well,' said the *bravo*, speaking into the priest's ear quietly, but in a tone of impressive command, 'that wedding is not to take place. Not tomorrow, and not any other time either.'"

Don Abbondio tries to talk his way out of it, deploying the elaborate rhetoric with which the educated bamboozle the uneducated, one of the book's main themes. The thugs are having none of it. "'*Orsù,' interruppe il bravo, 'se la cosa avesse a decidersi a ciarle, lei ci metterebbe in sacco. Noi non ne sappiamo, né vogliam saperne di più. Uomo avvertito... lei c'intende.*'" Moore: "'Enough talk!' interrupted the *bravo*. 'Running your mouth isn't going to fix this. Not another word out of you. Consider this fair warning... Have we made ourselves clear?'" Penman: "'Come, now,' interrupted the *bravo*, 'if these things had to be settled by talk, you'd make rings round us. We don't know all these things, and don't want to know them. A warning's a warning... and I'm sure you understand us.'" This more or less gives the measure of the two translations: Moore always shorter and

sharper, at the risk of straying into paraphrase or the conspicu-
ously contemporary, Penman a little more laboured, tending to
explain and expand.

Although at first glance the story seems a black-and-white tale
of good and evil – two despotic foreigners, Don Rodrigo and
his cynical cousin Count Attilio, destroying the lives of a whole-
some Lombard couple – the characters are more interestingly
distinguished along a polarity that runs from extreme fearfulness,
through pondered courage to the thoughtlessly rash. Early critics
noted that the comically cowardly Don Abbondio had an earlier
model in Boniface, the monk in Scott's *The Abbot*, but no one
doubts the superior psychological depth of Manzoni's portrait.
"When he was forced to choose between two contenders," we
hear of the priest, "he always sided with the stronger party, but
always cautiously, taking care to show the other party that he had
no choice in the matter, as if to say, 'Why couldn't you have been
the stronger man? Then I would have taken your side.'"

Other commentators saw an affinity between Manzoni and his
creation: the author suffered from panic attacks, found it almost
impossible to leave his home unaccompanied and was extremely
cautious about making political statements. While other Italian
novels of the period featured bold declarations of patriotism
(Foscolo's *Last Letters of Jacopo Ortis* being the most distinguished
example), *The Betrothed*, for all Manzoni's heartfelt support for
the Risorgimento, has none. It's telling that the most important
event in his life, his conversion to Jansenist Catholicism, came
in response to a moment of intense fear. He and his wife were in
Paris during the celebrations for Napoleon's wedding when they
were separated in a riot caused by exploding mortar shells. Taking
refuge in a church, Manzoni made a vow that if the two were safely
reunited he would convert. In *The Betrothed* it is precisely when
matters of faith become confused with issues of fear and courage
that the text becomes something more than melodrama on the one
hand and historical essay on the other.

Afraid that Don Rodrigo will try to abduct Lucia, the young couple turn to Fra Cristoforo for help. Years before, this Capuchin monk had killed a man in a moment of angry daring, then converted and dedicated his life to making amends. In an act of great courage he had knelt before the vengeful brother of the victim, and now he shows courage again, going to warn Don Rodrigo of God's vengeance should he touch Lucia. In vain: despite a "remote and mysterious dread", the Spaniard is determined to have his way. Rash as he is well-meaning, Renzo seeks to persuade Lucia to trick Don Abbondio into recognizing a sort of citizen's marriage: they must simply appear in his presence and declare themselves married. Terrified that this may be sinful, the virtuous Lucia risks a major quarrel with her boyfriend, and at the crucial moment hesitates long enough to allow an equally terrified Don Abbondio to push a tablecloth in her mouth and prevent her pronouncing herself Renzo's wife. Aided by Fra Cristoforo, the youngsters escape across the River Adda, Lucia with her mother to Monza, Renzo to Milan, where he immediately becomes involved in a hunger riot, and once again shows courage trying to stop the mob from lynching the commissioner responsible for supplying the city's food.

Something similar had happened in 1814 when the Lombard minister of finance, Giuseppe Prina, was lynched by a crowd close to Manzoni's house, "so that for many hours we heard the shouts of those going after him". Ugo Foscolo risked his life defending Prina; Manzoni locked himself away, fearful that the rioters would come after other targets. But if Renzo is given the courage that Manzoni perhaps wished he had himself, his boldness leads to disaster. Led on by an agent provocateur, he gets drunk and pronounces rabble-rousing speeches denouncing tyranny, greed and the subversion of justice, as a result of which he becomes the object of a manhunt that forces him to escape to Bergamo and live in hiding, far from Lucia. Understanding the proper use of courage seems far more difficult than distinguishing good and evil; in a period when patriotic rebellion against the occupying power was in the air, this was a theme Manzoni's readers understood.

Meanwhile, the ever-alarmed Lucia finds refuge in a monastery and comes under the protection of Gertrude, known as the "Nun of Monza", perhaps the greatest of Manzoni's characters. Her story is based on that of Marianna de Leyva (1575–1650), the daughter of a powerful noble, who as a mother superior had a ten-year affair with a rich hoodlum that produced two children and led to various murders, as the couple sought to conceal their relationship. Manzoni tones down the historical events, but gives a disturbing back story in which, as a young girl, Gertrude is groomed by her father for a life for which she had no vocation so he can save himself the expense of a dowry. Here Manzoni was able to draw on experiences close to home. He would have heard from his mother how her father, under the influence of his second wife, had more or less abandoned her in a convent against her will. Gertrude is frightened at the prospect of being locked up in a religious community, and wants to resist, but her father's anger is such that her "terror at the sound of his footsteps can be neither described nor imagined". Over thirty pages, Manzoni gives a powerful psychological study of a proud, conflicted woman yearning for an intimacy that, in the context of a convent, can only be considered shameful. She is envious of Lucia, who can expect fulfilment with Renzo, yet also protective of her, in the hope of atoning for her own sins. Lucia, on the other hand, never begins to understand the complexity and instability of the woman she now depends on.

This episode reveals the novel's great weakness: its central characters are its least interesting. We see this again when, following Lucia's escape, Don Rodrigo turns to a greater and more powerful sinner than himself, a "fearsome man", and asks him to arrange for the girl's abduction. Since this character was based on a historical figure with living descendants, Manzoni, ever anxious to avoid offence, imagines that everyone, out of dreadful respect, refers to him throughout as the Nameless One, a ruthless bully who has withdrawn from Milan to a castle in the hinterland, where, assisted by an entourage of thugs, he murders, rapes and plunders, "feared by all". Soon enough Lucia is seized and brought trembling and quaking to the evil lord's castle, where, in a night of anguish, she makes a vow that if the Madonna saves her, she will live a virgin. What she cannot know is that the Nameless One, now very much in mid-life, is experiencing a religious crisis. The idea of death, which once "instilled in him a courageous rage, now gripped him with panic". He is overcome by "the terrifying idea of being judged before God". Lucia's abduction proves one crime too many: after a night of "tormented contemplations" that bring him close to suicide, he takes advantage of the visit to a nearby village of Federigo Borromeo, Archbishop of Milan, to confess his sins. Fear prompts religious conversion: Lucia is released and sent off with a hundred gold scudi, a small fortune.

Here, at the halfway point of the novel as we now have it, Manzoni had considered ending his story with Lucia keeping her vow and a disappointed Renzo going off to fight in foreign wars. But how instructive would that have been? A fervent believer in divine providence, Manzoni was determined that his book be "useful", which meant convincing people of the value of prayer and the proper use of such things as religious vows. Father Tosi meantime, who was about to become a bishop and anxious that Manzoni get back to writing his *Observations on Catholic Morals*, implored him to tone down all references to sensuality, which, during the revision process, he did, depriving his lovers of the effusions and fleshliness that might have made them more compelling. They never so much as peck each other on the cheek. "One shouldn't write about love in order to encourage this passion in the reader," the author later defended himself, but also asked a friend, "Don't you think, for a peasant girl, I've idealized Lucia a bit too much?"

In any event, he now embarked on the second half of the book, in which the young couple's faith would be rewarded. At the same time, his interest was shifting towards historical fact rather than fictional creation: there is a long hagiographical digression on Archbishop Borromeo and many pages on the bewilderingly complex wars of succession that led to the Holy Roman Empire invading northern Italy. This conflict brought with it the plague that in 1630 wiped out more than half the population of Milan. The city's foreign rulers failed to respond properly, and a collective panic ensued, leading people to believe that the disease was being deliberately spread by evil conspirators – a situation described by Manzoni in great and, in this instance, fascinating detail. In a letter to Fauriel he describes his struggle to be faithful to historical fact rather than manipulate it for the purposes of his story, as he felt other novelists tended to do. Years later he would theorize the incompatibility of the poetic truth of fiction and the historical truth of chronicle, concluding that the historical novel was a flawed genre. Certainly he would never attempt to write another, and when the 1840 version of *The Betrothed* was published, he would add, in appendix, a lengthy, straightforwardly historical account of the trial of two men accused of spreading the plague. Nevertheless, despite his concern that the historical interludes were now too long and occasional grumblings to friends that he was exhausted and bored with the whole project, the final scenes of the novel, as Renzo goes to Milan and finds Fra Cristoforo, Don Rodrigo and, above all, Lucia in the plague hospital where thousands are dying, ministered to only by a heroic priesthood, is a breathtaking tour de force with a feel-good denouement that guaranteed the novel's popularity: Providence at the last provides, if only for our two chaste protagonists, amid a waste of corpses.

"A work of religious reactionism… written only to glorify priests," complained the influential patriot Luigi Settembrini. "You're often aware," commented the poet Giovita Scalvini, "that you are not under the great firmament that covers all multiform existence, but rather under the roof of the temple that covers the faithful and the altar." "I'm glad you enjoyed Manzoni's Christian novel," Leopardi wrote to his father, unimpressed. But arguably it was exactly this determinedly orthodox Catholic aspect of *The Betrothed* that, together with its linguistic achievement, guaranteed its centrality in Italian culture. Aside from a brief interlude during the revolutions of 1848, the Vatican had been implacably opposed to Italian political unity, knowing that it could come only at the expense of the sovereignty of the Papal State. Patriotism and religious loyalty were set at loggerheads, causing a deep wound at the core of Italian identity. After unification, the Church forbade Catholics from participating in political elections, and would refuse to recognize the Italian state until the Lateran Pacts with Mussolini in 1929. In these circumstances, the existence of a substantial, beautifully written novel that was at once wholeheartedly Catholic yet clearly patriotic in its sympathies, entirely suitable, in its chasteness, decorum and gentle, wry humour, to be taught to the children of those on both sides of the political divide, was a precious instrument of social consensus. It is not that other fine novels were not written in the Risorgimento period. Ippolito Nievo's 900-page *Confessions of an Italian*, written in the 1850s and published posthumously in 1867, is a marvellous, picaresque account of the first decades of the century. But it teems with lively north-eastern regionalisms, and is raucous, provocatively liberal and sexually explicit – not qualities suitable for the classroom, which is where *The Betrothed* is now mainly (if not exclusively) read.

GIACOMO LEOPARDI

(1798–1837)

Is Literary Glory
Worth Chasing?

Is writing worth it? Does it make any sense at all to pursue literary glory? Are the writers we praise really the best anyway?

In 1824, the Italian poet and philosopher Giacomo Leopardi decided to take on the subject in a thirty-page essay, of kinds. In fact, he puts his reflections somewhat playfully in the mouth of Giuseppe Parini, perhaps the finest Italian poet of the eighteenth century, a man from a poor family who spent all his life seeking financial and political protection in the homes of the aristocracy. Leopardi imagines Parini – "one of the very few Italians of our times who combined literary excellence with depth of thought" – responding to an exceptionally talented and ambitious young writer seeking advice. What follows here is nothing more than a brief summary of what he says. I take no responsibility for the ideas expressed. Readers can decide for themselves how much of this rings true today.

Young man, literary glory, or the fame that comes from learning and then writing, is one of the very few forms of glory presently available to the commoner. Admittedly, it's not as impressive or satisfying as the glory that derives from public service, since action is much worthier and nobler than thinking or writing, and more natural. We weren't made to spend our lives sitting at a table with pen and paper, and doing so can only be detrimental to your health and happiness. All the same, as I said, this is a glory that can be achieved without initial riches and without being part of a large organization.

Theoretically.

In reality, the obstacles are many and daunting. Let's leave aside the rivalries, envy, calumny, bias, intrigues and malice you're bound to come across. And, likewise, mere misfortune. The truth is, even without enemies and bad luck, it's perfectly possible to write wonderful books and be denied glory, while more mediocre authors are universally admired. Here's why.

First, only a tiny minority of people are able to judge great literature. Since literary achievement depends largely on style, and style is intimately tied to language, anyone who isn't a native speaker won't be able to appreciate the immense efforts you've put into developing a refined style. So that puts most of mankind out of the picture. Then those who do share your language will have to have put in the same effort that you have if they're going to enjoy your achievements. Only people who have learnt to write well themselves can really judge writing. There are only two or three such experts in Italy today, and don't imagine the situation is much better in other countries.

Second, perception of literary achievement is very largely a question of celebrity. I am convinced, for example, that the reverence felt for the best writers of the past mostly comes from blind tradition rather than individual judgement. We enjoy the classics in part for their celebrity as classics, the same way we admire a princess to a degree because she's a princess. A poem as good as the *Iliad*, written today, would not give the pleasure of the *Iliad*. We wouldn't feel the warmth of its centuries-old celebrity. Similarly, if we were to read a great classic without knowing it was a great classic, it wouldn't please us so much.

This makes things tough for a new book by a really serious author. Without the assurance that they're reading a classic, most readers prefer coarse and obvious beauties to real quality, and special effects to substance. So the success of a truly fine new writer, when it does miraculously happen, will be more the result of accident than merit. You need a lucky break to overcome the obstacles.

Because we've barely begun.

Obstacle three. It's not enough to have your work read by the handful of people capable of admiring it. You have to get them on a good day. Literary judgements, alas, depend on the effect of a book on an individual mind, not on any inherent or scientifically demonstrable quality in the book. So even the best critics may miss the point, especially if you've done something new. Even the critics who could get it may simply be in the wrong mood. Perhaps they just read something else that deeply impressed them and took them in a different direction. Or they may be dealing with personal issues that distract them. Pleasure in art is intermittent. One day the critic is super-receptive, on a high, full of enthusiasm. So he finds himself enjoying, and thus, of course, praising, something entirely mediocre, having mistaken his positive feelings for some quality in the book. Another day, he's dull and unreceptive, he can't see your book's genius – but being in a dull mood won't stop him judging it! As dull. We all have days when even the best classics seem a great bore. But we don't write them off because everybody agrees they're great classics. With a new book, we feel free to be as harsh as we want.

So sound literary judgement is an elusive animal. This without even mentioning the onset of age and mental decline, which is bound at some point to cloud the mind of the famous critic, whose judgements will nevertheless continue to be taken seriously for an awfully long time.

Nor will pessimism and scepticism help, even though nothing could be more reasonable or more grounded in reality than pessimism and scepticism. Readers have to have a certain baseline optimism in order to appreciate a book. They have to believe that greatness and beauty are possible and that what is poetic in the world is not necessarily all fantasy. Otherwise, nothing is going to impress.

Let's add, in passing, that the buzz of city life is a huge dampener of literary sensibilities – yet, for reasons of convenience and networking, most critics live in the city, and therefore in places of maximum distraction where people in general are more susceptible to fashions than real quality.

But onward, now, to the huge problem of obstacle four. Any literary work staking a serious claim to glory is not going to reveal itself entirely on a first reading. It will be better the second time around. And better still on third and even fourth readings. But who has time for this? The ancients could do it because they had so few books to read.

These days, a writer's lucky if his work's read once. With the mad abundance of books we have today, the only things people will read twice are the things everyone agrees are good. The classics, of course.

To make matters worse, your moderately but not seriously good book tends to work well on first reading. It's superficial, smart, fun. And when we have as many books coming at us as we do today, this is exactly what most people want: something that leaps to the eye, something right in your face, not the hard-earned subtleties of the dedicated stylist. However, a first reading will already give you everything this kind of book has to offer. Pick it up again and it's a bore. And this puts readers off second readings in general.

But why do the best books require a second reading? Because fine literature is attached to the notion of accruing deep insight for future application, and this takes effort, study even. The pay-off in pleasure comes, eventually. But the vast majority of readers want instant pleasure with no effort, from one superficial book after another. They're not going to admit this, of course. On the contrary, it's important for them to believe the books they read are great literature – it increases their pleasure to believe so. The result is a situation in which writers are praised to high heaven for a couple of months, then swept away. If a fine book is appreciated on first reading, it won't get a second, so can't put down roots in the culture, and soon enough sinks with the rest.

Who stays afloat, you ask, amid this general shipwreck of the moderns? Got it: the classics.

Finally, obstacle five. A work of great literature, like a great work of philosophy, will have something profoundly new about it. Some new insight, new attitude, new position with regard to the human condition or to present times, the result of deep reflection. But the crowd wants to be confirmed and reassured in the opinions its members collectively hold. They want surface novelty, not revolution, old ideas glossily repackaged. They take refuge in their numbers. Over time, little by little, they may come to change their opinions, and even endorse ideas diametrically opposed to those they held before. But for the most part, they won't notice this has happened. There won't be a moment where they say, "Hey, I'm wrong, I need to change my position." On the contrary, they will feel a deep suspicion and antipathy towards someone who lives, thinks and feels differently than they do. Our author seeking glory, for example. They can't understand. They feel provoked. The more we live in the age of the herd, the less likely great literature (and, above all, the recognition of great literature) becomes.

But enough of the obstacles! Let's imagine that, despite everything, you've somehow made it. You've achieved literary glory. You've done it thanks to the most serious literary achievement – and you've done it in your lifetime. Bravo!

What do you actually get out of it?

Well, people will want to see you and know you, to come and admire you in the flesh. Of course, if you live in a big city, they will also be wanting to know and admire all the impostors who have won the same celebrity with quite mediocre works extravagantly overpraised. So you may not be impressed by the company you're keeping. And if you live out in the provinces, people will very likely have no notion of literary glory at all. Writing? I could have done that perfectly well myself, if I'd had time, if I'd wanted to turn my mind to it. You'll get a lot of this.

Only a handful of people will really appreciate what you've done, so that, in general, it's hard to think of a commodity that comes at a higher price and brings fewer benefits than literary glory.

In response, you'll withdraw into solitude. You'll try to believe that the work itself is sufficient reward for your efforts. It isn't. Then, since we all have to have something to hope for in the future, you'll start to seek consolation in the notion that posterity will finally give you the true recognition you deserve. I'll live on in the minds of generations to come, you tell yourself. But honestly, there's no guarantee of this. Why should those who come after us be any better or any more receptive and perceptive than our contemporaries? On the contrary, the world will most likely have moved on and people won't have any time for you at all.

I'm sorry. I see impatience on your face. You want my final word on this. The decision of a lifetime: should you give up or should you go on striving for it – for literary glory? My straightforward opinion?

Well, without wanting to flatter, let me say that I do see who you are and what you might do. Your mind is wonderfully sharp; your heart, your imagination, are young and warm and full of ideas; you're deeply sensitive, noble even. These qualities can only bring you suffering and pain. But really, there's nothing you can do about that. You are who you are. So just as some unfortunate people, deformed and handicapped at birth, learn to make the most of their disabilities, using them to arouse pity and generosity, you might as well put your qualities to work and go for the one goal, however uncertain and unrewarding, that they're possibly good for: literary glory.

After all, most people actually envy these personal qualities of yours. They don't see that, if they had them themselves, they wouldn't be able to live as sensibly as they do, acting only as the times allow and enjoying themselves as much as they can. A serious writer, on the other hand, will be giving up all kinds of pleasures and living a life that looks like death to most people, all for a sup-posed life, maybe, after his death, courtesy of some improbable posterity. But there you are, this is the card fate has dealt you. You owe it to yourself to give it all the enthusiasm and courage you have!

*   *   *

Such is the advice that, nearly two centuries ago, Leopardi put in the mouth of Giuseppe Parini, addressing a young person of talent who doubtless must have gone away deeply perplexed. One notes in passing that the piece was written a few years too early for the poet to have appreciated the immensely damaging effects of literary promotion, hype, political correctness, creative-writing courses and global publication strategies. In 1862, Victor Hugo was to receive one of the largest advances ever for *Les Misérables*. It should be sold, he advised his publishers, stressing its championing of the poor and moral goodness, with translations prepared for simultaneous publications in a number of countries and aggressive poster campaigns in all major cities. Such high jinks, no doubt, Leopardi would have put down as obstacle number six. Or six, seven and eight. Depending on how he parsed it.

GIACOMO LEOPARDI
(1798–1837)

A Sublime Bearer of Bad Tidings

Imagine you spend your childhood almost entirely in a library, your father's library. There are thousands upon thousands of volumes, most of them old, many in foreign languages. Your native language is Italian, but by age ten you are reading in Latin, Greek, German and French. English and Hebrew are next on the list.

Why are you doing this? Your father is ambitious for his first-born son. He wants you to be a priest. At twelve you receive the tonsure, meaning your hair is cut like a monk's to dedicate you to God. You are dressed in a cassock. More than a priest, or even a bishop, your father wants you to be a champion of Christianity, a theologian: you will use your learning to refute false doctrines, liberalism, atheism.

Your progress is astonishing. At fourteen, your tutors tell you they have nothing more to teach you. Left to your own devices, you limber up with translations from the classics, philological commentaries, philosophical dissertations, tragedies, epigrams, *A History of Astronomy* and a *Life of Plotinus*, until, at age seventeen, you embark on your first major work: an *Essay on the Popular Errors of the Ancients*. "The world is full of errors," you write in the opening line, "and man's first task must be to know the truth." Your father is delighted. But the truth, as time slips by among the "sweat-stained pages" in the book-lined rooms, is that the more you write about gods and ghosts and mythical monsters, the more attractive these stories begin to seem, especially when compared to the Christian rationality that was supposed to sweep them away.

A crisis is approaching. At some point you look in a mirror and discover your back is crooked. Your youth has been wasted in "seven years of mad and desperate study". Your eyesight is weak, you have asthma, you are constipated. So unlikely are you ever to marry or have children that your younger brother is declared heir to the family estate. You have lost your birthright. But, most of all, you think too much. "Thinking about how one breathes", you find you can hardly breathe. "Thinking and ruminating on the act of urination", you find you can't urinate. "Thought," you later reflect, "can crucify... a person."

How can you know that it is precisely this insight into the dangers of compulsive thinking, the psychosomatic nature of your ills and the hubris of grand philosophical systems that will make you so important to readers two hundred years hence?

In any event, you don't want arid erudition any more: you want poetry. So you translate the *Odyssey* and the *Aeneid*, and even start to write poems yourself. You will call this your "literary conversion". It is followed at eighteen by your "political conversion". Suddenly you turn against your father's support of papal power and absolutist monarchies, and become a patriot and a liberal. You want Italy to be united and free. You want revolution. And you start writing patriotic hymns. Your father is appalled. But the real bombshell arrives at twenty-one: your "philosophical conversion". All at once it's obvious to you that Christianity is as much an "error" as believing in Zeus or Apollo. Because the world is "a solid nothing". It has no meaning and no direction.

So what on earth are you going to do now?

The you of this story, as any Italian schoolchild would immediately recognize, is the great poet and thinker Giacomo Leopardi. The place is Recanati, a small town near the Adriatic coast south of Ancona, then part of the Papal States. The time is the early nineteenth century. Leopardi was born in 1798 and completed his three "conversions" in 1819. So in one of the most neglected areas of perhaps the most backward and reactionary state in Europe, a young man arrived at the conclusions that were then driving the early writings of Arthur Schopenhauer and would later underlie the works of Friedrich Nietzsche, of twentieth-century existentialism and absurdism, of Samuel Beckett and Albert Camus, Thomas Bernhard and Emil Cioran.

Trained all his life to pursue knowledge, Leopardi's simple intuition was that, once found, it did not help you to live. On the contrary, it brought despair. And once learnt, it could not be unlearnt. His enormous contribution, in the eighteen years that remained to him, would be to explore this modern, godless state of mind in all its ramifications and implications, to reflect on how it had come about, and to look for strategies on how to live with it. In an age when so many people, particularly young people, are at a loss to give life meaning and direction, Leopardi is essential reading. "No one," Schopenhauer would observe, had handled the theme of life as "tragic farce" so "thoroughly and exhaustively" as Leopardi. Yet he did so "in such a multiplicity of forms and applications, with such wealth of imagery, that he never wearies us, but, on the contrary, is throughout entertaining and exciting".

Boredom and inertia, Leopardi understood at once, would be the arch-enemy of a world freed, or bereft, of all illusions, all belief. "If I were to go mad this moment," he writes in 1819, "I think my madness would be always sitting with my eyes wide with bewilderment... neither laughing nor crying, never moving from where I was unless forced.... This is the first time boredom hasn't merely oppressed and wearied me, but actually plagues and racks me like a terrible pain."

How did the heroes of the past do what they did, he wondered? How did anyone find the will to achieve anything? Illusion. They were driven by beliefs that were demonstrably vain, by the very errors he had trained himself to smell out and deconstruct. On the other hand, how wonderful to believe in such things and to act with energy and intention! No sooner had Leopardi undergone his philosophical (essentially nihilist) conversion than his thinking began to revolve around this central paradox: one studied and educated oneself under an imperative to find the truth, but to live a happy life, which necessarily meant a purposeful, active life, one needed to be impelled by illusion, not truth, or certainly not ultimate, philosophical truths.

So was "illusion" a positive quality? And was it actually better not to know things, at least certain things? In his first major, but very brief poem, 'The Infinite', written in 1819, the poet, sitting on a hillside, rejoices in the fact that his view is mostly blocked by a hedge. Not seeing the landscape he can imagine all kinds of things out there beyond the hedge, imagine the infinite, and hence write poetry, something he would not be able to do if he saw the landscape plainly. Freed of a stream of hard information, the imagination is stimulated, which is a pleasure. "All that is fixed and certain," he commented in his diary, "is much further from contenting us than that which, by its very uncertainty, can never content us." Vagueness has a value in itself. One hundred and fifty years later, the great aphorist Emil Cioran would have this text framed and hang it in his Paris apartment.

What rapidly began to accumulate, in a diary Leopardi called his *Zibaldone* (meaning "commonplace book"), was a vast psychological study of how man in the past, individually and collectively, had defended himself from existential emptiness, and at the same time an exploration of how in the present it might be possible both to know the truth about life, yet still to cultivate illusion and so find the impetus needed to live. Crass as it may seem, there was a self-help impetus behind his thinking. "I wish the best for my species," he wrote laconically. In fact, he was the poet most read by Italian troops in the misery of the First World War trenches.

The key to a positive state of mind, Leopardi soon decided, might lie in inducing a temporary forgetfulness. In 'To a Winner in the Ball Games', written in 1821, the poet watches a game of *pallone col bracciale*, a traditional team sport, and likens its impassioned players to the heroes of ancient times: "Has human effort / Ever been but a game?" he wonders. "Is truth any less / Empty than falsehood?" In the absence of nobler beliefs, the absurd notion that it might be of supreme importance to win a game of football is offered as a solution, albeit temporary, to existential crisis:

What's life for? To be despised:
Blessed then when by danger
Beset, it forgets itself, doesn't measure
The damage or heed the flow
Of slow and putrid hours –
Blessed when the foot,
Pushed to the ultimate limit,
Comes back the happier.

There could be no sport for Leopardi. Almost an invalid and with no private income, he was trapped in Recanati with his reactionary father and an ultra-Christian, penny-pinching mother, who had no intention of paying for her son to travel to the centres of learning, where he might be corrupted and fall into sin. "I once knew very well the mother of a family," Leopardi remarked in a thinly veiled autobiographical note, "who was not in the least superstitious, but devout and unswerving in her Christian faith and in the practice of her religion." Believing that the only thing that mattered was getting to heaven, this mother deliberately talked down her children's capacities and ambitions, to help them avoid the sin of pride, and "sincerely envied" parents who lost their children young, "because such infants had flown safe and sound to paradise, and had freed their parents from the inconvenience of supporting them". An illusion like Christianity, Leopardi concluded, could be genuinely comforting, until you started to apply systematic reason to it, after which it could only lead to aberration and disaster.

In an extraordinary paragraph that attacks the core of Western thinking from Plato onwards, he suggests that man had been happier in a distant past trusting the truth of direct but always relative experience, and ran into trouble only when he went looking for metaphysical absolutes. "We were fine just as we were... But we have sought out the good as a thing separate from our own essence, distinct from our own natural and original intellective capacity, as a thing consisting of abstractions and of universal forms." All too often the end result was persecution and torture.

In November 1822 Leopardi finally managed to leave home for Rome, where he stayed with an uncle, met other philologists, academics and clerics and looked for some kind of work. But he hated Rome. He found his interlocutors pompous and crass, and realized at once that it had been an illusion to imagine that travel might cure his despair. "All the greatness of Rome," he wrote to his sister Paolina, "has no other purpose than to multiply the distances and numbers of steps you have to climb to see anyone at all." "The ugliest, crassest Recanati tart was better than all the streetwalkers of Rome," he informed his brother. In April 1823 he was already back home. Years later he remembered, "When I went to Rome, the need to live with others, to give myself outwardly... made me stupid, inept and dead inwardly... I lost almost all self-esteem and all hope of... achieving anything in my life."

Self-esteem, Leopardi now reasoned, would be one of the most crucial of illusions for modern man, and something we all need help with. The English and French, he noticed, had an unwarrantedly high opinion of themselves, something that sustained their collective self-regard and created a shared sense of complacency. The Italians on the contrary had a very low opinion of each other, with each person trying to build up his or her own self-esteem by talking down others. Public conversation in general in Italy, he decided after the trip to Rome, was little more than "raillery and insult". At this absolute low point of his life, Leopardi set about turning the very exploration of despair into his salvation. First in poetry, then in a series of prose pieces known as the *Operette morali*, or *Moral Fables*.

The strategy of his finest poems is simultaneously to dramatize some absolutely inconsolable fact of private loss or tragedy, yet redeem it, as least aesthetically, by turning the narrative savouring of catastrophe into a pleasure, a wondering over the individual's capacity to feel and suffer and transform that suffering through language, an achievement that then becomes a source of self-esteem and encouragement for both writer and reader. In 'The Dream' the poet is visited by "the girl who first taught me what love is, then left me in tears". "Are you alive?" she asks. "Do you remember anything about us?" She herself is dead, she says. The poet is appalled. She died young:

> Cut off in the flower of my years
> When life is sweetest, and before the heart
> Can know how human hopes are all
> In vain.

While the history of their relationship is left absolutely vague, and hence intriguing, the anguished conversation between the two unfolds with crisp colloquial directness, but in a style that is curiously archaic, as if heard across a vast divide of time that, as it were, silvers the underlying hopelessness. "Works of genius, have this quality," Leopardi commented in his diary, "that even when they capture exactly the nothingness of things or vividly reveal and make us feel life's inevitable unhappiness, or express the most acute hopelessness... they are always a source of consolation and renewed enthusiasm." "Momentarily," he adds. Elsewhere, he reflects that one might expect a poem to induce this state of mind "for about half an hour". What makes Leopardi superior to so many other thinkers and poets is his refusal to deceive himself about the power of art and aesthetic consolation. Managing despair is a day job. Never imagine the problem is solved.

In the *Moral Fables*, written in 1824, whimsy and irony stand in for lyricism. The book opens with a 'History of the Human Race' that has Jove first inventing an easy, painless, rather restricted life for man, then constantly having to make changes in response to his creature's tendency to feel bored and dissatisfied. Natural phenomena are multiplied and diversified, different climates and races are introduced, new desires and ambitions are stimulated, and with them the concept of work and achievement. Eventually, illness is conjured up to give man something to overcome and a reason for feeling happy for the mere fact of good health. But none of this is enough. Men are "avid for the infinite, but incapable of it". Irritated by their endless whining, Jove finally lets the human race have what it has always been clamouring for: truth. He knows it will be devastating.

So the content is grim, but the form full of fun. As in the best of Borges's *Fictions*, we amuse ourselves with our tremendous predicament. Atlas and Hercules play ball with the world and drop it. An elf and a gnome discuss the extinction of the human race and agree that the planet is better off without it. Fashion and Death, who turn out to be sisters, debate which of the two is the most usefully destructive. A progressive academy that believes in the betterment of man offers three prizes for breakthrough inventions: a robotic best friend to build up the owner's self-esteem, a steam-driven man to perform "virtuous and magnanimous deeds" (since no one else will) and an ideal woman along the lines drawn up by Baldassarre Castiglione in *The Courtier*.

Essentially, Leopardi is creating a playful mythology, whimsical illusions that nevertheless deliver the truth that sweeps aside all illusion. The operation is all the more engaging for the multitude of sly references to Greek and Christian myth that allow the reader to feel pleased with himself for recognizing them, while nevertheless swallowing the bitter pill: life is empty and absurd. In 'Copernicus' the Sun suddenly decides he is fed up of turning round the Earth and asks the philosopher to inform the planet that if it wants to go on enjoying evenly distributed light and warmth it will have to do the turning itself from now on. Copernicus is hesitant: the change might be possible, he says, but the fact is that with the Earth fixed and the other planets all orbiting around it, man, despite his misery, has been able to imagine himself the centre of the universe and the acme of creation. Reduce the Earth to spinning around like any other planet and man will lose his self-importance and be left with just his misery. Not to worry, the Sun tells Copernicus, if they don't like the new situation, men will have no problem living in denial and *imagining* they are still the masters of the universe anyway. Then who cares what men think? So Leopardi satirizes human delusions of grandeur, but simultaneously reminds us how attractive it was to think of the Sun being pulled across the sky by a chariot, and how uninspiring is our mechanistic knowledge of the universe. If our condition is dire, we do have our imagination, he suggests, which we dismiss in favour of scientific fact at our peril.

These antithetical energies in Leopardi's vision, at once unmasking illusion and regretting its loss, inevitably led to conflicting responses to his work. His poems, where the underlying nihilism could be overlooked in favour of their extraordinary lyrical intensity, were soon loved and admired. But in the *Moral Fables* the poet's atheist message and his mockery of all science-driven optimism were inescapable. Rather than being moral, the stories destroyed all morality, observed one judge of Italy's main literary prize in 1830. Needless to say, Leopardi didn't win that prize, and he knew why: "The perpetual and total denial of the vanity of things," he wrote, was an obligation in society: how else could people trick reason and sustain their illusions? In short, no one wants a bearer of bad tidings.

One of the fables, describing the life of an imaginary philosopher, begins "Filippo Ottonieri... lived most of his life in Nubiana ['Cloudland']... where there is no memory of his ever having injured anyone, in word or deed. He was generally hated by his fellow citizens..." Hated simply because he didn't like what they liked, didn't share their opinions, hence became a threat to their collective denial. And as the illusions on which society was based became more fragile, Leopardi goes on to suggest, insistence on conformity can only increase. It's hard not to appreciate his clairvoyance in this regard, and when he has Ottonieri claim that one can measure the extent of a society's civilization by the diversity of opinion it is willing to countenance, we can't help feeling our modern times stand condemned.

The poet departed Recanati again in 1825, living first in Milan, then Bologna, where the papal authorities refused him a job because of his ideas, then Florence, then Pisa. Working freelance for publishers, he was always short of money, his health always poor. Three times he fell in love and each time had to recognize that for him this was the most unlikely illusion of all. "My dear, he stank," was how the last object of his affections explained her refusal of the poet. "Now you'll rest for ever, worn-out heart," Leopardi wrote in the late poem 'To himself'. "The ultimate illusion that I thought was eternal died. It died."

Even more galling than being denied work for his subversive ideas was the constant insinuation that his negative thinking was merely the result of his twisted spine and poor health – based, what's more, claimed the Catholic critic Niccolò Tommaseo, not on reason but on a few "incomplete observations". "I wish it were so," Leopardi replied to his publisher, who had told him of the remark. He added new pieces to the *Fables* to counter the criticism, but knew it would stick. "Two truths that most men will never believe," he remarked in his diary in 1832. "One that they know nothing, the other that they are nothing. Add the third, which depends a lot on the second: that they have nothing to hope for after death." Again, he proved clairvoyant. Although Leopardi has always been read in Italy, and although in recent years English and American publishers have at last retranslated and republished all his work, there remains a resistance to his thinking. Perhaps the time has come, though, when we are so genuinely used to the bad news which is Leopardi's premise that we can now begin to appreciate the strategies for survival he developed to deal with that news.

In 1833 he moved with a friend to Naples, living in poverty and giving up any attempt to become part of literary society, even discontinuing his diary, as if that too had been an illusion. In 1836 he wrote his last great poem, 'The Broom, or the Flower of the Desert'. Walking on the slopes of Vesuvius where a whole civilization had been buried under burning lava, he takes comfort in the scent and yellow flowers of the broom. Soon we realize that the shrub is an image of Leopardi's own endeavour: it thrives on the destruction of man's illusions, but without any pretensions to immortality, quite resigned to being swept away itself by the next lava flow. All the same, it does adorn "this abandoned countryside with fragrant bushes". The poem was published posthumously in 1845, Leopardi having departed this world aged thirty-nine in 1837.

Why read Leopardi now? And what Leopardi? If you're feeling robust enough for a major reality check, go to the *Moral Fables*: nobody will tell you more truthfully the predicament you are in, or put such a big smile on your face as he does it. If you want the company of someone who thought long and hard outside the box about almost every aspect of human behaviour, mental life and language, get the huge *Zibaldone* and keep it by your bedside. If, finally and unhappily, you are facing a personal crisis or suffering some tremendous loss, Leopardi's poetry is waiting for you. It is telling that Iris Origo, who wrote the only biography of the poet available in English, turned to the project soon after the death of her seven-year-old son in 1933. Nobody more than Leopardi could look disaster in the face, never denying that it was disaster, yet at the same time turning unhappiness itself into a colour or fragrance that would help you through the day. For "the recognition of the irredeemable vanity and falsity of all beauty and all greatness is itself a kind of beauty and greatness that fills the soul, when it is conveyed by a work of genius. And the spectacle of nothingness is itself a thing in these works, and seems to enlarge the reader's soul, to raise it up and to make it take satisfaction in itself and its despair."

LITERARY TRIESTE

Worth a Detour

Trieste is hardly on the beaten track for Italophiles. Almost a hundred miles east of Venice and on the wrong side of the Adriatic, it seems to gaze back at the *bel paese* instead of being a part of it. It has no great art galleries, museums or monuments. The weather is notoriously harsh – even identity is a problem: a windswept stone's throw from the Slovenian border, Trieste is home to three distinct ethnic groups: Slav, Germanic and Italian.

"I am Slavic-German-Italian," wrote the writer Scipio Slataper, the first to claim (around 1910) that there was in fact a "Triestine type".

From my Slav blood I have within me strange nostalgias, a desire for novelty, for abandoned forests, a sentimentality (or sensibility) that demands caresses, praises – an infinite, limitless dreaming. From my German blood I have my mulish obstinacy, my dictatorial will and tone, the certainty of my plans, the boredom I feel at having to accept discussion, my desire for domination, for exertion. These elements are fused in the Italian blood, which seeks to harmonize them, to balance them out, to make me become "classical".

The local intellectual Roberto Bazlen was more sceptical: "A melting pot," he writes, "is a utensil into which are put the most disparate elements, which are then melted. What is produced is a homogenous fusion, with all its elements proportionately distributed, with constant characteristics. But in Trieste, as I know it, a fused type has never been produced, nor any type with stable characteristics… And since a unique Triestine type does not exist, so a Triestine creative culture does not exist either."

His contemporary and fellow citizen Giani Stuparich agreed: "There is something in this city of mine that blocks any initiative designed to give it a cultural character of physiognomy, not only in its disintegrative atmosphere, but in its individuals, who willingly isolate themselves or go elsewhere. It has a bitter air…"

Yet in the early years of the twentieth century, the small and troubled town of Trieste was home to three writers who would later be designated "great": Italo Svevo, James Joyce and the poet Umberto Saba.

Of course writers and above all groups of writers tend to encourage mythologies about themselves, their lives and achievements: Gertrude Stein and her school, Ezra Pound, Ernest Hemingway. And readers too are often eager to surround the texts they love with anecdotes, and to attribute remarkable qualities to the authors they admire.

In Trieste, a port city with an uneasy history of difficult allegiances and blurred racial boundaries, the question of identity and ethnicity was bound to play a part in the formation of such mythologies. Hence it's hardly surprising, for example, that both Svevo and Saba are pseudonyms, and that the names should be the starting point for a great deal of literary speculation. Was Ettore Schmitz, alias Italo Svevo, who was educated in German, grew up speaking Triestine dialect, and indeed lived most of his life under Austrian rule, really an Italian writer? Was his style, as some contemporaries suggested, perhaps more Slav than Italian? Would he have done better, as Umberto Poli, alias Umberto Saba, thought, to have written in German? And did Saba's own problems of identity (he changed pseudonyms more than once) arise not only out of the early desertion of his father, but partly from the curiously mixed ethnic origins of the Jewish mother and aunts and the Slovenian nurse who brought him up, and from the uncertain identity of a city he was so determined should be Italian? Finally, could it have been precisely the uneasiness of this local situation and the fierce desire of the local people to be liberated from an imperial power that made the Irish exile, Joyce, feel at home in Trieste for ten long years?

These are questions that loom large in Joseph Cary's book *A Ghost in Trieste*. Behind them lies that more general but ever intriguing conundrum: how much does the spirit of a particular place at a particular time inform and shape the novels and poems written there, and how could such influence be measured and savoured?

Yet Cary's book is slow to home in on its subject. As a guide and critic he proceeds on the principle that indirections will eventually find directions out, and although some of the consequent meandering does have its charm, it must be said that much is sentimental and self-regarding. "I went to Trieste because I hoped to find my business there," he tells us in his "Preliminary" chapter.

A notion for a book, *Literary Trieste*, was in my head, and I felt that going there would translate this notion into a clear and spurring idea...

I drew a beautiful equilateral triangle in my notebook and wrote "Trieste 1905–15" beneath it. Trieste was the key.

All too soon, however, he discovers that Trieste is a modern town which in many ways resembles many others, that Joyce and Svevo's relationship was not after all very much more than that between young language teacher and older pupil, that Svevo met Saba only rarely and with no more than tepid cordiality, and that Saba, so far as we know, never met Joyce at all. His desire for an easy mythology, or literary salon, to exhume so immediately thwarted, Cary then embarks on pages of wistful self-irony which tell us little about either Trieste or the writers whose relation to the city we are interested in, and rather more than we would wish to know about his sense of himself as travel writer manqué:

In the Cinema Eden I sat through *101 Dalmatians* wondering what they made of it in Dalmatia. Ghost-wise I petered past as a pretty blonde peered through a crack in the green canvas at a tennis match on the court behind Villa Necker. For hours and hours, the louvres of my darkened hotel room cut street-lamp light into thin orange stripes across the ceiling. They rippled when a car passed.

Finally, it occurs to him to see himself as a ghost wandering through Trieste in search of an ever elusive literary past, a quaint image but hardly an encouraging one for those of us expecting to hear more of Saba, Svevo and Joyce. At other moments Cary seems to forget his literary interests altogether:

This is a book about Trieste – its curious history, some of its residents, some of my stumbling steps to get a view of it.

How long exactly did this adventure last?

My three weeks in Trieste have been distributed over five years with long intervals at home…

If readers were puzzled by the adjective "beautiful" used to describe the hand-sketched equilateral triangle earlier on, they will no doubt be even more perplexed by that "long intervals at home". More surprising still is the way it does not occur to Cary that to acquire the kind of deep sense of place and local character which might shed some light on the way the city influenced its writers, one might want to stay three months, or three years, rather than three weeks.

One feels bound to mention these irritations, but once Cary has got his self-indulgent comments on travel out of the way and begun to concentrate on the history of the city and the relationship of that history to its artists and writers, then his book becomes fascinating.

We hear of Trieste's early development as a Roman garrison town, its struggle to survive through the Dark Ages, and its unusual decision to offer itself to the Austrian crown in return for protection. We discover that it was the enlightened if never altruistic strategy of successive Austrian emperors that led to the city's rapid development as a southern port for central Europe, to the point where, in the late nineteenth century, it was second only to Marseilles. Most of all, Cary gradually and thoroughly establishes the huge irony that whereas Trieste's economic welfare depended on its connection with Austria and the north, the predominantly Italian identity of its people and the rising tide of nationalism which swept through Europe in the mid-nineteenth century inevitably pushed the city towards union with Italy in the west.

The first decade of the twentieth century, when Joyce and Saba and Svevo were all in the city together, was thus a fascinating one.

Trieste was at the height of its commercial success, but the very energy generated by that wealth went to feed a passionate Italian nationalism which, in achieving its end, would ultimately destroy the city's prosperity by cutting it off from Austria and its hinterland. Cary is at his best here in patching together an excellent series of quotations showing how artists, poets and novelists reflected this nationalism in their writing. From Giosuè Carducci through the predictably flamboyant D'Annunzio, the rumbustious critic Scipio Slataper and futurist Filippo Tommaso Marinetti, what is extraordinary is the vehemence, eloquence and, sometimes, even the wit with which this nationalism was expressed. Slataper, who died fighting on the Austrian-Italian frontier in 1915, is particularly impressive when he describes Trieste's discovery of its national and cultural identity as that of an ingenuous young Parsifal

who awakened one day between a crate of lemons and a sack of coffee beans thinking that, for his own good, he ought to modulate his life to another rhythm than that of a snorting or puffing engine, treat it to another melody than that of silver clinking in the pockets of some capacious waistcoat.

That is, he should look to Italy. Marinetti, on the other hand, is merely frightening. In the amazingly titled *War, Sole Hygiene of the Western World* (1910), he apostrophizes Trieste as follows:

> You are the scarlet, violent face of Italy, turned towards the enemy!... Trieste! You are our sole shield!... Do not forget, O Trieste, that the Italian peninsula has the form of a *dreadnought*, with a squadron of torpedo-boat islands.

The passage vaguely echoes D'Annunzio's notorious ode *To a Torpedo Boat in the Adriatic*, written almost twenty years earlier:

> Steel ship, straight, swift, flashing
> beautiful as a naked weapon,
> alive, palpitant
> as though metal enclosed a terrible heart...

By the end of the poem D'Annunzio leaves us in no doubt that that naked weapon is pointed in the very specific direction of Trieste. But it is not so much the warmongering of the literary intelligentsia that is surprising and sobering here as the realization that only a hundred years ago European culture was still based primarily on the written word, and a poet could still see himself as having a formidable, central and immediate political part to play. Just a few years before the movies would become ubiquitous, a few decades before television, the time of Joyce and Saba and Svevo in Trieste marked the last years of the word as unrivalled manipulator of public feeling. As if in a last homage to that power, or demonstration of the prophetic and political vocation of the poet, the transfer of Trieste from Austrian to Italian sovereignty was effectively confirmed by the arrival in the port of the torpedo boat *Audacious*.

So much for the fervid literary and political scene. But what makes a reading of Cary's carefully chosen quotes so intriguing is a growing awareness of the absence of any contribution from Joyce,

Saba or Svevo. True, Joyce, while in Trieste, gave one or two lectures on Irish history, where clear parallels were drawn between Britain and Austria as imperial oppressors. True, Svevo remarked that it was the coming of Italy to Trieste that gave him the inspiration to write his last and greatest novel, *La coscienza di Zeno*. True, Saba later spoke of having "married [Trieste] to Italy for ever with my song", but he was clearly speaking more of having been the first to write poetry on the city in a "proper" Tuscan Italian than of having contributed to nationalist propaganda. For the fact is that none of these writers had anything at all to say in their creative work about the political issues that were exciting the other writers round about them.

In his indirect style Cary thus appears to stumble on the central point of his book when remarking that a literary history of Trieste and Istria, written in 1924 by a professor at the newly established University of Trieste, includes neither Saba nor Svevo. Cary comments: "It is the total absence of *anima patria* in the novels of Svevo… and in the poetry of Saba… that accounts for their absence from the pages of *Storia letteraria di Trieste e dell'Istria*."

Exactly. One begins to see that it was the creative isolation of these three writers that distinguishes them. For all their living in a very particular place at a very particular moment, they had nothing in common with the local literary scene and very little in common with each other. For Joyce, the most important thing about Trieste, surely, was that it was not Dublin. He arrived there by accident. He found he was able to borrow money and to work (teaching English). It was enough. He was obsessed with words, with style, with the extent to which words can evoke a world, create a world, many worlds, including the Dublin he never wanted to live in again. To a very great extent he must have lived in that world of words (as in another way he never left Dublin). Svevo's description of his teacher, written as an English homework assignment, is pertinent here:

When I see him walking on the street I always think that he is enjoying a leisure, a full leisure. Nobody is awaiting him, and he does not want to reach an aim or to meet anybody. No! He walks in order to be left to himself. He also does not walk for health. He walks because he is not stopped by anything. I imagine that if he would find his way barred by a high and big wall he would not be shocked in the least. He would change direction, and if the new direction would also prove not to be clear he would change it again...

Thus when Trieste was closed to Joyce with the arrival of the First World War, he continued his walks in Zurich, and later Paris. Nor is there any indication that leaving Trieste affected his writing. If Molly could say of Leopold just before she decided to take him, "well, as well him as another", certainly Joyce could have said the same of the cities he lived in after he left Dublin.

For Svevo, on the other hand, as Cary sensibly points out, Trieste was merely home, a place he had no particular quarrel with, a place above all for work. If the city comes through at all in his novels, which despite being set in Trieste hardly ever mention or describe it, it is in the world of work, the commerce that all his characters are involved in, as indeed was Svevo himself. The observation points up the wonderful irony underlying the now traditional linking of Joyce and Svevo's names. For the two could hardly have been more different: the Irishman living in Trieste but meticulously describing, re-creating his home town of Dublin, the Triestine happily at home but apparently uninterested in the city around him. Joyce the avant-garde aesthete, the stylist par excellence, was searching for new techniques, new games, new languages. Svevo, for his part, is quite embarrassingly inept as a stylist, to the point where, on reading him in Italian one occasionally has to look at a sentence very hard indeed before understanding it, and this is not because of some effect the writer was aiming for, but out of sheer clumsiness.

Was this perhaps the essential aspect of the Triestine influence on Svevo, this writing in a language that was not truly his own? Certainly of all the serious novelists I have read Svevo seems the least interested in drawing on the resources of language to enrich his vision. Rather, Italian is a medium he uses as best he can to get across a brilliantly comic and perceptive succession of thoughts and actions that continuously unravel the perversity of his characters. When Joyce apparently told Svevo that "there are passages in *Senilità* that even Anatole France could not have improved", he was either lying (to flatter) or simply had not appreciated why he liked the book, or his words have been misreported. And if *La coscienza di Zeno* is Svevo's best book, it is perhaps because by adopting the first person he makes the clumsiness of his Italian, and the constant strain in it, a reflection of Zeno's own curious mix of effort and buffoonery, the confusion of a man who tries so hard, and so hopelessly, to be morally healthy. The final irony, however, of all the criticism of Svevo's Italian is that he is now by far the most readable, particularly in translation, of all his Italian contemporaries. Their D'Annunzian grandiloquence seems so egregious beside his simple, if sometimes awkward, dispatch.

Umberto Saba, a lyric poet who moved to Florence precisely to improve his Italian, but then wrote many of his poems about Trieste and eventually returned to live there, is a very different, perhaps even "opposite" case. Towards the end of his book Cary offers translations of extracts from the writers he has talked about, plus two of Joyce's *Pomes Penyeach*, translated by Montale. One is struck how well Svevo and Slataper come across, how badly Saba. "Poetry," as Paul Celan said, "is the fatal uniqueness of language" – and for Saba the exact register and semantic range of each word, the exact rhythm of the line and arrangement of the syntax, are all important. Read in the Italian, which Cary wisely leaves alongside, the spareness and hard-earned intensity of his verse is immediately apparent. Transferred into a would-be poetic English, it disappears. (In contrast, Saba's fine prose writings come across excellently in the 1993 volume *The Stories and Recollections of Umberto Saba*, translated by Estelle Gilson.) The subject of the poems Cary chooses is Trieste, its streets, its bars, its people, but one soon appreciates that the city is above all a mirror for the poet's mood, a source of consolation for his suffering, material for the constant reinvention of that wisely dying fall which is Saba's voice.

Apart from the space and time of Trieste and Triestine politics in the early twentieth century, there is also of course the less provincial, if more elusive, world of ideas, of changing aesthetics and literary movements. So, as Cary remarks towards the end of his book, each of the three writers was more influenced by, and influencing of, incipient literary modernism than the city they lived in. "Conscience", or the Italian catch-all, "*coscienza*", are useful words here. In his poetic manifesto, *Quello che resta da fare ai poeti*, Saba speaks of the poet's responsibility as lying precisely in *coscienza*, his "moral awakeness", as Cary puts it, his determination to write nothing and use no technique that is not profoundly felt. Hence the hard-won precision of his language, the difficulty of translation.

Svevo, on the other hand, in *La coscienza di Zeno*, seems to be engaged above all in revealing, sincerely, the impossibility of such sincerity. Every resolution his hero makes is immediately overwhelmed by an opposing appetite, every appetite is thwarted by moral awareness. In this tragicomic demonstration language need not be precise – on the contrary all the better if, being the writer's second language, it is inherently mendacious. Commenting on his analyst's ingenuousness in imagining his confessions sincere, the hyper-conscious Zeno remarks: "With every Tuscan word we use we lie. If he knew how much we enjoy saying those things we know the words for and how we avoid anything that would oblige us to resort to the dictionary!"

Meanwhile, Joyce was inventing his "stream of consciousness", amorally following thoughts wherever they and language would lead, during his Trieste walks perhaps. Behind all three writers one can't help feeling the presence of their near contemporary, Freud. Svevo translated him and presented *Zeno* as an exercise in self-analysis.

Saba got himself analysed, discovered all about his identity crisis and dedicated a book of poems to his analyst. Joyce pooh-poohed Freud and confirmed his importance in almost everything he wrote. Trieste, as Cary points out, for the obvious reason of its daily commerce with Vienna, was one of the main entry points by which Freud's ideas came to Italy.

GABRIELE D'ANNUNZIO
(1863–1938)

The Virgins

Nothing drives a narrative better than repression. When we hear in Shakespeare's *Measure for Measure* of Angelo's ruthless purity, we are already determined that it be corrupted. This man must be humiliated by lust. Nothing else will satisfy us. When we see a story entitled *The Virgins*, we are tensed for the deflowering. All the stories in this book are essentially tales of awakening, but not the kind that brings enlightenment. Rather, the lucid mind is overwhelmed by a compulsion before which every rule and taboo is suddenly obsolete. A river, usually no more than a distant murmur, has broken its banks. The everyday world is submerged in sensuality, utterly sexualized. Sensory perceptions fantastically enhanced, the will drowns in a flood of feeling.

Transgression is usually taken as a hallmark of vocation in a writer. The poet's sins assure us that he is the real thing. Not so with D'Annunzio. On the rare occasions when he does nudge his way into the Anglo-Saxon consciousness, it is always for the wrong reasons. He is the rabid nationalist who urged Italy to join the First World War. He is the egocentric adventurer whose mad volunteers, in defiance of international law, occupied Fiume on the north Adriatic coast in 1919. He preached the "superman" (along with Carlyle, Nietzsche and Shaw) and became friends with Mussolini. Even his sexual trespasses win him little credit. There is something farcical about the ageing man who orders the bells of his villa to be rung whenever he achieves orgasm with his umpteenth mistress. An old alliance between piety and caution, between Church and socialism – something we have recently learnt to call political correctness – has written off D'Annunzio as a monomaniac. His style, they tell us, is excessive, verbose. They don't want us to open his books. I was kept away for years.

A dozen pages of *The Virgins* will dispel these prejudices. D'Annunzio surprises us. One of two spinster sisters is dying of typhus. These young women have given up their lives to God and to the community, teaching catechism and basic grammar to young children in their home. The priest arrives to give extreme unction. The host is placed on a tongue dark with blood and mucus. The evocation of a suffocatingly religious peasant household, of a mortal sickness in all its ugliness, stench and mental stupor, is dense and marvellously paced. Sentence by sentence, we are waiting for the woman to die, begging for it to be over.

Giuliana doesn't die, and D'Annunzio is not just another practitioner of nineteenth-century social realism. Far from cancelling out the old Adam and ushering another soul through the pearly gates, the last rites appear to have returned Giuliana to a state before the Fall. She is back from the dead and intensely sensitive to the mystery of her healing body, as if experiencing the throes of a second puberty. A subtle symbolism informs the plot, but, as with Hardy's or Lawrence's finest work, it springs naturally from the world we know, offering but never imposing a possible order. In the shameless hunger of first convalescence, Giuliana searches the house for food while her sister is away at mass. She finds an old apple and bites deep to the seeds. A heady, rosy perfume is released. Giuliana laughs, as anyone returning to health would laugh, and laughter is of the Devil. She finds a mirror, studies her face, then, more boldly, her naked body. All at once we have a fiercely sexed young woman, adult and virgin, dangerously innocent, living and sleeping beside a sister who, in her repressive religious devotion, seems "the corpse of a martyr". It is Camilla who is dead. Not Giuliana.

At last the convalescent goes to the window and draws back the curtain. The smell of fresh bread drifts up seductively from the bakery below, the blast of the trumpet sounds the hours from the nearby barracks where the soldiers whistle to the passing girls. The reader is gripped by a powerful sense that something terrible is about to happen.

Place is important. Pescara is at the same height as Rome on the Italian peninsula, but on the opposite coast, the Adriatic. Busy, provincial, backward, the town forms a ribbon of chaotic life between coastal pinewoods and rugged hills that rise steeply to the high plateaux of the Abruzzo mountains. Winter rains and snow fill the streets with rushing water. Spring is an explosion of rich smells. The violent summer sun glares off white limestone, tortures the dark vegetation, glitters on the sea. Himself in love with extremity, D'Annunzio has an uncanny ability to capture every manifestation of climate and landscape, bucolic or grotesque, threatening or lush. Far from being superfluous, his descriptions set in motion the brooding drama of a huge and inexorable natural process, against which the moral pretensions of religion and society are increasingly felt to be meaningless. In one of these stories a bleeding woman stumbles into a house to collapse and die, while a solitary blind old man taps uncomprehending about the corpse with his stick. Nothing could better express D'Annunzio's sense of the fatal elusiveness of life and death to rational enquiry.

Altered states of mind, sickness, passion, delirium are the norm in these stories. A woman and her husband's brother are pampering her young daughter in the presence of his elderly mother. Adult fingers meet by chance in the child's thick blond hair; unplanned and unwanted a passion begins that sweeps away the claims of parenthood, the duties of son to dying mother. "Aren't you afraid of enchantments?" one character asks in another story. "You should be," is D'Annunzio's answer. It is this apprehension of the subjection of the mind to the magic of the world, or to organic processes if you like, coupled with a conviction that established prescriptions for good behaviour are quite obsolete, that will ultimately lead D'Annunzio to his cult of the superman, the figure whose will is so strong that he can stamp new patterns of value on life. That dangerous figure is absent from these stories, which present us rather with life's victims, yet latent all the same, and understandable.

Teaching proper Italian to their infant pupils, the two virgin sisters broke up the language into its constituent parts – *la, le, li, lo, lu,* they made the children repeat *nar, ner, nir, nor, nur...* Returning to new life after her terrible illness, Giuliana listens to her sister repeating these formulae – *ram, rem, rim, rom, rum* – and finds them intolerable. She sobs and beats her fists on the pillow. These rigid patterns and divisions are death to those truly alive. The moment can be considered emblematic of the birth of modernism. From now on everything is to be mixed and fizzing with life: male and female, ugly and beautiful, sacred and profane, poetry and prose – above all, good and evil. The most unexpected words appear together, sacred images disclose all their eroticism, erotic gestures are made in complete innocence. Decades before their day, this is the world of Lawrence and Joyce.

LUIGI PIRANDELLO
(1867–1936)

Characters in Search
of a Conflict

"It's not true at all," we hear in Pirandello's story 'Romulus', "that men come together to offer each other comfort and assistance. They come together to wage war."

Born in Agrigento, Sicily, in 1867, Luigi Pirandello grew up in a family that had a certain intimacy with conflict. His maternal grandfather had been involved in the 1848 Sicilian uprising against the Bourbon king in Naples. His uncles and his father had fought with Garibaldi when he captured Sicily with an army of volunteers in the 1860 campaign that led to the unification of Italy.

There were also struggles closer to home. The wealthy owner of a sulphur mine, Pirandello's father roughed up a man who came to demand he pay protection money, then survived a murder attempt when the man returned to shoot him. Pirandello spoke of his father as a tyrant, fought him over his educational aspirations, and, when, in his early teens, he caught him with a mistress, who was also his niece, spat in her face. Almost all the thirty stories in *Stories for the Years* (translated by Virginia Jewiss) are tales of conflict, accounts of winning or more often losing. What changes is the nature of the struggle.

The stories are not arranged in chronological order, but editor and translator Virginia Jewiss has provided publication dates, which range from 1901 to 1934, shortly before Pirandello's death in 1936. However, twenty-seven of the stories were written after 1903, when Pirandello's father lost his fortune after his mine flooded, obliging his son to write more urgently for money, and all but two of these before 1922, by which time the extraordinary success of the play *Six Characters in Search of an Author* (1921) freed him from such immediate needs. Written for journal or newspaper publication, almost all the stories present the same carefully crafted ten pages, moving rapidly through an opening *in medias res*, a predicament defined by some turbulent relationship, unexpected complications, ingenious machinations, extreme emotions and a dramatic twist, often a death, to close.

Influenced by the *verismo* of Pirandello's fellow Sicilian Giovanni Verga, whose longer novellas sought to get close to the voice and spirit of Sicilian peasant life, the early stories oscillate between pathos and what the Italians call the *beffa*, an ironic, unexpected, crushing reversal. In 'The Raven of Mizzaro' (1902) some peasants mistreat a raven and tie a small bell round its neck. The tinkling sound as the bird flies alters its behaviour. It leaves its nest and roams far and wide, pestering other peasants. In particular, it steals the lunch of poor Cichè as he labours in his almond orchard. Fatally, Cichè sees this as a personal affront and decides to get his revenge, threading twine through some beans to capture the raven, then torturing it. But when he ties the bird to his mule to take it home, its crowing prompts the animal to bolt, and Cichè ends up dead in a gully, the raven once again "ringing his bell in the air, blissful and free".

Constant in all Pirandello's conflicts is the total incomprehension that reigns between antagonists – the raven squawked "but in raven language, so naturally he wasn't understood". In 'The Fly' (1904) the deadly enemy is an insect. Two brothers rush through the most arduous Sicilian landscape to beg the help of the village doctor. Their cousin is dying. Overwhelmed by the demands of his multitudinous and sickly family, the doctor is reluctant. But the young men are persuasive and optimistic, planning even bigger families with their pretty *fidanzate*. One man runs to the barber for a shave to please his girl as the doctor prepares himself and a mule is found.

On the journey nature is implacably hostile.

The heat was tiring, the sun so hot it split the stones. Every now and then a sparrow's shriek or a magpie's laughter would come from beyond the dusty hedges of prickly pear, which made the doctor's mule prick her ears.

"Evil mule, evil mule!" the doctor would moan.

But melancholy and unsympathetic as the physician is, he recognizes that their cousin is dying of anthrax: an insect must have brought it from a dead animal. On the wall of the barn a fly "could be seen to extract its tiny proboscis and pump it up and down, then quickly clean its slender front feet rubbing them together, as if in satisfaction". And that fly inexorably finds the bleeding nick on a freshly shaved chin. If this seems wilfully macabre, it's worth remembering that in the year Pirandello was born an outbreak of cholera killed 53,000 people in Sicily out of a population of around 2,400,000.

Three early stories – 'The Little Fan', 'On the Mark', 'The Brazier' – offer the familiar trope of the poor young woman abandoned by the man who made her pregnant. One story ends with a revenge shooting, one with a suicide, one with fingers unbuttoning a blouse in the piazza on a sultry evening as, "fanning her nearly bare breasts, laughing and with shining, inviting, provocative eyes, [Tuta] looked brazenly at the soldiers going by". Some awareness of Pirandello's own dealings with women will inevitably affect the way we read these cautionary tales, and indeed his whole oeuvre.

His first awareness of sex, he claimed, came when, as a young boy, curious to see a corpse, he stole into the local morgue and surprised a couple making love. Later there was the showdown with his father over his mistress/niece. In this case, when the girl fell pregnant, the father married her off to a compliant young man. In his last year of school in Palermo, Luigi started a relationship with a cousin, Lina, a popular girl five years older than himself. The two became engaged. Hostile to the prospect of a marriage, the families insisted they wait. Luigi's father brought him back to Agrigento to work in the commercial side of the mine. Luigi was inept. He believed he had a vocation for poetry. He wanted to study. His father agreed and financed a university education, first in Palermo, then Rome, whence Luigi sent poems back to Lina. But in a pattern of behaviour that would recur throughout his life, Pirandello made scathing remarks about the incompetence of the professor tutoring his thesis. An argument ensued, and he was encouraged to switch to the University of Bonn, even further from Lina, who grew hysterical. Pirandello rushed back to Sicily to be with her, felt suffocated, and rushed back to Germany again.

In Bonn the young Sicilian was impressed but also shocked by the openness and freedom of the young women. When his friendship with his landlady's daughter led to sex, he lost his respect for her. Returning to Italy after completing his studies, he chose to settle in Rome and asked his father to talk to Lina's family for him and end the engagement. The man's forceful practicality had its uses: aside from anything else, he was financing his son's attempts to become a writer. A year later, his father wrote proposing he marry Antonietta Portulano, the daughter of his closest business associate. Her large dowry could then be invested in his sulphur mine.

It was a strange marriage. Pirandello had been experiencing a period of intense depression. Life was meaningless. He had no work, no relationship. He wasn't publishing. The story 'The Light in the Other House' presents a man, Tullio Buti, similarly alone and depressed, lodging in a melancholy room, rejecting all the attempts of his landlady and her daughter to cheer him up. "The savageness he had witnessed growing up, from a most tender age, of his father's brutality and ferocious tyranny, had extinguished every spark of life in his soul." But one day Tullio notices the happy family life going on through the window across the street. He falls in love with the young mother. Spying through the keyhole of his room, the landlady's daughter guesses what has happened and tells the woman. The two run off together, procuring unhappiness for all concerned.

Pirandello was twenty-six, Antonietta twenty-two. They had never met. She had spent her youth in a convent. Her obsessively suspicious father had never allowed her to be alone with a man. Relatives were present whenever the *fidanzati* met in just two months of courtship. Antonietta was beautiful. Pirandello bombarded her with letters. He was lost, he said, before he met her, sad without knowing why. "Life was a maze with no way out." "Art was the only rock in the general shipwreck." Now she will save him. "You are my sunshine." "I am cured." "I will make a real woman of you."

Antonietta has nothing to say as Pirandello piles up airy castles of epistolary romance. Art is a religion, but he needs her to cheer him up. "Your heart will expand at the vision of my high ideal." Then he warns that actually there are two Pirandellos, "a big me and a small me", who "are always at war". "One is taciturn and self-absorbed… one is jokey and playful." Pathos and *beffa*. Constantly solicited, the bride-to-be at last pens an awkward response and is immediately told she will one day "become the most perfect writer on earth" – her husband will be her guide. In short, the relationship betrays exactly the mutual incomprehension that reigns between Pirandello's characters. Years hence the two will be referring to each other as "the enemy".

Arguably, it was the exhausting battle this marriage became that provided Pirandello with the intuitions on which his most important writing was built. Raising three children, Luigi and Antonietta inhabited different worlds. In 1897 he took up a post at a women's teacher-training college. Dressed as a dandy for lessons, he was much loved by his students, despite his low opinion of them. Antonietta, inheriting her father's obsessions, became insanely jealous. Pirandello, who could not have been more monogamous, acquiesced to her paranoia, completing a daily diary to justify every moment of his absence from home. When his father lost his money and with it her dowry in 1903, her condition worsened. There were fits of paralysis and hysteria. She would abandon the house, or demand that he leave, then the two would be reunited in a blaze of romantic passion, which fed her concern that he was obsessed with sex. As their daughter Lietta grew into adolescence, Antonietta accused her husband of incest. Lietta tried to kill herself.

Year by year Pirandello's stories became more explicit in their exploration of incomprehension. Each character projects his or her own reality, entirely unaware of the inner world of those closest to them. In 'The Cat, the Goldfinch and the Stars' (1917), an elderly couple, having lost the orphaned granddaughter they were bringing up, transfer all their affections to the girl's pet bird. The old woman believes it is forever mourning for the dead girl. They trap the struggling creature in their hands and kiss it. But each interprets its behaviour differently. They argue. The man keeps freeing the bird from the cage so it can fly round the house, as the granddaughter had encouraged it to do. The old woman complains, but cleans up after the bird, as if it were a toddler needing to be toilet-trained. The windows have to be kept closed in case the neighbours' cat gets in, not a trifling matter in a hot Sicilian summer. The two are shut off from the wider community by their folly. The man fears being laughed at, and is determined to strike whoever mocks them.

These violent thoughts would make his blood boil every time, and he would get up, goldfinch often on his shoulder, go to the window and glare at the windows of the house across the way.

The old man had no reason to doubt that those things across the way were houses… or that those things above were roofs, with chimneys, tiles and gutters, just as he knew who owned them and who lived in them and how. The problem was that it never once crossed his mind to ask what his house and those other houses across the way were to the goldfinch perched on his shoulder.

Eventually, the cat gets the bird and the old man picks up his gun. Meantime, the stars hang brightly above, but "do not – of this you can be absolutely sure – see at all the poor roofs of that little mountain village". All the same, "so brightly did they shine, you could almost have sworn that they saw nothing else that night".

These sudden acts of narrative distancing offer irony and control, making the author and the reader, if not winners in the conflict, then at least superior people who have understood the dynamic driving it. This is now a far cry from Verga's *verismo*, and prompts the reflection that when one is trapped in a drastically dysfunctional relationship, the solution might indeed be distance. In 1903, in the midst of urgent domestic and financial crises, Pirandello explored that possibility in the novel *The Late Mattia Pascal*. A bizarre set of circumstances compel the ingenuous but always opportunistic Mattia into an unhappy marriage with the ex-mistress (and niece) of the man who has deprived his family of their fortune. Oppressed by a wife and mother-in-law who resent his poverty, he flees to Monte Carlo, where the roulette table transforms him from disconsolate loser to confident winner. But while returning home to impress his family with his money, he happens on a newspaper announcing that Mattia Pascal has killed himself. In fact, another man's corpse has been mistaken for him.

Here is the opportunity to break free from domestic conflict. He changes his name and moves from town to town living on his winnings, only to discover that such a life condemns him to a state of isolation, since to form a relationship involves disclosing one's past. Isolated, identity dissolves, life become meaningless. One is reduced to staring into mirrors, pitying one's shadow. After various improbable attempts to construct a new life, Mattia returns to Sicily to avenge himself on the family whom he blames for reducing him to this state. But by now his wife has remarried. "Outside of the law," a friend observes, "and those circumstances, happy or sad as they may be, which make us who we are, dear Signor Pascal, it is not possible to live."

This is the dilemma at the core of Pirandello's vision. We live in separate worlds; incomprehension breeds conflict – nevertheless, what identity we have is entirely relational. Hence to abandon conflict is to destroy oneself. In 1918 Pirandello and his elder son Stefano tricked Antonietta into visiting a mental institution and had her locked up. There was no other solution. Immediately, Luigi longed to have her back. Three years later, in *Six Characters in Search of an Author*, the Father observes of his separation from his wife: "My house, without her... suddenly seemed empty. She was my nightmare, but she filled my home."

If all this was deeply unhappy, writing about it brought success. Indeed, writing became part of the conflict. "Art is a revenge on life," Pirandello observed. Antonietta became upset when she recognized that allusions were being made to their marriage. Her paranoia was inflamed. Many contemporaries were shocked by the openness of the references. Invariably Pirandello's alter egos appear as losers, enslaved by unhappy circumstances, but their brilliant depiction in witty prose made the author himself a winner.

Acts of vengeance are everywhere in these stories. In 'The Revenge of a Dog' (1913) a poor shepherd is identified by a speculator as owner of a barren stretch of land. Hitherto unaware of the possession, the shepherd is happy to sell the land which he can see no use for. The speculator builds expensive homes on it. The shepherd realizes he could have had much more. Furious, he chains a starved dog at the bottom of the gully under the houses. The dog keeps people awake with its howling. The house owners fight over how to respond. "Killing a Sicilian peasant's dog means getting yourself killed," the narrator observes. For the reader it is simply a question of how cleverly catastrophe will be served up.

Moving closer to the author's life in Rome, 'The Cathar Heresy' (1905) gives us a pathetic professor whose book on a gnostic heresy of the twelfth century has been ignored while an inferior (he believes) work by a German professor has been extravagantly praised. Reduced to misery when his brother's death obliges him to support his sister-in-law and her seven children, the professor eats his heart out at the thought of the German's success and, although only two students attend his classes, plans a devastating lecture to destroy his rival's book.

Both the Pirandellos whom the author had identified in his earlier letter to his wife, the taciturn and the playful, come together in this story in a formula he theorized as "humorism". Essentially, the comic depiction of grotesque figures – "Professor Lamis's bald patch peaked out like a leathery half moon between his hat and the nape of his neck" – was to be qualified and complicated by an awareness of their unfortunate circumstances: the meringue, we hear, that the professor keeps in his pocket will be all his food for the day. Whatever the case, there is a cruel glee in the description of the revenge lecture. Neither of the professor's pupils can attend, but other students have left their coats on chairs in the gloomy classroom. Believing he has an audience, the professor destroys his rival with relish, while passers-by gather at the door to snigger in silence. As Gaspare Giudice observed in his fine biography of Pirandello, suffering gives one "the right to make one's characters suffer".

In 1915, in the final phase of his marital impasse, Pirandello wrote 'Mrs Frola and Mr Ponza', a story he transformed in 1917 into the breakthrough play *Così è (se vi pare)* – literally, "That's how it is (if that's how it seems to you)". A small community is shocked when a new arrival, Mr Ponza, keeps his wife locked up in the top floor of his home while setting up his mother-in-law, Mrs Frola, in another house some distance away and not allowing the two to meet. Aware that the locals are gossiping, Mrs Frola assures them that Mr Ponza is a wonderful man, but morbidly possessive of his wife, who is happy with the situation.

Mr Ponza then comes to tell the same people that, actually, Mrs Frola is mad. Her daughter, his first wife, died four years ago. Unable to accept the death, the distraught mother came to believe that his second wife was her daughter, still alive. He is saving her from the truth by this pretence of an excessive love that prevents them from meeting. Mrs Frola then returns to explain that her daughter did not die at all, but had to be put in an institution to save her from Mr Ponza's obsessive love. When the wife returned, he was so convinced she was a different woman that a new wedding ceremony had to be arranged.

So it goes on. Each character "has for the other's presumed madness the most exquisitely piteous consideration". Only thus can conflict be avoided. But the result is that "the entire city" – desperate to know the truth – has been drawn into "this nightmare", unable "to tell the difference between fantasy and reality". This is "an endlessly alarming agony".

The genius of *Six Characters in Search of an Author* (1921) was to bring this unhappy vision into the very mechanisms of theatre. Exasperated with the family of characters he has created, an author gives up on them. But since their conflict has been set in motion, they are determined their story be staged, if only to get revenge on one another. At the heart of the drama are a troubled marriage and a moment when the father, "not so old as to be able to do without a woman", visits a brothel and is offered his daughter, who is prostituting herself to make ends meet for the destitute mother.

The characters burst in on a theatre company during rehearsals and plead their case. Actors and characters can't agree. The play is always on the edge of mayhem. What may or may not actually have happened, how these or those words were originally spoken, this item of clothing worn, this or that gesture made, can never be known. The world multiplies, brought into being by any number of subjective visions. "A person believes he is 'one', but it's not true: he is 'many', sir, 'very many'." The English censors decided the play would disturb viewer's minds and banned it.

From this understanding of life as conflict and chaos it is a short step to Pirandello's politics. The theatre director in *Six Characters* struggles to impose order. "We are in need of a great captain," Pirandello announced in 1909, "for tomorrow's war." Democracy could only bring more confusion. He was opposed to emancipation for women, sceptical of women writers. Success in the theatre came exactly as Mussolini stepped up to impose order on an anarchical Italy. When writer and politician met in 1923, it was as two winners. In 1924, after the assassination of the socialist parliamentarian Giacomo Matteotti, just as support for Mussolini was wavering, Pirandello declared in the Duce's favour and joined the Fascist Party. "I've been a Fascist for thirty years," he announced in 1926.

With Fascist funding Pirandello set up the Teatro dell'Arte, a theatre company in Rome. He chose the plays, inviting his actors to enter entirely into their characters and their extreme emotional states. It was a hallmark of his dramas that at some fatal moment the protagonists would lose control, drawn into the collective folly of conflict. In 1934 he was awarded the Nobel Prize for Literature, and in 1935 gave his gold Nobel medal to be melted down for Italy's war effort in Ethiopia. "The Author [Mussolini] of this great work of ours [the war]," he argued "is himself a Poet who knows very well what he is doing." Art and conflict were one.

On the other hand, Pirandello often declared that his own work was apolitical: to be above or outside conflict was another kind of victory. In 1924 he wrote the novel *One, No One and One Hundred Thousand*, his strongest statement on systematic mutual incomprehension and the desire to subtract oneself from other people's controlling narratives. It ends with the protagonist isolated in extreme poverty but enjoying a quasi-Buddhist ecstasy of self-annulment. But there was no danger of Pirandello himself following this course: he went on writing and arguing, being praised and insulted, insulting and praising, fighting hard to sustain success and celebrity with scores of plays, stories and novels.

Stories for the Years is a fine sampling of the author's world, convincingly translated by Virginia Jewiss, who negotiates the problems of bringing Pirandello's vivid, colloquial prose and effortless storytelling into English with great skill. One of the finest stories is 'A "Goy"'. Its main character, Daniele Catellani, has one unpleasant habit: before agreeing with anything you say, however offensive, "he laughs, deep in his throat". A Jew determined to shed his Jewishness, Daniele has married into a traditional Catholic family, where his rigid father-in-law – "cold, cadaverous and cosmeticized" – does everything to remind him (and his children) that, as a Jew, Daniele is "an enemy of the Christian faith", a deicide. Daniele's infuriating laugh betrays his enormous effort of repression.

The story was written and set in 1916. Pirandello had enthusiastically supported Italy's entry into the First World War, then been shocked by the scale of the carnage. In the story, Daniele is increasingly dismayed by his father-in-law's insistence on the superiority of Christianity at a time when Christians are massacring each other. At last he fights back. The father-in-law has planned to surprise his grandchildren, on return from midnight Christmas mass, with a spectacular nativity scene:

> many little terracotta shepherds, who bring their humble offerings to the manger in Bethlehem... straw baskets of pure white ricotta and panniers of eggs and raviggiolo cheese, and flocks of fluffy lambs and little donkeys laden with even richer offerings, followed by farmers and peasants. And on camelback the three kings...

While the others are at mass, Daniele "trembling all over with crazed joy", replaces the nativity scene figures with

> armies of tin soldiers, of every nationality, French and German, Italian and Austrian, Russian and English, Serbian and Romanian, Bulgarian and Turkish, Belgian and American and Hungarian and Montenegrin, all with their rifles levelled at the grotto of Bethlehem... Then he hid behind the platform.

Pirandello didn't live to see the Second World War, or Italy's Race Laws of 1938. Nevertheless, some believe that the instructions he gave for his funeral suggested he was at last distancing himself from Fascism. The norm would have been for the state to appropriate the international celebrity in a display of public pomp – instead, the author ordered that there must be no procession and that no political figures were to attend: "Burn me. And no sooner burnt, let my remains be scattered. I don't want anything, not even ashes to remain of me." Whatever the case, in one final *beffa*, he removed himself from the fray, leaving his readers in search of their author.

CESARE PAVESE
(1908–50)

The House on the Hill

Pavese's titles always offer hints on how we are to read his stories: there is a complex experience that demands unravelling, events that cry out to be understood, and the title points the way. So *The House on the Hill* suggests the importance of position: from start to finish this is a novel about finding one's place in the world – or perhaps it would be more appropriate to say, about failing to find one's place.

At first it appears the problem is simply a product of historical circumstances. The narration opens in June 1943. Night after night Allied aircraft are bombing industrial Turin. Fascist Italy is on its knees. Corrado, our narrator, who grew up in the hills of Le Langhe some 80 km away, is working in the city as a science teacher in a secondary school. But he has the good fortune to be lodging just outside town, on a hill immediately to the south-east. Here his landladies are a spinster, Elvira, about his own age, approaching forty, which was also Pavese's age at the time of writing, and the spinster's elderly mother. The two women are not in any sense "family", yet they would clearly like to become so. Elvira sees a chance to find a man at last; the mother would be happy to marry her daughter off. Corrado insists he is merely a lodger. But is it possible, when times are so dramatic, to maintain a merely economic relationship with those one lives with? Is it noble?

The hill, we hear in the opening paragraph, "wasn't just any old place... but an aspect of things, a way of life". The claim begs more questions than it answers. "Rough, rolling land," Corrado goes on, "farmed and unfarmed, everywhere roads, ravines and farmsteads." But how does this make the hill "an aspect of things"? The novel will gradually explain, but a little context may help.

Throughout his writing career, first as a poet, then a novelist, Pavese would set town and country in opposition to each other. Like Corrado, the author was born in Le Langhe, but to a middle-class family based in Turin. The long hot Italian summers would be spent in the village of Santo Stefano Belbo, his grandparents' home, then the school year in the city. At school, in an urban environment, the young Pavese was competent, in control, effective. He had intellectual friends. He could please his teachers. But there was something missing: the intensity of country life, the rough contact with soil and corn and vineyards, oxen and donkeys, streams and ravines, music, dance and drink. And – most of all – girls, women. Eroticism is always out in the country in Pavese's personal topography. Only there are you really in life. Yet sex is as crude and dangerous as it is absolutely necessary.

In the poem 'August Moon', published in 1936, a husband is stretched out dead in a field while his wife gives birth beside him.

> Long shudders come over the naked hills
> from afar, and the woman can hear them behind her,
> like when they'd run through that sea of wheat...
> The woman runs forward, beneath the moon's horror,
> chased by the rustle of wind on the stones,
> by a shadowy form that gnaws at the soles of her feet,
> by pain in her belly. She returns, bent double, to the shadows,
> collapsing onto the stones and biting her lip.
> Beneath her, the dark earth darkens with blood.

Sex both obsessed and terrified Pavese. "A man," he writes in his diary, "does everything outside, in the light of day, but you've got to penetrate a woman, rummage in there, and everything happens in her bowels in the roots of her flesh." Living in the country one was close to life, to roots, to naked hills, yet women remained an impossible mystery for Pavese. He yearned for but could not sustain a relationship. City life, city competence, success at school, university, and later as a translator, editor and writer, were a refuge from that failure, but could not substitute for it. Very early he began to feel that there were two parts to his character that could not be reconciled. Without that reconciliation he would not be able to grow up, to become a man. Aged eighteen, he writes a poem where he describes going into the woods with a gun. First, he shoots it into the ground, then,

> Thus walking
> among the naked trees, I imagined
> the tremendous jolt it will give
> on the night when the last illusion
> and the fears will have abandoned me
> and I will place it against my temple
> to shatter my brain.

Failing the gun, "Most probably I shall masturbate myself to death," he wrote, only half humorously, in a letter to a friend. At the beginning of *The House on the Hill*, Corrado seems to be beyond such adolescent torments. His work life is the school in the city, science, facts. He has no attachments, and claims to be happy that way. His family, far away, write him only cursory letters and rarely. Living up on the hill allows him to get a smell of life's intensity, walking in the woods with his landladies' big dog, Belbo. So a kind of melancholy balance is established: town and work by day, hill and recreation in the evening and at the weekend. Besides, Corrado reflects, "With the war it was acceptable to withdraw into yourself, take things one day at a time, stop regretting the missed opportunities." On the morning after a heavy bombing raid, he describes seeing soldiers looking at women in the city.

> The war was lost, it was obvious. But the soldiers marched along at an easy pace, circling round holes and turning to sneak looks at the houses like everyone else. A pretty woman walked by, and

they all called after her. The soldiers were the only ones who seemed aware that women still existed. In the tense, chaotic town no one looked at yesterday's women any more, no one followed them around, not even in their summer dresses, not even when they laughed. It was another side to the war I had foreseen. That risk was long over as far as I was concerned. Desires I might still have, but illusions no.

This detached complacency is abruptly challenged one evening when, returning home from the city, Corrado hears singing from another part of the hillside, a part where he has never been. The voices remind him of something, "like an echo from the past, a call from youth". He decides to explore, if only to escape the clutches of his two landladies. He is "safe" with them, because he feels no sexual desire for Elvira. At the same time, he is irked by their warm concern for him, and consequently their feeling that they have a right to know where he is, particularly during the air raids. Again, although this novel is never straight biography, such feelings were an ordinary part of Pavese's life and of the dilemma his characters always find themselves in. On 21st December 1947, in the middle of writing *The House on the Hill*, he jotted this note in his diary (the sudden shift in frames of reference is typical Pavese):

> To know that someone is waiting for you, that someone can ask you to account for your behaviour, your thoughts, that someone can follow you with their eyes, expecting a word from you – all of this is a burden, an embarrassment, an offence. Perhaps that's why believers are healthy people, carnally as well – they know that someone is waiting for them, their God. You are celibate – you don't believe in God.

On the other side of the hill Corrado finds a farm which is also a tavern, Le Fontane ("The Springs"). Working-class men and women, some from the country, some taking refuge from the city, are drinking outside in the dark of the wartime blackout, laughing, dancing, joking and smoking. This is life. If Pavese is very much the intellectual, life, in his writing, is always with ordinary people – people who act, love and hate, rather than think and write. Corrado laps up their easy happiness; he feels at home with them. At the same time, he immediately registers the fact that these people are anti-Fascists. They are waiting for the moment when the regime will be sufficiently weak for them to strike. They, unlike him, are committed. Then, as the revellers chat in the dark, Pavese plays the narrative card that will bring political and private life together:

A voice spoke to me: "And you, what are you doing here? On holiday?" I recognized that voice. Now, thinking back, it seems obvious. I recognized it, and didn't ask myself whose it was. A slightly hoarse voice, alluring and brusque. What you'd expect, I thought, in a woman in a place like this.

It is his old girlfriend Cate. And she has a child with her, a boy, Dino. Six years before embarking on *The House on the Hill*, in 1941, Pavese had written but not published a story entitled 'The Family'. Its main characters are Corrado and Cate. Corrado is spending a lonely summer in Turin while all his friends have gone off to the sea or the mountains. He is thirty, bored with himself and his inability to change, hoping that something will happen to cause him "to become someone else", but without his having to take any initiative or actually do anything. Women are part of the problem. He has just ended one desultory relationship and is hesitating before beginning another that hardly promises to be different. In these circumstances he runs into Cate, whom he'd left seven years before. They had been lovers – they would regularly take a boat down the Po into the country and make love in the fields. Sex always requires this atavistic placing for Pavese's characters: they find it difficult to bring sex into domestic or social routine. In fact, when Corrado had tried to introduce Cate to his intellectual friends, he immediately found her vulgar, ingenuous, embarrassing. Disenamoured, he failed to turn up for an arranged date, and they never spoke again. Now, on seeing her after so many years, he is fascinated. She is a mature, self-contained adult. She has achieved the transformation he can only long for. Arranging to meet her in the park, he is astonished when she brings a child, Dino. She is a mother. And Dino is a short form for Corrado (through Corradino). The child, she eventually confides, is his son. Corrado is appalled and concerned that she is trying to make claims on him. But he is also fascinated. This is the maturity, the fatherhood, that should have been his. It is staring him in the face, but has eluded him. Things get worse when it becomes clear that Cate wants nothing from him: she has someone else, she is self-sufficient. When Corrado offers to marry her, she tells him it would be impossible: "I have changed since those days, but you are still the same."

The 1941 story works well enough as an account of one man's private angst, his fear of remaining for ever excluded from life. What makes its recasting in *The House on the Hill* infinitely more powerful is the wartime context. This time Cate insists the child is not Corrado's, though the timing of his birth suggests otherwise. She won't tell him who the father is. She works as a nurse in Turin, a city under bombardment. She is part of a band of anti-Fascists preparing for a partisan war. How can she take seriously a forty-year-old man lodging with two doting landladies, a man working as a teacher and hence the holder of a Fascist Party card, a man who doesn't even own the dog he always has beside him, a man uncommitted on any front? Corrado has no place, no position, in the play of forces that are shaping Italy's destiny. He is irrelevant.

Here we are getting close indeed to autobiography. Pavese did not fight, either in Italy's regular army, from which he was exempt for health reasons, or with the partisans. He had friends who were involved, but he did not commit himself. Working for the publisher Giulio Einaudi through the 1930s, he had been friends with the editor and anti-Fascist Leone Ginzburg, who was arrested in 1934 and would die in prison during the war. In the same year Pavese started a relationship with Tina Pizzardo, an active anti-Fascist, and agreed that a fellow conspirator could send messages to her by writing to him at his address. Tina, like Cate, had a "hoarse voice", indeed she was known among friends as "the woman with the hoarse voice". In 1935, the police raided Pavese's lodgings (in his sister's house) and arrested him. Pavese could hardly tell the truth without betraying a woman he hoped to marry. Tried and condemned, he was sent to the remote Calabrian village of Brancaleone Calabro, nearly 1,500 km away. But when, after many months, Tina had not written to him or commiserated in any way, Pavese eventually got in touch with the Fascist authorities, explaining the situation and asking for clemency. No sooner was it granted and he had returned to Turin than he found Tina was engaged to be married to an old boyfriend. Pavese was devastated and ashamed of himself.

Perhaps the most difficult moment for Italian men in the war came in September 1943, three months into the story of *The House on the Hill*. In July, in response to the Allied invasion of Sicily, Mussolini had been deposed and imprisoned. People hoped the fighting would soon be over, and there was much rejoicing when, on 8th September, an armistice was signed with the Allies. But Hitler responded rapidly: German forces poured into northern and central Italy, Mussolini was freed by German paratroopers, and a puppet state, the Italian Social Republic, was set up under the Fascist dictator. It was at this point that many men took to the hills to fight a partisan war. Pavese was not among them. When the Einaudi publishing house was placed under Fascist control, he escaped to the country, eventually taking refuge in a monastery (which was also a private school) until the end of the war. After which he expressed enormous regret that he had not fought.

Pavese was never easy on himself, and it may often seem that he invents his alter egos, their failings and tribulations, as a form of self-castigation. But that is not the whole story, and *The House on the Hill* is not a lament that Pavese did not fight. Things are more complicated.

Corrado becomes a regular visitor at Le Fontane. He gets to know the anti-Fascist group. He renews his friendship with Cate and takes an interest in Dino, who is now a young teenager. He is an acute observer of the air raids, the situation in Turin, people's reactions to the increasingly chaotic and dangerous situation. Unlike others, he has no illusions as to a rapid end to the war, and no confidence at all that the partisan struggle will lead to anything but more violence and hatred between Italians. The war, if it ever does end, will do so when the Allies break German resistance. Nor does he join in an easy condemnation of the Fascists. The Fascists took power because people let them, he points out; everyone was complicit, himself included.

The book becomes a plea, or apology, for pacifism – but with an understanding that there is simply no place for a pacifist in Italy in the winter of 1943–44. The young conspirators at Le Fontane look up to the science teacher – they respect his intelligence, his evident moral concerns, his clear-sighted analysis of the situation. Cate admires him immensely. But they naturally want to be involved in life and in history, they want to fight for their rights and their freedom, while he seems to be looking for a place of neutrality, or hibernation, a sort of safe waiting room which simply doesn't exist. Even his work as a teacher, under the Fascist republic, could be seen as a form of collaboration. Corrado recognizes this. He doesn't condemn his friends for their military projects – quite the contrary: he envies them. Yet he argues strenuously against them. When the Nazis come to round up the partisan group, of whom they believe Corrado is one, his theorizing will be put to the severest of tests. Life, the maturity to which he aspires, demands that he dirty his hands, and this is something he simply cannot do. What, in his relationship with Cate, seemed merely a problem of private sentiments now becomes a great moral dilemma that involves us all.

Pavese's style is very much the product of the preoccupations that haunt all his protagonists. If life was of its nature ugly and violent, art, he believed, was pure. And if he personally could not commit to relationships or to conflict, as others did, he could at least produce art. The position of the artist, detached from events, became the only possible position for him, but it was important that he make no compromises, never sink to opportunism or crowd-pleasing. So his writing is terse, thorny, elliptical, rapid, full of apparent non sequiturs, unexpected plot developments and oddly heterogeneous lists. Just as Corrado never seeks to please his friends at Le Fontane and never tells anyone what they want to hear, so Pavese never offers the reader lush descriptions, easy entertainment or straightforward pathos. We are kept constantly on our toes, often fumbling after a sense that is only hinted at. The narrative voice is colloquial but brings together both a dialect earthiness, typical of country folk, and a city man's cool reasoning. This does not make things easy for the translator. Very often one looks up unusual words and usages only to discover that Pavese was the only person ever to have committed them to print. Sometimes it is only on a second or third reading that one sees the deeper sense of what has been said, which then has to be rendered in English with the same caution. It is as if our writer were hiding or avoiding our company somehow, as Corrado is so often escaping other people's company.

Yet precisely because of all this *The House on the Hill*, as one proceeds, is immensely seductive, full of pinpoint description, wry humour, a generous acceptance of human weakness and a genuine striving to come to terms with life – all of which eventually produces a far more powerful pathos than any ingenious novelistic contrivance. What we have is a man contemplating, in extreme and intensely evoked circumstances, the impossibility of his finding any way forward. Many readers will begin to feel, as Elvira and Cate do with Corrado, or as friends did with Pavese, that they want to get close to the author, to understand him, perhaps in some way to help. In fact the brilliance of the novel is to construct in our regard the same kind of relationship that Corrado constructs with those around him.

Sadly, in the end, there was no getting close to Pavese. In August 1950, two years after completing the novel, he booked a room near Turin's central station and took a fatal overdose of barbiturates. A note left on the bedside table read:

I forgive everyone and ask forgiveness of everyone.
OK?
Keep the chit-chat brief.

ELSA MORANTE
(1912–85)

Arturo, *C'est Moi*

With all the present enthusiasm for the practice of literary translation, one might suppose there was little point in learning a foreign language to engage with another culture's literature. From the press release for the recent Society of Authors' Translation Prizes we learn that Gini Alhadeff's translation of Fleur Jaeggy's *I Am the Brother of XX* "equals, and sometimes even surpasses, this twenty-first-century Italian classic", while Helen Stevenson's translation from the French of Alain Mabanckou's *Black Moses*, "[captures] all the vitality, drawing out all its layers of jokes and puns, different cultural references and registers, all the battles for meaning that lie under its witty surface". The verb "capture" is used seven times in the press release. Apparently, we have this nailed.

Yet some styles remain elusive. Elsa Morante's masterpiece, *Arturo's Island*, is largely about the dangers and pleasures of being captured, seduced or obsessed by place, ambition or romance. Its characters are all and always bewitched and bewitching, in thrall to someone or some idea, and very likely, simultaneously, enthralling to someone else. In describing all this, Morante herself flagrantly, joyously, looks for the same kind of relationship with the reader: her lush, generous style, so rich in spoken idiom, yet so far from standard usage, wills us to succumb to its strange and gorgeous pessimism. A translator is thus asked to be first an object of enchantment, as reader, then to reproduce that spell for new readers in another language: first captured, then capturing. It's a tall order. Published in 1957, *Arturo's Island* quickly worked its spell on the literary establishment, winning Italy's most prestigious literary prize, the Strega, and going on to achieve best-seller status in the USA in Isabel Quigly's 1959 translation. Now the book appears again in a new translation by Ann Goldstein.

Comparing their versions, one is struck by how differently two people can read the same text. Morante begins her story with Arturo remembering his childish enthusiasm for his name. The chapter is called "King and Star of the Sky". Here is Quigly:

> First of all, I was proud of my name. I'd found out early on (from *him*, I have a feeling) that Arturo is the name of a star – the fastest and brightest in the figure of the herdsman, in the northern sky. And ages ago there was some king called Arthur as well, who had a group of loyal followers; and as they were all heroes like himself, he treated them as brothers and equals. The pity of it was, as I later discovered, this famous old king of Britain wasn't proper history at all, but just a legend; and as I thought legends were kids' stuff, I dropped him for more historical kings.

And here is Goldstein:

> One of my first glories was my name. I had learnt early (*he*, it seems to me, was the first to inform me) that Arturo – Arcturus – is a star: the swiftest and brightest light in the constellation of Boötes, the Herdsman, in the northern sky! And that this name was also borne by a king in ancient times, the commander of a band of faithful followers – all heroes, like the king himself, and treated by the king as equals, as brothers.
>
> Unfortunately, I later discovered that that famous Arthur, king of Britain, was not a true story, only a legend; and so I abandoned him for other, more historical kings (in my opinion legends were childish).

These are quite different registers. Quigly, English though she was, goes for a voice that has hints of Huckleberry Finn or Holden Caulfield – "And ages ago there was some king called

Arthur as well... and as I thought legends were kids' stuff, I dropped him for more historical kings." This is a long way from the elaborate, exclamatory rhetoric of Morante's (or Arturo's) Italian, which Goldstein follows almost word for word, and without dropping the exclamation marks. She starts with "glories" not "pride" (the Italian is "*vanti*", "boasts", suggesting something verbal and vainglorious); she tells us, as Morante does, that Arturo is a star, not merely the name of a star. She gives straight dictionary translations for "learnt early", "inform me", "borne by a king" and "commander", the last being particularly important, since to be sovereign is to command, and we are entering a world where people command each other, but also where Arturo longs to be treated as an equal by the person who commands him, his father, the "*he*" who first told the boy the meaning of his name.

Goldstein also respects the paragraph breaks of the original, something Quigly frequently alters. This seems crucial on the novel's first page, where Morante sets up three short paragraphs, the first establishing the boast of the name, which is then dismissed with the "Unfortunately" opening the second paragraph. This second paragraph then speaks of the adoration Arturo feels for the person who chose that name, his beloved mother, who was "to me more than a queen". However, this excitement in turn is deflated with the opening of the third paragraph: "In reality, I knew almost nothing about her, since she wasn't even eighteen when she died" (giving birth to Arturo). So the book's rhythm, of a mind always ready to be excited, to imagine parents as kings and queens, then promptly disappointed by a reality that cannot live up to these imaginings, is established in the opening page.

At first glance, then, Goldstein's version seems the more reliable, though there is a price to pay for shadowing the Italian so closely: the clumsily repeated "me"s, for example, in "*he*, it seems to me, was the first to inform me". The Italian here is more emphatic, but also more fluent: "*fu lui, mi sembra, il primo a informarmene*"

– it was *him*, I think, who first informed me). Goldstein also adds the explanatory "Arcturus", not in the original, breaking up the excitement of "*Arturo è una stella*" – "Arturo is a star" – perhaps because she is afraid that the English reader won't get it. The explanatory "Herdsman" is also added (as in Quigly), and draws attention away from the glamour of exotic names and kings (there is really no place for a herdsman in this royal text). Despite all this diligence, which may of course be editorial intervention, Goldstein then misses the insistent possessives when Arturo talks about the king's loyal men: "*tutti eroi, come il loro re stesso, e dal loro re trattati alla pari*" – "all heroes, like their king himself, and treated by their king as equals". This is a world where belonging, family and community are supremely important. A king is not "the king", he is "*my* king". He commands me. I possess him. Arturo's father commands his son's mind, but he cannot escape being the boy's father. The relationship is two-way.

Considering Morante's work as a whole, one might say her signature achievement is to conjure raptures of fantasy from miseries of circumstance. Arturo is born on the tiny island of Procida in the bay of Naples. Having lost his mother at birth, he grows up mostly alone in the so-called Casa dei Guaglioni (literally the "House of the Boys"), a dilapidated ex-monastery turned eccentric, filthy home that Arturo's vagabond father inherited from an inveterate misogynist, Romeo the Amalfitano, in return for having kept the man company, so to speak, in his dotage. Wilhelm, the father, himself an only child let down by self-obsessed parents, is bitter, spiteful, vain, distracted, interminably sardonic when not viciously scathing, and very handsome. Born of a German mother to an itinerant Neapolitan, he is blonde in a world where everyone is dark. Arturo reads that blondness, which he doesn't share, as a sign of his father's nobility and sees nothing of his faults. He understands his long absences as quests of exploration and gallant endeavour, and his one ambition is to grow up and be worthy of joining his father on his travels. In return, the father calls Arturo "moro" – "Blacky", Quigly gives; "dark-haired kid", offers Goldstein. "He scorned to conquer my heart," Arturo observes with wistful awe.

Morante was writing at the height of Italian neorealism. In the early 1950s Carlo Cassola, Beppe Fenoglio, Vasco Pratolini, Morante's husband Alberto Moravia and her friend Natalia Ginzburg were all in their different ways seeking to describe a disoriented post-war desolation in spare, chastened prose. Morante was having none of it. Her own writing is more reminiscent of the *fin de siècle* grandiloquence of D'Annunzio. And she is scarcely interested in the nitty-gritty of Arturo's physical survival. Could a baby really grow up bottle-fed on goat's milk by an older boy? Could a child learn to speak and read so well with just the occasional help of an old family retainer who stops by once a day to leave him some food? Could an infant live alone in an isolated house whose dozens of rooms are never cleaned, whose roof is falling in, whose central courtyard is a damp jungle of untended vegetation and discarded furniture? Could he really spend his entire childhood exploring rocky cliffs and beaches with his dog? Morante doesn't answer these questions. What matters is Arturo's imagination, his evocation of an island Eden that simply *is* his childhood, and that like everything we powerfully imagine threatens to become a prison, a place he must escape from if he is to achieve maturity. In fact, at the centre of Procida, high above the House of the Boys, stands a fortress prison, establishing all too clearly the island's status as both paradise and penitentiary.

From the roof of the house, one can see the full shape of the island, which resembles a dolphin, its small inlets, the penitentiary and, not far away, on the sea, the bluish purple form of the island of Ischia. The silvery shadows of more distant islands. And, at night, the firmament, where Boötes the Herdsman walks, with his star Arturo.

That was Goldstein. Quigly's versions are always a little shorter.

> From the roof you can see the dolphin shape of the island lying below, with its small gulfs, its Penitentiary and, not very far out at sea, the purple-blue shape of Ischia; silvery shadows of islands farther off; and at night the firmament, where the herdsman wanders with his star, Arturo.

If this seems the stuff of fable, or existential theatre, the deeper psychological reality of Arturo's relationship with his father is convincing and implacable. Wilhelm never writes when he is away, which is most of the time, and the boy marvels at his own certainty of the man's continued existence, and dreams of the "glorious", "blessed" companions who enjoy the "aristocratic privilege" of his presence. Briefly back on the island, Wilhelm shouts angry German words at a rock face to hear the echo, and Arturo, who can't understand German, feels they must be "terrible, rash words" and imagines "we're at Roncesvalles, and suddenly Orlando will erupt onto the plain with his horn. We're at Thermopylae, and behind the rocks the Persian knights are hiding, in their pointed caps."

How could a fourteen-year-old boy with no formal education produce these (and many other) erudite references? Romeo the Amalfitano, who used his monastery-cum-house to throw wild, men-only parties, who abhorred women and swore that if any female ever entered his abode a curse would fall upon her, also kept a library stocked with classical literature. Arturo reads voraciously, in thrall to a culture of male values, male heroism and female inadequacy. The only "female being" the boy knows as a child is his dog Immacolatella, a name recalling the Christian tradition of pious and devoted femininity. In fact the dog is as besotted with her master Arturo as Arturo is besotted with his father, or again as the old Amalfitano was besotted with the young Wilhelm to whom he left his house. So Morante exposes but also seems to take pleasure in capturing and performing the engrained misogyny and machismo of one strand of Mediterranean culture, forgivable in the young Arturo, who has no other reference points, but disgraceful in the old Amalfitano and the opportunist Wilhelm, who in ten lavish pages pronounces a terrifying anathema on womankind in general and possessive mother love in particular. All women, he declares, are ugly; a woman's love is a curse, and of all women a mother is the worst. Arturo listens, rapt, adoring his father, but at the same time longing for the mother love he has never known.

It is into this poignantly toxic atmosphere that Morante introduces the sixteen-year-old Nunziatella, whom Wilhelm brings home as a bride from Naples. Just two years younger than his new stepmother, Arturo watches, contemptuous yet spellbound, as, fresh off the ferry, this illiterate girl, the first woman he has ever known, unpacks a dozen images of different Madonnas from her suitcase and places them for protection around her bed. Her air of loyal submission to a husband who seems to have married her only in order to have someone to mistreat, reminds Arturo of his dog. In the night he is shocked by her animal cries. Quickly falling in love, but at the same time intensely jealous of Nunziatella for having stolen his father's attention, Arturo decides to spurn and humiliate her in every way he knows, becoming of course more hopelessly attached to her in the process.

The drama is beautifully drawn, at turns hilarious and shocking, full of startling but seemingly inevitable reversals as Nunziatella proves far less vulnerable than she initially appeared, her unshakeable Christian superstitions casting their own enchantment to challenge Arturo's more bookish fantasies, her simple affections effortlessly trumping the men's misogyny. When the drunken Wilhelm falls asleep after a long rant against her, she picks up a blanket to cover him against the cold, and Arturo is stunned, "as if a mysterious, double-edged weapon had pierced my heart". By the end of the book, he will be acknowledging that Nunziatella is not just a queen, but "worthy of a true king".

Making all this possible is the peculiarly flexible voice and ambiguous point of view that Morante invented for the novel. In an interview in *Publishers Weekly* Goldstein speaks of the author as "writing in the voice of a fourteen-year-old boy", but in fact Arturo is speaking long after the events he describes and begins his narrative with a distancing past-perfect tense that neither translator chooses to follow: literally, "One of my first boasts had been my name." The narrator is simply too eloquent to be fourteen, but he employs that eloquence to evoke fourteen-year-old emotions and, above all, the adolescent's limited awareness of the world he is growing up in, never making explicit what the reader all too soon intuits about the lives and predatory sexual habits of Wilhelm and the Amalfitano. Every enchantment is built on denial and taboo; each character has things they do not want to know and cannot speak of, issues that the writing flirts with and circles around, preparing the reader for the grand clashes when some truth is finally brought into the open and change becomes inevitable.

This fine balance, or blurring, between maturity and childhood – and above all Morante's insistence on language as the vehicle of fantasy – puts her translators under pressure. For the book to work, the prose has to be captivating, quirky and lush. Quigly lowers the register, sometimes to the point of plainness, often skipping a nuance or flourish, and generally trusting in a faithfully delivered content. Goldstein, as she does in her other translations, sticks tightly to the letter and syntax of Morante's original. One wonders about the wisdom of this. "The letters of the Latin alphabet make it pretty hard to speak good German," observed Luther of his translation of the Bible, and the same is true when rendering elaborate Italian prose in English. Or even simple Italian prose. Here are a couple of examples. When Nunziatella goes into labour one night while her husband is away (very likely in the fleshpots of Naples), Arturo rushes to the house of the island's only midwife. It's a walk of half an hour, but he's frightened and runs fast. "I don't think I took more than ten minutes," he tells us in Quigly's version. In phrases like this, Italian places the negative not with the verb "to think" but with what is thought: "*Credo che non impiegai più di dieci minuti.*" Goldstein follows this formula, giving the more unusual English, "I think it didn't take me more than ten minutes." Arturo bangs furiously on the midwife's door, and she appears at the window. "Oh, so there's only one of you!" she exclaims in Quigly's version, having supposed from the noise that there must be an army out there. Again, Italian constructs the question of how many people there are in a group rather differently, in phrases like, "we are three", "they are four". And again Goldstein follows the ordinary Italian, "*Eh, guaglió, sei uno solo*", having the midwife say the improbable: "Hey, kid, you're just one."

Far from giving the "flavour of the Italian" this approach, constantly deployed over 350 dense pages, creates an atmosphere of quaintness where everything is uniformly odd, a little awkward, vaguely "literary". So Arturo is "closed in my thoughts" (Quigly: "thinking my own thoughts"); a young man's possession of a ring is "a clear document of his person" (Quigly: "an obvious proof of his identity"); Arturo hides in "my usurped room" (Quigly: "the cave I had taken over"); Nunziatella's chin trembles, "like a real girl's" (Quigly "like a little girl's"); the house where Arturo fears Nunziatella has died in labour looked as if "already not a soul were alive within its walls" (Quigly: "nothing [were] left alive within its walls").

When so little of the prose reads like standard English, it becomes hard to spot where Morante's writing is adventurous and unusual. The problem is compounded by Goldstein's attachment to English cognates of Italian words. So she frequently has "sojourn" for "*soggiorno*", "zone" for "*zona*", "land" for "*landa*", "historic" for "*storico*", "vile" for "*vile*", "piety" for "*pietà*", "exaggerated" for "*esagerato*", "negation" for "*negazione*" – the list could run on and on – often in instances where the meaning or register is quite different in the Italian. When Arturo tells us that someone "*mi riusciva... antipatico*" – a fairly ordinary Italian expression for "I didn't like him" or "found him irritating" – Goldstein gives "[he] was antipathetic to me".

Words that signal imagination and fantasy, which is what the novel is largely about, are particularly thorny. Morante frequently uses the adjective "*fantastico*", but the word is more complex than it might seem. When Nunziatella's mother demands to know why Wilhelm is always away travelling, leaving the girl alone with a tiny baby, her daughter answers: "*Lui... viaggia perché è fantastico!*" Goldstein has this as "He travels... because it's fantastic!" The pronoun "*Lui*" – he – is not strictly required in Italian, and its introduction here is emphatic; we're contrasting Wilhelm's reasons for travelling with other people's. And "he" is the subject of both verbs. The sense is "he travels because *he* is *fantastico*", where the adjective does not have the banal modern sense of "wonderful", but the idea, now largely lost in English, of someone extravagant, someone with imagination. Nunziatella says this, Morante tells us, "*alteramente*" – proudly, haughtily even – because she is pointing to her husband's superiority, his special quality. Since she has spoken of her own fear of travel, it's unlikely she would say that travelling was "fantastic", even if the syntax could be made to fit this. Quigly more credibly gives "he travels because he's imaginative".

Although Quigly often paraphrases and simplifies, she always seems to understand Morante's Italian. She had, after all, unlike Goldstein, studied languages at university and lived in Italy – indeed she married and rapidly divorced an Italian in circumstances that, as she describes in her novel *The Eye of Heaven* (1953), led her to understand the vagaries of passion and disillusionment all too well, and the vocabulary Italians use for it. At the climax of Morante's novel, when Arturo finally realizes that his father is infatuated with a young delinquent in the island's prison, he confronts Nunziatella with her husband's homosexuality. "HE LOVES HIM," the boy shouts. And Nunziatella protests, "*Tu... non dici parole giuste*" – which Goldstein translates as "You... are not speaking true words."

Aside from the unlikeliness of anyone expressing themselves like this in English, *giusto* doesn't mean "true", but "right", "proper", "appropriate". "You shouldn't say that," Quigly paraphrases, but she has the sense of it. Nunziatella is defending a taboo: in her world you don't talk about love between men.

There is a lot of autobiography in *Arturo's Island*. Morante spoke of having always wanted to be a boy, of a childhood spent playing games of princes and princesses with three younger brothers who were in thrall to her, of a possessive, competitive mother who dreamt of an upwardly mobile daughter achieving aristocratic status, to the point of persuading a noblewoman to take Elsa into her home for some months of the year. "Arturo, *c'est moi*," Morante declared of her narrator. Those who like to draw parallels between life and fiction will find plenty of material in Lilly Tuck's biography of Morante or Alberto Moravia's account of their relationship, or again the recent *MoranteMoravia. Una storia d'amore*, by Anna Folli. Morante was deeply attracted to the gay community that revolved around Luchino Visconti and Pier Paolo Pasolini, had an affair with Visconti and later with the young gay American painter Bill Morrow. She was fascinated by the way homosexuality was seen and experienced in Italian society. In his book, Moravia tells how Morante once played dead for hours to force herself on his attention, a trick Arturo plays on Nunziatella in the novel. On a more positive note, Moravia speaks of Morante's extraordinary inventiveness when they hid together from the Nazis in a shepherd's hut high in the hills of Lazio and had to choose between pages of Dostoevsky or the Bible for toilet paper. In a comic aside, Arturo too reflects on the nobility or otherwise of the paper one uses to wipe oneself. His father, he says, found newspapers so full of "*roba fetente*" (literally, "stinking stuff", but meaning also "bad stuff") that it irked him even to use them in the toilet. Goldstein has: "My father said [newspapers] were disgusting, so full of cheap nonsense and idiotic gossip that one felt compelled to use them in the toilet." Quigly resourcefully and correctly gives: "My father said that [newspapers] stank... and it was an insult even to use them in the toilet."

In her interview with *Publishers Weekly* Goldstein explains how she came to translate *Arturo's Island*: her editor and publisher had so enjoyed collaborating with her on the complete works of Primo Levi that he wanted to work with her again. "He looked into the Morante situation, and this was the one that was available." Coming after "'Ferrante fever', it seemed like this was a good time for translating Italian women writers." Perhaps she was not aware of Morante's complaint that "the generic concept of women writers as a separate category harks back to the society of the harem". In short, this match of translator and writer was not a question of elective affinity. Goldstein found the novel "astonishing and difficult". "Morante's sentences are very complicated and full of words – there are so many words!" Indeed. Putting her version down, one's feeling is that many of them eluded her. This twentieth-century masterpiece is yet to be captured in English.

GIORGIO BASSANI
(1916–2000)

The Novel of Ferrara

The Holocaust must be mentioned, but it will not be talked about. It must be mentioned because it is the single most conditioning fact in Giorgio Bassani's life and in the life of the Jewish community in the northern Italian town where he grew up: in 1943, 183 of Ferrara's four hundred or so Jews were rounded up and deported to Germany, whence but one returned. It will not be directly talked about because Bassani himself was not among the 183, and apparently had no inclination to describe the horror itself. "Buchenwald, Auschwitz, Mauthausen, Dachau and so on," reads a line from one story, and leaves it at that.

Considered one of the finest Italian novelists of the twentieth century, Bassani wrote and published four novels and two collections of stories between 1937 and 1972, later editing and combining them into a huge composite work, *The Novel of Ferrara* (1974), now published for the first time in English as a single book, with a single translator, Jamie McKendrick. Reading it, we contemplate the people of Ferrara over some sixty years, Jews and gentiles, rich and poor, before and after the great convulsions of the Holocaust and the Second World War. Each story is self-contained, but with characters and events that return and call to each other, illuminate one another, so that reading the whole oeuvre together we have the powerful impression of having seen three generations consume their lives, or all too often be consumed by violence.

Despite its evident emotional and intellectual complexity, Bassani's work is frequently reviewed as if his writing were primarily an analysis and denunciation of Fascism. We mix aesthetic appreciation with complacent political approval, and that is it. In reality, his fiction is by no means circumscribed by its focus on a particular historical moment or its dramatization of the predicament of Italian Jews in the 1930s. Nor can his vision be so easily aligned with straightforward liberalism as many commentators would have us believe. True, in his masterpiece, *The Garden of the Finzi-Continis* – a novel about a wealthy Jewish family who choose to live in genteel seclusion behind the high walls of their villa, ignoring the rapidly rising tide of anti-Semitism in the community at large – the whole drama is anchored by the pathos, announced in the opening pages, that the Finzi-Continis will eventually be deported to the death camps. Yet the individual members of the family remain deeply enigmatic, and their choices open to question. Through them Bassani explores the relationship between fear and conformity, individually and collectively, what it means to be civilized and what role art might have in the matter. For readers today, with our own civilization looking increasingly precarious – and the urge to withdraw from it ever more enticing – these are pressing issues, hence the immediate allure of these stories. But great writers do not offer easy answers or uncomplicated sentiments.

Giorgio Bassani was born in 1916 to a moderately wealthy Jewish family in the small town of Ferrara, about thirty miles north-east of Bologna. His father would be an early and enthusiastic member of the Fascist Party, formed in 1921, and Giorgio himself, like many Italian intellectuals, would become a member of the GUF, the Gruppo Universitari Fascisti, when he studied literature in Bologna in the mid-Thirties. Here one must remember that the Jewish community in Italy had only been permitted to live outside the ghettos as recently as 1861. Given that this liberation was granted soon after Italian unification was achieved, it was understandable that many Jews associated the two events and were eager to be part of the mainstream of the new nation. Indeed many fought and died for Italy in the First World War, including, for example, the seventeen-year-old Roberto Sarfatti, son of Margherita, Mussolini's mistress and first biographer.

So successful, in fact, was Italian Jewry at integrating with the wider community that a non-practising Jew like Primo Levi would remark that he was barely aware of being Jewish right through the 1920s and early '30s, his Jewishness being merely a "cheerful anomaly", and his family feeling ninety-five per cent Italian and only five per cent Jewish. The 1938 Racial Laws, with which Mussolini followed Hitler in discriminating against Jews, essentially excluding them from public life, were thus doubly shocking. Jews had gone trustfully towards the national community, apparently been accepted, then found themselves inexplicably repulsed.

Rather than the calamity of the death camps, it is this experience of betrayal that profoundly shaped Bassani's fiction. In his world all involvement in human relationships of whatever kind is experienced as exposure to risk, the risks of rejection and cruelty. Romantic love is no exception: "something cruel, atrocious, to be spied on from a distance or to be dreamt of beneath lowered eyelids", we hear in one early story. And in *The Garden of the Finzi-Continis*: "Love... was something for people who were determined to get the better of each other – a cruel, hard sport... with no holds barred..."

As a result, many of Bassani's characters live in constant fear of any involvement in life at all – hence the pressure to conform, keep one's head down, or simply, and despite an intense longing for company and affection, to opt out of life altogether. The author began his writing career as a poet, and in a late collection, *Epitaphs*, wrote:

No, no I won't bring fresh wood
to the fire let's leave
the wood already there to burn
itself out little by little
the flames to transform
it little by little to embers
while you and I sitting silently
side by side watching
from the deep dark of the room
as even that, at last,
goes out.

Sitting beside the author watching a fire blaze – destructive, beautiful and, above all, compelling – is largely how it feels reading Bassani's work. Published to great acclaim in 1956, the five long stories of his first collection, *Within the Walls*, lay down the kindling with precision, drawing on Bassani's intimacy with his home town and wartime experiences, dramatizing the yearning of the young, the complacent blindness of the old and the urgent question: how do I react to threat and calamity – with involvement or flight?

In the opening story, 'Lida Mantovani', set in the 1920s, Lida, abandoned by her Jewish lover, David, after giving birth to their illegitimate child, returns to her mother's house where she finds "a sense of peace and protection". The two work together at home, as seamstresses, cocooned in tedium. Emotionally, the young woman lives off the passion she had shared with David, but this can never be mentioned to her mother, both women understanding "that their harmony could only... be preserved on condition that they avoided any reference to the sole topic on which their closeness depended".

Complicity in denial is the coal that smoulders throughout Bassani's fiction. It is always what is unsaid that most matters. Not to speak may make a relationship possible, but it also prevents life from flaring up and moving on. And it can mean simply refusing to talk about the catastrophe that is about to overwhelm you.

In this first exquisitely domestic story, an older man, Oreste, begins to hang around the two women, but despite his evident interest in Lida nothing is said. When after some years a proposal of marriage is finally made, she is "stricken by a wave of anxiety" and rushes out into the street with a desire to "mingle with the crowd, happy, dressed in a pinafore and holding an ice cream". The yearning to be spared adult experience is another familiar emotion in this writing. Only much later will Lida understand that it makes sense to accept Oreste's offer of "a new, modern house equipped with everything necessary for a comfortable life of modest luxury". The unremitting sadness of the story is made beautiful by the silvery evenness of its telling, as if everything had happened an enormously long time ago, and was thus, however painful to its protagonists, somehow possible and even pleasurable to the reader now.

The second story, 'A Stroll before Dinner', makes this framing of events in a remote past explicit. Just as his central characters are intensely attracted to life but fearful of moving towards it, so Bassani approaches his material with painstaking indirectness. The narrator finds an old postcard "crammed with details" of a busy street in the Ferrara of decades before: a horsemeat butcher's, a schoolboy in danger of being run over by a carriage, a man in a bowler hat pulling down an awning. In the centre of the photo "things and people merge together in a... luminous dusty haze", so that "a girl of around twenty years of age, at that very moment walking quickly along the left-hand sidewalk" remains quite invisible to "us contemporary spectators".

Thus Gemma Brondi, a trainee nurse from a working-class family, is conjured from a photo where she doesn't even appear, accompanied by Elia Corcos, a young and gentlemanly Jewish doctor. Despite class and religious divides, the couple are evidently in love. The narrative point of view shifts to Gemma's older sister, Ausilia, who hides by a bedroom window to spy on the two as they arrive at the girl's home each evening – their relationship is so exciting, so scandalous.

Will this be a replay, the reader wonders, of Lida's story, the single mother abandoned by the Jewish lover?

No, when Lida falls pregnant, Doctor Corcos bites the bullet, enters her home and asks her "old drunkard" of a father for his daughter's hand. The Jewish community is appalled that this promising young man should compromise his future marrying a poor goy. Ausilia, destined for spinsterhood, switches her spying from the lovers to the rumbustious, intimidating Jewish family who gather around the couple.

Elia Corcos, who appears in other sections of The Novel of Ferrara, works hard at his career and is successful despite his "baffling" marriage, until decades later he disappears into the crowd as suddenly as he earlier emerged from the photograph. Typically, Bassani tucks away the crucial information in an aside at the end of a long parenthesis in an overall sentence of almost a hundred words. Nothing else is said on the matter, but in the final lines of the story we learn that from the moment the doctor took his decision to marry his pregnant girlfriend, he also decided to dedicate his life entirely to medicine, looking "at things and at people... from above, and in some way from beyond time". That this cool, detached attitude seems to align with Bassani's narrative approach makes us wonder about our own engagement with the characters: are we "contemporary spectators" closer to the morbid voyeurism of Ausilia or the defensive indifference of the doctor? Is there a proper position?

In the two stories that deal more directly with war experiences, Bassani focuses on diametrically opposed responses to the community's determination to live in denial. At the very moment, in 'A Memorial Tablet in Via Mazzini', that a decorous and distancing plaque goes up to commemorate the 183 Jews who didn't come back from Germany, Geo Josz, the sole survivor, does in fact return and simply will not stop talking about the loved ones he has lost, upsetting the townsfolk, who are "so fearful they might unexpectedly be called to account". By contrast, in 'A Night in '43', Pino Barilari, a paralysed syphilitic confined to a room that overlooks the very wall where eleven citizens were gunned down during the war, will not admit, even under oath, that he saw what everyone knows he must have seen: the killings and the perpetrators.

As always, in Bassani, great attention is paid to the function of domestic and public spaces, houses and bedrooms, cafés and clubs. Geo Josz plasters the walls of his room with photos of his dead family – it is a place of witness – and he constantly stands at a high window commanding a view of the main street, as if to remind his fellow citizens that he is watching them. Worse, he takes to dressing in his old death-camp rags to buttonhole people in the smart restaurants and dance halls, where they are trying to return to normal life.

The paralysed Barilari also watches from his window, staring through binoculars at the point where the atrocity he witnessed took place and shouting vague warnings at whoever passes by. But his room, unlike Geo's, is a lair of regression and denial, and he sleeps on a child's bed, surrounding himself with crossword puzzles and adventure stories.

Geo's refusal to let the past go, his obsessive bearing witness, becomes intolerable for his fellow citizens, who ban him from all the places where he comes to bother them, until one day, to a great sigh of collective relief, he leaves town for ever. If Pino, on the other hand, is able to stay on in Ferrara, it is because he keeps his mouth shut. Intriguingly, the closer Bassani comes to describing the massacre this man saw but will not speak of, so the more indirect and contorted his narrative and syntax become, as if the prose itself were driven by the antithetical energies of telling and not telling, and the whole construct that is literary Ferrara were at once an elaborate refuge from the truth and a bold *j'accuse*.

It's quite a challenge for the translator, and Jamie McKendrick's new version often runs into trouble when the prose gets knotty. Negotiating the complex syntax seems to distract his attention from any number of errors. The *punto supremo* – last moment – of the lives of the massacred citizens in 'A Night in '43' thus becomes "the lofty vantage point" from which Pino sees them. Of Doctor Corcos we hear that "it was clear that when he'd converted [to Christianity] he'd hardly even considered it". The Italian gives: "It was clear he wasn't even thinking of converting." This is not a minor detail in a story looking at the relationship between Christian and Jewish communities. Geo Josz is described as a "sixteen-year-old survivor" when in fact he is a "self-styled survivor" – *sedicente* ("self-styled") has been mistaken for *sedicenne* ("sixteen-year-old"). In fact, the figure of Josz was based on a cousin of Bassani's who was in his mid-twenties at the time and is clearly no longer an adolescent in this story. The previous translation by William Weaver had these details right. At one point McKendrick skips a whole paragraph. Of course one wishes to congratulate the publisher for bringing out all of Bassani's fiction in a single volume: these are works that are stronger together, and fortunately they can be enjoyed in this translation. Nevertheless, it would be good to see it carefully revised before the next edition.

Within the Walls was a remarkable debut. But Bassani wasn't satisfied. If he was to continue as a writer, he now felt, some new ingredient would be required. "I would have to include," he tells us in the autobiographical reminiscence that closes *The Novel of Ferrara*, the person who had so far remained "hidden behind the screen of pathos and irony" – himself. So in the short novel that followed, *The Gold-Rimmed Spectacles* (1958), an anonymous Bassani alter ego narrates in first person the story of Athos Fadigati, who arrived in Ferrara from Venice shortly after the First World War to practise medicine. With his elegant, inoffensive manner, his modern and clean surgery, the good doctor "attracted and reassured" people. When, years later, the still unmarried Fadigati is rumoured to be homosexual – though no one will actually pronounce that awful word – it is felt that so long as he remains discreet this will be okay.

But Fadigati is desperate for human contact. Commuting to Bologna, he shares a train compartment with a group of students, anxiously seeking to be part of their company. And one of those students is our narrator. At this point the pay-off of Bassani's introducing an alter ego into the story is clear – for the narrator has trouble knowing how to respond to Fadigati. He is disturbed by his homosexuality and neediness, but also upset when one student repeatedly insults him. Does one get involved or not? We feel the author simply does not know, and the story flares into life.

Madly, Fadigati begins a relationship with the very boy who despises him. In a week of folly on an Adriatic beach, this ambiguous lover first forces the doctor out into the open, then runs off with his money, abandoning him to inevitable public disgrace. It's a terrible betrayal. And all this occurs exactly as the Racial Laws are introduced, so that the doctor's downfall coincides with the Jewish narrator's growing sense of vulnerability. The two become uneasy friends, unwilling allies against prejudice and blindness, the narrator being furious with his father, who, in pathetic denial, simply won't accept that Mussolini has turned his back on Jewish Fascists like himself, and that, for a Jew, the easy option of conformity is no longer available.

"From my exile, I would never return," vows the narrator of *The Gold-Rimmed Spectacles* in response to the Racial Laws. "Never." And he is talking of a psychological or spiritual exile, a refusal ever again to look for acceptance from the wider community, as his father so ingenuously had. Certainly Bassani himself, after publishing these stories, which were hardly designed to make him popular in Ferrara, or indeed among its Jewish community, never went back to live in the town and would spend the rest of his life in Rome. But he would often return in his mind, not least for the setting of his great masterpiece, *The Garden of the Finzi-Continis*, published in 1962 and in every way more substantial than anything else he wrote.

This time Bassani's signature distancing device, in the novel's opening pages, takes the form of a family visit, years after the war, to some Etruscan tombs. The necropolis is presented as a place of peace and tranquillity, "so well defended, adorned, privileged", a place of "perpetual repose" where you feel "nothing could ever change". It is here, we are told, that the author finally decided to write about the Finzi-Contini family, who were never to lie in any cemetery.

All the familiar Bassani themes and polarities – to engage or not engage, yearning for love and defence of privacy, fear and courage – are reshuffled and deployed for maximum effect so that the novel lends itself to being told through a series of sharply focused vignettes, each entirely realistic yet dense with deeper meaning. The unnamed narrator, again a Bassani alter ego, tells of his youthful fascination for the children of the wealthy Finzi-Continis, who, quite unlike his own family, lived in "absurd isolation" in a large house and huge garden just inside the town's imposing walls. The only time these home-educated children, Alberto and Micòl, can regularly be seen is at synagogue, where they sit directly behind the narrator, whose father has to constantly forbid him to turn and stare. At the end of the service, as the children are gathered under their fathers' prayer shawls, they peep at each other through chinks in the fabric, each yearning to be admitted to the other's different world. Micòl in particular is "strangely inviting".

But like any object of desire, she is also dangerous. Years later, feeling miserable after failing an exam, the narrator is riding his bike at random when he comes across the now teenage Micòl perched on the high wall of her family's garden. She invites him to climb up. Excited, he is held back by a fear of heights, fear of Micòl and fear that his new bicycle will be stolen. Why can't he come in through the gate? Mocking, she climbs down and shows him where he can hide the bicycle in an underground chamber in the city wall opposite the garden, a place that looks "a bit like the Etruscan *monterozzi*" – which is to say, "tombs". Advancing alone into the dark, the boy spends so long looking for a safe place for his bike, while simultaneously fantasizing about an erotic encounter with Micòl, that when he returns from the tomb she is gone, at which he feels he has escaped "the greatest danger a boy of my age... might ever meet". Years later again, Micòl fondly suggests a commemorative plaque be placed on the wall to record that encounter, at which nothing happened. This pattern of a before and an after with nothing in the middle is a constant in the lives of Bassani's fearful characters.

When narrator and reader finally enter the garden of the elusive Finzi-Continis, what they find is at once richly imagined, intriguing, entirely credible and, above all, impossible to pin down. Does the family, in its remove from society, represent the apex of civilization or a pathetic aberration? However many times one comes back to the book, the puzzle remains unsolved, both for us and, one feels, for Bassani too.

Owning thousands of acres of land farmed by thousands of workers – something they themselves would never be so tasteless as to mention – the Finzi-Continis are astonishingly self-sufficient. "They have everything": well-stocked libraries of books in many languages, all sorts of recreations, a tennis court, every kind of food and drink (they do not restrict themselves to kosher meats). The house comes complete with a lift. Proud and dutiful goy servants make domestic life as easy as it can be. A telephone extension in each bedroom is a "safeguard" for "personal liberty". The vast garden includes trees and plants from all over the world.

Who would ever want to leave such a place? Indeed, the Finzi-Continis seldom do. Each is a collector in his or her own way. Alberto has his records, his stereo, and obsessively controls background music and ambient lighting; Micòl fills her bedroom with scores of *lattimi*, tiny Venetian glass ornaments. She studies the supremely hermetic Emily Dickinson. Their father, Professor Ermanno, has collected all the inscriptions on the tombs of the Venice Lido's old Jewish cemetery, where he met his wife. They possess the world in safety. Isn't this what civilization is about? Isn't it admirable that the professor has refused Fascist Party membership?

But can one live a full life without mixing with others, without addressing the political realities that threaten to destroy you? In so many ways the garden of the Finzi-Continis resembles a well-kept cemetery. Nothing can happen here. Speaking a bizarre family idiolect to each other, brother and sister never seem to talk about anything that matters. Old furnishings decorously decay. When the Racial Laws are introduced and Ferrara's Jews are expelled from the local tennis club, the Finzi-Continis seem glad of the chance to invite their co-religionists to play on their own court. Some of the young people in Bassani's previous stories turn up.

Playing tennis deep into an Indian summer as Europe hovers on the brink of war, the narrator falls in love with Micòl, who gently flirts yet equally gently repels him. The two sit in the dark of the old coach house in an antique horse-drawn carriage, and, to the reader's dismay, fail to kiss. Micòl flees to her university studies in Venice, but encourages her would-be boyfriend to keep visiting her lonely brother, while her affable father suggests he use the family library for his own studies. So, for months, the narrator enjoys a highly cultured environment where the rising tide of anti-Semitism is ignored or simply accepted as a confirmation that the only thing one can do is withdraw. There is no talk of resistance or escape, or a response of any kind. Yet, as the plot thickens, the tennis games drag on and the Finzi-Continis become ever more amiable, the reader senses that this is a terrible trap, a Gothic nightmare. We want our lovesick boy to get his girl, and at the same time we fear for his future if he does. With great stealth, the novel has drawn us into the conflicted state of mind that is its subject: should we go towards life or defend ourselves from it? Is civilization "safe" if it involves denying ugly reality?

Brothels appear frequently, if marginally, in Bassani's fiction. They are where young men go when desperate for contact but unable to approach a real object of desire. Tennis likewise provides a way of engaging without real exposure or risk. Nor is any Bassani protagonist without a bicycle, which offers an illusion of freedom and reduces the danger of unpleasant encounters in the street. It's hard to think of a writer more adept at the embarrassed conversation where something needs to be said but never is, or more capable of creating moments of catharsis when two people do at last communicate, as in the moving conversation between father and son at the end of *The Garden of the Finzi-Continis*. More frequently, though, Bassani's characters have to make do with the voyeuristic gaze, fascinated but excluded, as when the *Garden*'s narrator rides his bike slowly past lovers making out and feels like a "strange... ghost, full both of life and death".

All these elements would turn up again in the author's later works. Accused, absurdly, in the mid-Sixties by a group of experimental writers (Umberto Eco among them) of being a conventional sentimentalist, Bassani changed style drastically in

The Heron (1968), assuming a third-person stance to deliver a driving inner monologue and an existential drama that unfolds in a single day. A Jewish landowner, Edgardo, who has never come to terms with the post-war world – alienated from wife, family and workers – decides to take up hunting again, booking a scout to meet him in a nearby town and take him to a hide in the marshes to shoot duck. Bodily needs and unexpected developments force Edgardo into a series of unwanted encounters and phone conversations with old acquaintances and relatives, all of whom seem as enviably at home in this new world as they were under Fascism. Ensconced in the hide with his shotgun, concealed and watching, he finds himself unable to shoot, while his guide, hidden nearby, brings down bird after bird, including a fine heron. The creature is inedible, the guide admits, but will look very good stuffed. Edgardo's immediate identification with the dead heron, useless as anything but a memento of past life, triggers a determination to end his own existence, something that paradoxically cheers him up immensely. The novel, Bassani later commented, served to get its author out of a long depression.

In *The Smell of Hay*, the closing work in this collection, we are watching a last glow of dying embers. The dangers of intense, youthful engagement with life behind him, or only savoured in memory, Bassani now feels free to emerge from the protection of fiction and reflect more openly on his life as a writer and the lives of the people he knew, many of them recognizably the characters in his Ferrara novels. The strongest piece here tells of a friend who passes from a determinedly dissolute youth to a wilfully conventional marriage – neither of which really convinces his friends – until one day, with life absolutely secure in a well-appointed home complete with caring wife and delightful children, he simply disappears, never to be heard of again. It seems that for all its attractions the bourgeois life at the core of our Western civilization can only come at the price of denial – of sexual desire, a will to cruelty, a constant yearning for change – and this, in the long run, is hard to sustain.

Married in 1943 to a girl he met at the Ferrara tennis club, bringing up a family of two children, Bassani chose neither to disappear nor to live in denial. During the war he carried messages for the resistance and survived a brief period in prison. Later he would be a founding member and president of Italia Nostra, an organization that seeks to protect Italy's culture and landscape. In this regard he was very much his father's son. At home, as we learn from his daughter Paola's memoir, he would discuss his mistresses with his long-suffering wife, complaining of them as people from whom he needed protecting. Certainly that would have brought fuel to the fire. Eventually leaving his marriage, Bassani spent the last twenty years of his life and a long slide into Alzheimer's with the American academic Portia Prebys, whom his daughter, in a gesture worthy of a character in her father's books, contrives never to mention in her biography. Bassani's family had tried and failed to sue Prebys for appropriation of his property. Paola does tell us, though, that her father enjoined her to take flowers regularly to his grave and "sustain a constant relationship with him after his death". Like the needy characters of his novels, he placed his daughter under obligations she found hard to sustain. She would have to marry and live in Paris, Paola tells us, to begin to free herself from her father's shadow.

All things considered, then, Bassani's life revolved around the same preoccupation as the novels, with the same passions and the same uncertainties – which, no doubt, is why *The Novel of Ferrara* is so captivating. It is easy, after its demise, to denounce Nazism – far more difficult to know how to behave from day to day.

PRIMO LEVI
(1919–87)

The Mystery of Primo Levi

Primo Levi was born in 1919 on the fourth floor of an "undistinguished" apartment block in Turin, and aside from "involuntary interruptions" continued to live there "like a mollusc" in the company of his mother until in 1987 he threw himself down the stairwell to his death. The longest interruption was from September 1943 to October 1945, and would provide Levi with the core material for his writing career. It involved three months on the fringe of the partisan resistance to German occupation, two months in a Fascist internment camp, eleven months in Auschwitz and a further nine in various Russian refugee camps.

In 1946, aged twenty-seven, despite working full time as an industrial chemist, Levi completed his account of his time in a concentration camp. Now widely considered a masterpiece, *If This Is a Man* was turned down by Turin's main publishing house, Einaudi, in the person of Natalia Ginzburg, herself a Jew who had spent the last years of the war in hiding and whose husband had died in a Fascist prison. It was also rejected by five other publishers. Why?

Even before his return, Levi had been overwhelmed by the need to tell what had happened. Prior to Auschwitz he had not felt that Jewishness was central to his identity. Like most Italian Jews, the Levis had long been assimilated into the community with little or nothing to distinguish them from other Italians. The introduction of the Race Laws in 1938, which discriminated against Jews in public education and excluded them from regular employment, thus created a predicament for Levi that went far beyond the immediate problem of completing his degree in chemistry and finding a job. It was a threat to his identity. Who was he if not an ordinary

Italian like his fellow students? The question "What is a man?", which would echo throughout his work, was never an abstract consideration, but a matter of personal urgency.

Until September 1943 it had been possible for Levi to live in "wilful blindness", to get round the rules and graduate in 1941, then find work unofficially – but with the Italian capitulation to the Allies and the German occupation of northern and central Italy this was no longer possible. Jews were being rounded up. Many were fleeing to the Americas. Levi himself was too committed to his Italian identity and indeed to his mother to contemplate this. In any event, he lacked the "fabulous capacity for initiative" that would be required.

Levi's insecurity was compounded by the death of his father in 1942, making Primo, at twenty-three, responsible for the well-being of his mother and younger sister. His father had been something of a womanizer whose betrayals of their mother were common knowledge. Here too there was a question of manhood: Levi himself had yet to have anything more than "bloodless female friendships", was believed by his companions to be terrified of women and feared himself that he was "condemned to a perpetual male solitude". He nursed his self-esteem with adventurous chemistry experiments and arduous mountain climbing in the Alps above Turin, and it was to the mountains that he fled in September 1943, taking his mother and sister with him and renting rooms in a small resort hotel high up near the Swiss border.

Was he a Jew on the run or a partisan? The Swiss border was closed. German occupation forces were climbing the valley. The would-be rebels whom Levi eventually associated with were poorly organized, had few weapons and were quickly infiltrated by a Fascist spy. The only shots fired in anger were those that served to execute two younger members of the band who had gone on a drinking and looting spree, putting the safety of the others at risk. How far Levi was involved in this killing is largely the subject of Sergio Luzzatto's mistitled book *Primo Levi's Resistance*. There was no resistance. To Levi's dismay, his sister had taken his mother from the hotel on 1st December to find refuge back in Piedmont. On 9th December the two undisciplined band members were dispatched with shots to the back. By the time Levi was arrested on 13th December, he was utterly demoralized and disorientated. Warned that to confess to being a partisan would mean certain death, he opted for the lesser evil of admitting his Jewishness.

The reader coming to *If This Is a Man* today brings with him the context of the scores of other books and articles he has read about the Holocaust, the dozens of films and documentaries he has seen. He is also in most cases free of any personal involvement in the war. Readers in Turin in 1947 were not so well informed, while their own intense war experiences were very much on their minds. The book opens, in first person, with a curious mixture of coolness and portentousness – coolness on Levi's part about his feeble involvement with the resistance, portentousness leavened with a certain evasiveness as he talks about deportation to Auschwitz. "I cultivated a moderate and abstract sense of rebellion," he remarks, and declares that given his half-heartedness and mistakes the "sequence of events" leading to his arrest were "justified". The tone changes when he talks about the moment, in the internment camp in Italy, when the Jews were informed that they were to be dispatched to Germany the following day:

> Night came, and it was such a night one knew that human eyes would not witness it and survive… Many things were then said and done among us, but of these it is better that no memory remain.

Today it is easy to imagine the young Levi searching for a voice, a manner, that would allow him to tell his tale without being overwhelmed by it and at the same time compel the reader's attention. Prior to studying chemistry he had been educated at a prestigious *liceo classico* in Turin. He knew his Dante and Manzoni and brought frequent references from them to his text, to enrich it, to get across a sense of extremity and profundity. But having lived through twenty years of Fascism, the literary establishment in post-war Turin were sworn enemies of all grandiloquence, which they tended to associate with inauthenticity. Thirty years later Levi would remark that his model for writing was now "the 'report' that is written in the factory at the end of the week. Clear, essential, comprehensible to everyone" – in fact, it has to be said that *If This Is a Man* is most powerful when most straightforward.

The difficulty telling people what had happened was intimately linked to the experience itself and the question of what it means to be human. Many inmates of Auschwitz, Levi tells us, experienced the same dream: they would be at home with their family, comfortable and well fed, and they would be telling of the awful deprivations of the Lager, the hunger, the cold, the beatings, the selections. Getting the story out of their systems like this would give them an enormous pleasure, until slowly they realized that their loved ones were not listening. "They are completely indifferent... as if I were not there."

Why this refusal to listen? Levi likened his need to tell people about Auschwitz to the compulsion of Coleridge's Ancient Mariner, who physically stops people and forces them to pay attention. Like allusions to the *Inferno*, the analogy suggests a sinner in search of redemption, or at least consolation, comprehension. But what sin had Levi committed? The worst aspect of the Lager was that it "was a great machine to reduce us to beasts". The victim was systematically brought down morally to the level of his torturers. Prisoners were encouraged in every way to fight one another, for the possession of a spoon, for sufficient space to sleep, to get the easier jobs, to avoid emptying the slop cans.

One had to... throttle all dignity and kill all conscience, to climb down into the arena as a beast against other beasts... Many were the ways devised and put into practice by us in order not to die:

as many as there are human characters. All implied a gruelling struggle of one against all... To survive without renouncing any part of their own moral world – apart from powerful and direct interventions by fortune – was conceded only to very few superior individuals, made of the stuff of martyrs and saints.

To give up this struggle against your fellow victims was to become a *Muselmänner*, an obvious candidate for the gas chamber, one of

an anonymous mass... of non-men who march and labour in silence, the divine spark dead within them, already too empty to truly suffer. One hesitates to call them "living"; one hesitates to call their death "death" – in the face of it they have no fear, because they are too tired to understand.

In her introduction to this three-volume collection of Levi's works (edited by Ann Goldstein), Toni Morrison remarks how "the triumph of human identity and worth over the pathology of human destruction glows virtually everywhere in Levi's writing". These are heartening words, but they are not true. Rather, Levi tells us about human identity crushed and corrupted by unspeakable evil. His work is powerful because it squares up to that reality. "The personages in these pages are not men," he tells us, and he includes himself in the cast. Everybody in the camp, from the most powerful commander to the most helpless slave, was "paradoxically united in a common inner desolation".

To tell this harrowing story was to confess to one's own degradation. You hoped a listener would say it was all right while communicating that it really was not all right, that you had been profoundly damaged and sullied. This anguish perhaps explains the strange shifts of tone throughout *If This Is a Man*, in particular the moments when Levi abruptly and defensively addresses the reader with the didactic "we":

We now invite the reader to contemplate the possible meaning in the Lager of the words "good" and "evil", "just" and "unjust"; let each judge... how much of our ordinary moral world could survive on this side of the barbed wire.

Rejections of his memoir must have come to Levi as confirmation of his recurrent nightmares. It was more than just a book that was being turned down: it was his way back into humanity. Fortunately, in the mean time there was love. Levi had started dating Lucia Morpurgo in early 1946. She was a year younger than him; both were virgins. Crucially, Lucia was happy to listen to Levi's story in all its terrible detail, so that as he had been writing his book he was also pouring out the experience in intimate conversation. It was the relief he sought. "I felt myself become a man again," he later wrote. Eventually *If This Is a Man* was published by a tiny publishing house in October 1947, a month after Levi and Lucia had married.

Levi had been cautious, diligent, conservative and prone to depression before his deportation, and continued to be so after his return. Always anxious about money, he quickly found a job as a chemist in a paint factory, briefly allowed himself to be seduced away from it into an adventurous freelance enterprise with a fearless friend, then in 1948, with his wife pregnant, he knuckled down to serious long-term employment with another paint and chemical factory, SIVA (Società Industriale Vernici e Affini). Good reviews of *If This Is a Man* did not convince him it was safe to take up a career in writing. Whether out of genuine financial difficulties or because he was in thrall to his mother, he did not move out of the family home, but brought his wife to live there, against her will. Arguments, incomprehension and resentments ensued.

On the other hand, Levi was quite changed. Auschwitz had humiliated and degraded him, but it had taught him a great deal: he was "more mature and stronger". After the Germans had abandoned the camp, he and other inmates had behaved with great resourcefulness to stay alive until the Russians arrived. During the long return through various refugee camps, he had practised all his newly learnt survival skills, and was proud of his accomplishments. So if the experience had initially stripped him of identity and manhood, it eventually led to a new confidence. Writing about Auschwitz he had published a book, talking about Auschwitz he had found a wife. His identity was now inextricably bound up with Auschwitz: it had been his coming of age, and for the remainder of his life Levi would spend a great deal of time tracking down people he had known there and corresponding at length with other survivors. His children Lisa Lorenza and Renzo were both named after the Italian worker Lorenzo Perrone, who had regularly brought him food at Auschwitz and thus, as Levi never tired of repeating, saved his life. It was "our finest hour," he would say of the last days at the camp. He referred to Auschwitz as his "university", an "adventure", "a rite of passage". His next book, *The Truce*, was written in this more positive spirit.

In 1958 Levi had finally managed to persuade Einaudi to republish *If This Is a Man*. This time sales were promising, and an English publication was planned. Bored with his job, disaffected with home life, in 1959 he became a regular contributor to Turin's newspaper *La Stampa*, and in 1961 he at last started to write a sequel to the first book. *The Truce* thus opens with the last days in Auschwitz, then tells of the confusion and vitality of Russian refugee camps in various parts of Poland and Ukraine, followed by an interminably roundabout return to Italy by train, through Romania and Hungary. The tone is immediately more literary than *If This Is a Man*.

In those days and in those places, shortly after the front passed, a high wind blew over the face of the earth; the world around us seemed to have returned to a primal Chaos, and was swarming with deformed, defective, abnormal human specimens; and each of them was tossing about, in blind or deliberate motion, anxiously searching for his own place, his own sphere, as the cosmogonies of the ancients say, poetically, of the particles of the four elements.

The pleasure of *The Truce* lies in Levi's account of his returning health and the dramatis personae of idiosyncratic companions and extravagant Russian soldiery involved in every kind of ruse, scam and jam. In particular there is Cesare,

> a child of the sun, a friend of the whole world. He didn't know hatred or scorn, he was as varying as the sky, joyful, sly and ingenuous, reckless and cautious, very ignorant, very innocent and very civilized.

Supremely shrewd, Cesare will buy, "fix" and resell absolutely anything – broken pens, ragged shirts, fish bloated with injections of water – always at a profit, and make love to any woman who crosses his path. But the tone of *The Truce* is so charmingly literary, the detailed events so distant from the time of writing, and some of the stories so far-fetched, that the reader begins to wonder how much is documentary and how much novel. In fact, though recognizably based on a certain Lello Perugia, Cesare's antics are much inflated, sometimes invented, and Perugia was furious with the way he had been presented. So were others who saw themselves described. It would have been "a much more important book", Perugia protested, if Levi "had got [his] facts right".

Why did Levi do this? There had already been some curious fact-twisting in *If This Is a Man*. Here a close friend, Alberto Dalla Volta, another companion in colourful bartering episodes, is described as having no German, a crucial factor in the struggle for survival at Auschwitz, when in fact his German was excellent, far better than Levi's. In his meticulously researched biography, Ian Thomson glosses this with the remark that "Levi, like most writers in their books, made life more interesting than it is". Leaving aside whether we agree with this, it's hard to see how describing Alberto as less well educated than he was, or, in a later book, speaking of another dead friend as coming from a "peasant" family when he didn't (and refusing to alter the adjective when the friend's parents complained), could enhance our interest in works that command our attention above all for their documentary status.

Two impulses seem to be at work. In his biography, Thomson notes Levi's tendency to form friendships with men less intelligent or less intellectual than himself, but also less fearful, more extrovert, energetic and engaged in life. There was a trade-off: the timid Levi could enjoy mountaineering adventures and female company in the protection of his lively companions, while they would recognize his intellectual superiority and learn from his store of knowledge, something that increased his self-esteem. Many of the changes in his writing shift the relationships described towards this preferred model, Levi's close associates becoming at once more animated and less cultured than perhaps they were. Never is anyone "elevated" or made more intellectual, or more proper, than Levi himself. Throughout *The Truce*, Levi seems to be the only sober figure hanging back from a wild post-war promiscuity, at one point declining an invitation to indulge himself with "twenty large girls... blonde, rosy creatures with... placid, bovine faces".

Related to these descriptions of his spirited companions were Levi's lifelong thirst for freedom and his difficulty achieving it. Work at SIVA had soon become a prison (in which Levi's boss was once again the energetic but rather crass associate). Home life with a quarrelling wife and mother was also a prison. Levi was loyal and responsible, and would never hurt others by going his own way, but the people he liked to associate with and describe were free spirits: they did as they chose. *The Truce* takes its title from the reflection, in the closing pages, that this period of time, between Auschwitz and the return to responsible life in Turin, had been, for all its harshness, a moment of respite and freedom, of "unlimited openness" before the need once again "to join battle, against still unknown enemies, within and outside us". The novel closes with Levi at home but dreaming a terrible dream that in fact he is back in Auschwitz and that nothing is real outside the oppression of imprisonment.

Levi was committed to bearing witness, but lifelong adhesion to the same harrowing story is constricting. In a later work, he speaks of encountering a man who pesters him with a manifestly fabricated version of his war heroics, but Levi admits to envying the "boundless freedom of invention of one who has broken down the barriers and is now master of constructing the past that most pleases him". Many critics have noted a struggle in Levi between commitment to fact and literary ambition, but perhaps deeper than the question of literature is simply the urge to be free of constraint, the need to feel that one can describe people as one chooses, make one character ten years older than he was, have another talk of spending a month in Genoa when he had never been to Italy, and so on. In a curious aside in *If This is a Man*, Levi remarks that if one message could be smuggled out of the camp to "free men", it should be "Be sure not to tolerate in your own homes what is inflicted on us here." As if he believed that even without all the horror and violence a certain kind of degradation and imprisonment could be experienced anywhere any time.

Whatever its status as documentary, *The Truce* is a hugely entertaining and moving book, and made Levi popular in Italy. However, he still feared he could not survive by writing alone, and not only stayed in his job, but accepted promotion to a managerial post that he found more depressing and constricting than his work as a chemist. Perhaps in response, he began to look for absolute freedom on the page with a series of light-hearted sci-fi stories – little transgressions, he later called them – published to general critical disappointment in 1966 under the title *Natural Histories*. Each piece offers a smart idea, ironic and potentially alarmist – a society where people are duped into believing they need to avoid physical contact and wear heavy armour at all times in order to avoid a deadly virus, an international telephone network that has developed its own intelligence and makes and interrupts calls as it pleases, a country where the duties of literary censorship are assigned to barnyard hens – but in general there is an abyss between these stories and the memoirs.

What is striking, and this is true for all the story collections in these volumes, is that despite the frequent references to sexual problems – a female spider discussing her consumption of males, a wise centaur torn apart by sexual desire who experiences "in the form of anxiety and tremulous tension" any sexual encounter that occurs in his vicinity – there is no attempt to dramatize however obliquely or discreetly what might have been the reality of Levi's life in his fourth-floor apartment with his increasingly estranged wife and ageing mother, nor to explore the many intimate but sexless friendships he was now in the habit of forming with women. To one of those friends, Hety Schmitt-Maas, Levi would confess his frustration with marriage, deep depression and sense of entrapment, but nothing of this emerges in the fiction. The better stories in the later and looser collections are almost always returns to the wartime period and Auschwitz.

Another undistinguished collection, *Flaw of Form*, followed *Natural Histories*, before in 1975 Levi returned to memoir with the remarkable *Periodic Table*. The breakthrough here was to use his experience and knowledge as a chemist to provide the frame or cover for explorations of earlier friendships and relationships. Each chapter recalls some episode that features a different chemical substance, whose qualities are allowed to take on a quiet symbolism. In a Fascist jail Levi speaks to a man who lived panning for gold, not in order to sell it, but for the love of engraving and hammering it, and above all "to live free" as an artist; a job that involves extracting phosphorus from plants brings Levi into contact with the charming Giulia, who despite her imminent marriage may or may not be a possible lover; a problem with a paint that won't dry, due to contamination with vanadium supplied by a German company, leads to Levi being in contact with the chemist who supervised his work in Auschwitz.

Crucial to *The Periodic Table* is that Levi knows everything about chemistry and we know very little. There is an ease and control throughout that isn't there in any of the other work. Many of the situations are presented as puzzles that Levi solves or sometimes fails to solve, but always with a wry panache. A man wants to know if a certain substance is pure sugar, and Levi finds arsenic. An employer asks him to find a way of extracting nickel from mine rubble, and Levi finds a way, but it isn't economically viable. Again and again the material world is presented as a canny guardian of secrets, possibly hostile, requiring patience, caution, practicality and knowledge, but not in the end intractable. By comparison, human relationships are even more mysterious and definitely less susceptible to the qualities Levi displays. He is unable to see how ready for love the flirtatious Giulia may or may not be, and unwilling to take the risk of challenging her. He is afraid to meet the German chemist from Auschwitz and disturbed that the man has read into *If This Is a Man* a message of Christian forgiveness, something he has no intention of granting.

Levi had always been concerned that his books might be admired more for their wartime evidence than their literary achievement. *The Periodic Table* settled any doubts as to his writerly credentials, though again there were complaints of distortion. The woman who recognized herself in Giulia protested that she had been turned into a mindless flirt. It was not true that Levi had come into contact with the German chemist through his work: he had tracked his man down through Hety Schmitt-Maas, who was upset how negatively Levi presented him in his book, since the German had been one of the few to give him some help at the camp. And again Levi had offended the family of his old Auschwitz friend Alberto Dalla Volta, alleging in the last lines of the story 'Cerium' that after Alberto's death his family had allowed themselves to be fooled by a man "half visionary and half swindler" who made them pay for "false consoling news". It wasn't true.

In 1977, following the success of *The Periodic Table*, Levi finally felt sufficiently confident to resign from SIVA. He was fifty-eight. Shortly afterward he was indicted for having caused involuntary injury to workers at the factory through failure to impose safety regulations over the use of toxic materials, and was described by the investigating magistrate as a "dangerously unprofessional man". Levi was concerned that the newspapers would publish something about the case and that his mother would find out. He suffered panic attacks and various psychosomatic pains. Eventually, in 1983 he was acquitted.

Free from "the treadmill of factory life", Levi produced in quick succession *The Wrench* (1978) and *If Not Now, When?* (1982). Both draw on the writer's special areas of knowledge for their authority, and both present themselves as fiction, free from the constraints of bearing witness. In the short stories of *The Wrench* Tino Faussone, a hugely energetic, incorrigibly womanizing engineer, intensely familiar with pylons, rigs, boilers and the like, tells the narrator, apparently Levi, of his adventures around the globe with every kind of dramatic technical problem. Having complained about his own thirty years of "forced labour", Levi now celebrated work, or at least work as experienced by one of his typical foils, a man of boundless energy and freedom who basks in the sure knowledge of his immense practical competence. In the Italian original, Faussone's earthy Piedmontese dialect alternates with Levi's more sober and sophisticated reflections, as if the two natures of a centaur (Levi would occasionally refer to himself as a centaur) were in happy harmony. It is by far Levi's most cheerful book.

If Not Now, When? – the author's only novel – is more ambitious. Covering the same time period and territory as *The Truce* – Eastern Europe in the last year of the war – it tells the story of a Russian Jew who joins a band of Jewish partisans to battle against the Germans and eventually fight their way to Italy, whence they hope to move on to Palestine and the nascent state of Israel. In *Primo Levi's Resistance* Sergio Luzzatto observes how much this novel draws on Levi's own unhappy partisan experience, transforming it into something triumphant and competent. The hero Mendel, a watchmaker, a man who can repair a radio and is prone to philosophical reflection ("Mendel is me," Levi said in one interview), boldly bears arms, engages in any number of skirmishes and sabotage operations, finds himself a woman, then betrays her with another (though he immediately feels trapped and threatened by her), and even executes a spy.

Ulybin handed the rifle to Mendel, without a word.

"You want me to…" Mendel stammered.

"Go on, *yeshiva bocher*," Ulybin said. "He can't walk, and if they find him, he'll talk. A spy never changes: he's always a spy."

Mendel felt bitter saliva fill his mouth. He took a few steps back, aimed carefully and fired.

"Let's go," said Ulybin, "the foxes will take care of this one." Then he turned to look at Mendel again, illuminating him with his flashlight: "Is this your first time? Don't think about it: it'll get easier."

Levi had spent much time researching Yiddish Eastern Europe and the exploits of Jewish resistance fighters whose war efforts he wished to celebrate, in part to dispel the notion that the Jews were somehow guilty of having passively submitted to Nazism. "It's important that there be Jewish partisans," Mendel observes, expanding on the debate in *If This Is a Man*. "It's important, but it's also horrible. Only if I kill a German will I manage to persuade other Germans that I am a man."

Unfortunately, the novel's dialogue comes across as wooden, the actions and setting are hardly credible, and those who knew Levi's previous work could not fail to see elements of fantasy and wishful thinking. Shortly after the book was published, Israel invaded Lebanon, and the writer found himself alternately praised and criticized for promoting militant Zionism, something that could not have been further from his mind. In response he called for Menachem Begin to resign over the invasion.

Constantly afraid that he would run out of subject matter or succumb to Alzheimer's, Levi stepped up production in his later years. Some two thirds of the almost three thousand pages of *The Complete Works* were written after he left his managerial job. Most of the writing was made up of articles and short stories published in *La Stampa*, and then poems that plumb Levi's darker moods. Spared the duty of providing narrative content, the poetry makes for stronger reading than the stories. On the occasion of his wife's sixtieth birthday, he wrote her this gloomy message:

> Be patient, my impatient lady,
> Pulverized and macerated, flayed,
> Who flay yourself a little every day
> So the raw flesh hurts you even more.
> It's no longer time to live alone.
> Please accept these fourteen lines –
> They're my rough way of telling you you're loved,
> And that I wouldn't be in the world without you.

A year later he wrote 'Arachne', spoken by a female spider who weaves a web from "a thousand spinning teats".

> I'll sit in the centre
> And wait for a male to come,
> Suspicious but drunk with desire,
> To fill my stomach and my womb
> At one and the same time.

Terrified of spiders since earliest childhood, Levi made a huge copper spider and hung it on the balcony of the family's flat. Warned by the Jewish community that people were gossiping about his relationship with a certain woman journalist, he immediately refrained from seeing her. Afraid the translators of his books would make mistakes, he bought foreign dictionaries and waded through them, Romanian included. Anxious that the world was reverting to Fascism, he was disturbed when his children became involved in extreme left-wing protest movements. Constantly drawn back to the experience of the camps, he took German lessons at the Goethe Institute and corresponded in German with German survivors.

Meantime, he visited hundreds of schools to tell the children about Auschwitz, yet felt more and more oppressed by this mission. Visiting New York for the launch of *If Not Now, When?* he protested he did not want to be labelled as a Jewish writer, and wondered why he was only being introduced to Jews. Yearning for celebrity, he did not enjoy it when it came. Eager to travel, he complained his "women" prevented him from "going anywhere". His mother had never given him "a single kiss or caress", he confided to a journalist in 1982. "I've known some Jewish sons," remarked Philip Roth after meeting him, "but Levi's filial duty and devotion was stronger than anything I'd ever seen. There was a pathetic edge to it." Levi was on antidepressants.

It was in this unhappy state – trapped, as he saw it, in his apartment with his wife, his mother and now his mother-in-law as well (the elder pair seriously infirm, "like Auschwitz victims") – that Levi chose to return to his core material in *The Drowned and the Saved* (1986), a book that must rank as one of the most powerful and upsetting attempts at moral analysis ever undertaken. The story of Auschwitz, he begins, "has been written almost exclusively by people who, like me, did not plumb the depths. The ones who did never returned, or if they did, their capacity for observation was paralysed by pain and incomprehension." Far from being "sanctified", victims were "degraded and assimilated". "Those who were 'saved' in the camps were not the best of us," he insists, rather they "were the worst: the egotists, the violent, the insensitive, the collaborators... the informers... I felt innocent, to be sure, but herded among the saved and thus in permanent search of justification... The best all died."

In unsparing detail Levi draws on other concentration camp memoirs to consider the facts in all their complexity and awfulness. The Sonderkommandos, he remarks, were "an extreme case of collaboration", Jews induced to lead other Jews into the gas chambers, to "remove the corpses... extract gold teeth from their jaws; shear off the women's hair; sort and classify clothing, shoes and the contents of the baggage; transport the bodies to the crematoriums; supervise the operation of the ovens; and remove and dispose of the ashes." Again and again the surreal collective cruelty of the Nazi regime is examined in relation to its effect on its victims; the lack of any toilet facilities in the train wagons into which Jews were packed and kept for days without food or water; the quite unnecessary deportation of the extremely old and terminally ill; the constant denuding of victims (without clothes "a man no longer feels like a human being"); the crazy obsession with bed-making in the camps, which involved "bed inspectors" (again "privileged" inmates) using a long string to check that all beds were exactly in line; the replacement of names with numbers tattooed on the flesh; the habit of forcing inmates to defecate in the open and very close to each other; the supremely ugly jargon of camp life; and so on.

At every point, Levi's declared enemy is denial in all its forms. "The intrinsic horror of this human condition... has imposed a kind of constraint on all testimony," he warns. On both sides of the divide people simply don't want to remember; they exploit slippages in memory to establish a comfort zone; artists offer portrayals that aestheticize or indulge in consolatory pieties. The book finishes with a selection of letters from German readers after *If This Is a Man* was published in Germany, many of them desperately offering spurious justifications. The whole book conveys a sense of the enormity of the task of keeping alive the truth of just how evil it all was.

No sooner had Levi committed suicide in 1987 than attempts were being made to, as it were, defend his work from his life, his death, as if admirers were afraid that by killing himself he might have undermined the positive side of his message, the supposed "triumph of human identity" over "the pathology of violent destruction". This is largely the subject of Berel Lang's *Primo Levi, The Matter of a Life*, which considers the interminable speculation as to whether Levi's motives for suicide had more to do with Auschwitz or his chronic domestic unhappiness, clinical depression and recent prostate operation. Whatever the truth, the views Lang records tell us more about people's relationship with Levi's work than about Levi himself. It is clear that many readers are eager to feel that behind the writing there was a saint, or at least a well-balanced man with an ultimately positive vision of life. There are even those who have denied that it could be suicide, something Levi himself, with his contempt for any denial of the obvious, would hardly have wished. "Suicide is an act of will, a free decision," he wrote to his German translator Heinz Reidt in 1959. "Suicide is a right we all have," he claimed in 1981.

Levi's best writing was about his life, about questions of freedom and survival, so it is inevitable that once we are aware of the manner of his death, it will always be there when we read him. On the other hand, it is hard to see why this should detract from his remarkable achievement, if only because there is no place in his writing, at least that I can find, where Levi suggests that life is likely to end well, nothing that his suicide, as it were, contradicts. If anything, the contrary.

GIANNI RODARI
(1920–80)

Have You Seen My Hand?

"Look both ways when you cross the street," Giovanni's mother tells him when he goes out. He's a careless boy, easily distracted. The reader is primed for pain. In the street, the boy is "so pleased with how careful he's being that he starts hopping along like a sparrow". A polite gentleman warns him that this is careless: "You see, you've already lost a hand." Looking for his hand, Giovanni is distracted by a tin can, then a limping dog. So much so that he doesn't notice he's lost "a whole arm". Fortunately, a passing woman picks it up and takes it back to his mother. Soon another woman is bringing a foot. Others arrive with a leg, an ear, a nose. Giovanni hops home, "cheerful as a sparrow, as he always is". His mother "puts him back together and gives him a kiss".

"Is anything missing, Mama? Have I been a good boy?"

"Yes, Giovanni, you've been a very good boy."

Gianni Rodari is considered the most innovative Italian children's writer of the twentieth century. His countless stories and rhymes tend to end well, but as it were in the teeth of the evidence. *Telephone Tales* offers sixty-eight of them ably translated by Antony Shugaar and lavishly illustrated by Valerio Vidali.

Rodari's childhood was not as carefree as Giovanni's. By his own admission "small, scrawny and anaemic", the author was born in the village of Omegna, some five miles from Lago Maggiore. His father, the local baker, died when he was nine. His mother, a factory worker and house servant, "poor, humiliated and overworked", was a staunch Catholic and sent him to a seminary. "I was such a submissive child," Rodari later wrote, "so needy of approval and praise, I'd obey anyone who gave me an order." Nevertheless, he baulked at the harsh discipline of the seminary, and was allowed to leave at fourteen. One of the *Telephone Tales* opens with a boy who, at his father's untimely death, inherits the blanket the man used as a soldier. "When he wrapped himself in it to sleep at night, his mother would tell him a long fairy tale" – and in the tale a fairy is seeking to weave "a blanket big enough to cover all the children in the world and to keep them warm".

The children's story for Rodari is always an act of generosity favouring a process of initiation and liberation. Thus the stories of *Telephone Tales*, published in 1962, are supposedly told by a travelling salesman who calls his daughter every evening from public phone boxes to tell her a bedtime story, the length of the story depending on the change in his pocket. Rarely more than two pages. Or the length of a newspaper article. Rodari spent his whole working life as a journalist, and his children's writing began on the pages of the Communist Party newspaper *L'Unità* at the height of post-war ideological tension.

In 'Elevator to the Stars', Romoletto, a delivery boy at Bar Italia, is sent with a tray of beers and an iced tea to the notoriously impatient Marchese Venanzio, who will "throw them all out of the window" if they don't arrive instantly. The Marchese lives on the sixth floor. The lift is forbidden to tradesfolk. Romoletto sneaks in anyway. But instead of stopping on the sixth, the lift accelerates into the sky. "Before Romoletto had time to be astonished, all of Rome lay spread out beneath him." "So long, Marchese Venanzio," he murmurs. "With his left hand, he was still carefully balancing the tray with the drinks. It seemed almost funny, since the elevator was surrounded by increasingly vast expanses of interplanetary space." *"At least I won't arrive among the Martians empty-handed,"* he thinks. The lift falls back to the ground floor. Chastened, the boy runs up the stairs to the sixth. "Yuri Gagarin... would already have landed on the moon," the Marchese fumes, but his drinks are still pleasingly cold.

Rodari's first engagement with children came in 1937, when he tutored the son and daughter of a Jewish family fleeing from

Germany. They would soon be fleeing Italy too. In the mean time, Rodari made the effort to learn German and read, in Novalis, "If we had a Fantastics as we have a Logics, we would have discovered the art of invention." Thirty-six years later, Rodari would publish his own extraordinary *Grammatica della fantasia*, an exploration of the art of inventing stories. One of the keys, he suggests, in a lively discussion of surrealism, is to find the right mutually illuminating tension between reality and fantasy. So one telephone tale opens: "Once upon a time, Giovannino Vagabond decided to travel to Rome to touch the king's nose." And with great comic aplomb we explore the distance between power and infant impertinence. What does it mean to touch a nose? Why does Giovannino want to do it? What does the king understand by it? Or again: "Once upon a time, in Gavirate, there was a little old lady who spent her days counting other people's sneezes." And now we are in the world of middle-class control. Eavesdropping. Gossiping. The unseemly vitality of the sneeze. The little old lady gets her comeuppance in a cloud of black pepper tossed from a victim's window.

When war came, Rodari was initially spared conscription: he was too small and sickly. A favourite character of his is tiny Alice, so small she can get lost in her grandfather's pocket. He taught in primary schools, then in 1943 was called up by the fascist Republic of Salò. He served briefly in a military hospital, then escaped to join the partisans, though much of 1944 was spent recovering from an appendix operation. After the war he joined the Communist Party, and was given the task of writing propaganda for the party's paper in Varese, before being invited to write for *L'Unità* first in Milan, then Rome.

In Vanessa Roghi's biography, *Lezioni di fantastica*, Rodari comes across as a fish out of water at the fiercely ideological paper, a country boy among city intellectuals, possessing only one suit for work, extremely reserved about his private life, living with his widowed mother. Yet always fun to be with, full of jokes, tossing off rhymes and doggerel. So in 1949 he was asked to write a humorous column for the Sunday edition, to give the paper a touch of levity. And failed. The pieces looked more like things for children, his superiors complained. They changed his brief. Write a column for children, he was told. It was a first for *L'Unità*. And an instant success.

Perhaps this explains an intriguing ambiguity one senses in Rodari's stories. It's never clear quite who they're for. "I wasn't writing for any old children," he later reflected, "but for children with a political paper in their hands. So I was pretty well obliged to move away from the traditional prescriptions for children's literature, to talk with them about the things of every day." At the same time he knew that the children's parents would be reading over their shoulders, and for the most part these people were farm and factory workers. He had to please a "double public". But there was an advantage: "With the excuse that these were 'things for kids', I could... say what I had in mind the way I liked to say it." As the Cold War set in, a Communist Party newspaper office could be a dour, embattled environment. Orthodoxy was at a premium. Files were kept on all employees. Writing for children offered a certain licence for a man who dreamt of freedom but urgently needed a job.

"A young crayfish wondered, 'Why does everyone in my family walk backward? I want to learn how to walk forward.'" His parents are shocked, the whole community appalled. The young crayfish is thrown out, to pursue his bizarre love of straight walking and straight talking far from home. Whether it is a critique of traditional society or the Communist Party hardly matters. It is rather as if Winston Smith had found a space to play in the Ministry of Truth.

But what were "the traditional prescriptions for children's literature"? Two hugely successful classics dominated the Italian scene: Carlo Collodi's *Pinocchio*, published in 1883, and Edmondo De Amicis's *Cuore* ("Heart"), published in 1886. The latter is a boy's diary of a school year, with occasional interventions from his father

and mother and long episodes – which the eleven-year-old Enrico
dutifully copies down – recounting the courage (and deaths) of
children in the Risorgimento wars. Beautifully told, drenched in
pathos, *Cuore* is an extended appeal to children to sacrifice their
own inclinations to the collective will of their nearest and dearest
and the good of the community in general. "Come to your senses,"
Rodari's crayfish is told by his mother. "Walk the way your father
and mother taught you, walk like your brothers and sisters who
love you so dearly."

Rodari admired *Cuore* and loathed it. In particular, he could not
forgive De Amicis for his invention of Franti, a boy who "hates
school, hates his companions, hates the teacher", laughs in everyone's face, steals and bullies. "It was a serious crime," Rodari felt,
"to have imagined a child so totally and irremediably evil." He
refused to believe such creatures existed. If there was a moral obligation in the grim years following a world war, it was to be positive:
"Utopia is no less educational than the critical spirit. One need
only move it from the world of intelligence... to that of the will."

Giovannino Vagabond chances one day upon the "country with
an 'un' in front". What could that mean? A citizen shows him what
looks like a pencil sharpener but is in fact an "unsharpener... to
make pencils longer when they're worn to a stub... very useful in
schools." There is also a conceptually more challenging clothes
"unhanger": rather than hanging up clothes that you have had to
buy, you simply take clothes for free from the unhanger. "We save
lots of money that way." There are also uncannons and unbugles.
"If there's a war, we blow the unbugle, we fire the uncannon, and
the war is immediately unwaged." So much for the heroics of De
Amicis's Risorgimento children.

In 1952 Rodari wrote to Italo Calvino, then an editor at the
Einaudi publishing house, proposing a critical work on *Pinocchio*.
The book's "ties with reality are deeper and more complex" than
those of *Cuore*, he claimed. It captures the child's "need of freedom
and his guilt" when seeking to achieve it. It speaks "to adults of

their own infancy" in "a constant dialectic of rebellion and accept-ance", a dialectic largely expressed in the back and forth between fantasy and reality.

But also in the adventurous use of language. Rodari is a great inventor of words, a connoisseur of the kind of orthographical and grammatical mistakes that unleash unexpected energies (to the point of writing *The Book of Errors*, a rhymed encyclopedia of common mistakes that children make in Italian). One of the finest stories of *Telephone Tales* has two children who have invented their own language. An old man and an old lady, sitting on opposite balconies, hear them saying "brif, braf" in the courtyard. And "Maraski, barabaski." "How silly these children are," the lady complains. "Not at all," the man says, and offers translations. The silliness escalates. The man goes on translating: "The first child said, 'How happy we are to be here on Earth.' And the second one answered, 'The world is beautiful.'" "Is it really so beautiful?" demands the old lady. "Brif, braf, bruf," the man answers.

On the back of his success in *L'Unità*, Rodari wrote *The Adventures of Cipollino* (1951), featuring a young working-class onion involved in a class war against Prince Lemon and Sir Tomato. As ever, what is at stake is liberty, with most of the plot revolving around imprisonment and flight. The book was hugely popular in the Soviet Bloc, with the result that Rodari would be making regular trips to Russia for the rest of his life. Like other illustrious compatriots, Calvino and Dario Fo included, he seemed blind and deaf to the anti-libertarian aspects of what was going on there. Socialism "for us means more liberty," he said. And the enemies of liberty were middle-class anxieties and proprieties.

In 'Dog Town' every one of the community's ninety-nine little houses has "a little yard with a little gate, and behind each gate was a barking dog". For protection. This is bad enough when a resident walks by, but if an outsider should venture into the street, the din is deafening and the ninety-nine housewives lower their shutters in fear. The dogs bark so loud people can't hear themselves speak, and eventually forget how to talk. "It's an epidemic," thinks Giovannino Vagabond, passing through, and he suggests to the mayor that they knock down all the fences and gates and let the dogs go off hunting and perhaps throw some street parties. "Bow-wow!" the mayor replies.

In 1950 Rodari wrote an article, 'Voltaire in Romagna', where he imagines the books of the Universale Economica, a collection of classics at low prices, on the shelf of a labourer. Side by side, Spinoza, Gogol, Feuerbach and others are arguing together, but mostly marvelling at their conversations with the labourer. Collodi is among them. "You would have man evolve from the trunk of a cherry tree, would you?" Darwin condescends as Pinocchio plays a trick on Hugo's notorious policeman, Javert. Rodari was claiming parity of seriousness for the children's writer. In 1960 he was vindicated when Italy's most prestigious left-of-centre publishing house, Giulio Einaudi Editore, offered to put his writings alongside those of the country's most serious intellectuals.

Throughout the '60s and '70s Rodari became ever more involved in a movement to reform Italy's school system. In addition to his journalism, now with the paper *Paese Sera*, he travelled widely, visiting school after school, in Italy and abroad, inventing ingenious ways to involve children in the process of storytelling, convinced that this was the key to liberalizing society. The old formula of discipline and punishment must be abandoned, he thought.

Running a children's weekly, he worked until five most mornings, then would stay out until at least six, smoking cigarettes in the Gianicolo, so as not to wake his baby daughter. There were polemics with left-wing intellectuals who were not happy to see cartoons in Communist Party publications: too American, too frivolous. And again with others who thought everything but gritty neorealism a bourgeois fraud. There were polemics with the Church, which had already excommunicated Rodari for writing *The Pioneer's Manual*, the Pioneers being the Communist youth organization. There was the trauma of acknowledging Russian repression in

Hungary in 1956 and again in Czechoslovakia in 1968. All the same, Rodari went on touring schools in the Soviet Bloc, inviting teachers to let children express themselves freely: one must never suppose, he insisted, that imagination was the exclusive prerogative of genius. Art must be democratized. In 1970 he was awarded the prestigious Hans Christian Andersen Prize, the international award for children's writing.

At the edge of a town, we read in 'The Road to Nowhere', among other roads leading to familiar destinations, there was one that led nowhere at all. Or so people said. But one little boy doesn't believe it. It must go somewhere, he says. Martino insists so much he's given the nickname Hardhead. And one day he takes the road, which goes on and on through a huge forest, but eventually brings him to a castle, a princess and a pile of treasure. After his return, others try to take the same way and find nothing but "a dense wall of trees in a sea of thorns".

The more Rodari promoted freedom and independence, the more he became imprisoned in the projects of his admirers. In 1968 he agreed to take on the editorship of the Communist-funded *Giornale dei Genitori*, the "Parents' Paper". Another enormous chore. *Grammatica della fantasia*, published in 1973, offers a range of fascinating strategies for stimulating the imagination, all entertainingly argued and theorized – "not," Rodari explained, "in order that everyone become an artist, but so that no one be a slave." Yet the book has no tips for saying no to onerous demands, or for forcing employers to pay you properly. Like other Einaudi authors, Rodari was paid scandalously little and criminally late. In 1976 he resigned his position at the *Giornale dei Genitori*, mentioning overwork and underpay. In 1977 he wrote to Giulio Einaudi complaining of hypertension, high cholesterol and nervous exhaustion. He took three months off to write the charming novel *Twice upon a Time There Was the Baron Lamberto*, in which, on the advice of an Arab sage, the moribund ninety-three-year-old Lamberto, owner of twenty-four banks but beleaguered by twenty-four illnesses, hires six people and pays them exorbitant wages to repeat his name without cease day and night in the attic of his island castle, something that causes him to grow younger and younger and less and less interested in money.

The affirmation of the author's own name had no such salubrious effects. In the autumn of 1979 a two-month trip to Russia proved fatal. Rodari was physically exhausted and, above all, deeply depressed. At last it was clear to him how grim the Soviet Union had become, and how far its people were from being free: "They put up with anything and everything without even protesting, expecting others, higher up, to act for them." And of the schoolchildren: "I did everything I could to stir them – in vain: they seemed frozen." Six months later, in hospital for an operation on an occluded artery that he would not survive, he told a friend: "The wind in Moscow cut right through my legs. That's where it started."

"He took stories apart and put them back together like toys," Rodari's wife remembered in a rare interview. Often it seems the reassembly is an attempt to construct the kind of relationship between protagonist and world that Rodari himself would have liked. It is this discreet private yearning, I suspect, that makes the stories so appealing. In 'On the Beach at Ostia', a "whimsical and most peculiar gentleman" finds every inch of sand already taken. So he opens the beach umbrella he has brought and immediately floats up a couple of metres above the crowd. Suspended in the air, he opens a lounge chair and settles down to read. The regular beachgoers only notice him when he drops his book and has to ask them to toss it back up. Books, it seems, constitute his only need for a relationship with them. "Who knows who he was or where he bought that beach umbrella?" the story ends.

PIER PAOLO PASOLINI
(1922–75)

Boys Alive

Ragazzi di vita, Pasolini's original title for his first novel – literally, "Boys of Life" – brings together youth and vitality. But in Italian a *"donna* ('woman') *di vita"* is a prostitute. So what are we to expect in these pages? Call boys? Hustlers? The title of Pasolini's second novel would again include the word "life": *Una vita violenta*. And again there is a dark side, as if life could hardly be separated from sinister and dangerous forces.

Both novels are set in Rome, both feature adolescents from the underclasses housed in the sprawling developments that sprung up around the city during the Fascist era and in the years immediately after the Second World War. Characters invariably speak the fierce and distinctive Roman dialect, whose mannerisms, blasphemies and obscenities spill over into the more literary third-person narrative. In an essay published posthumously, Pasolini described this dialect as the only "revenge" of the common people, "depository of a view of life that is... virile – uninhibited, vulgar, cunning, often obscene, free from any moral ballast". And he gives two examples of this ethos: "When I told a boy it was hardly polite to spit on the floor in a pizzeria, he shrugged and with his blonde, baby-Cain face told me: 'I do *my life* – I don't give a damn about anyone else.'" On another occasion, when the author complains about an old drunk urinating on the pavement, a young friend observes: "It's life."

Ragazzi di vita was published in 1955. Pier Paolo Pasolini was thirty-three. He had not grown up in Rome, and was not a native speaker of its dialect. Elder of two sons, his father a Fascist army officer and compulsive gambler, his mother a schoolteacher, he was born in Bologna. But the family moved about with his father's military postings, and for one period, when his father was jailed for gambling debts, they went to live in his mother's home village, Casarsa della Delizia, some fifty miles north-east of Venice. It was here that Pasolini would later escape, again with his mother, when Allied bombing targeted northern Italy in 1942. His father at this point was a prisoner of the British in Africa; his younger brother, Guido Alberto, had joined the partisans, fighting against Fascism. But Pasolini pursued his literary studies for the University of Bologna, researching a thesis on the nineteenth-century lyric poet Giovanni Pascoli. He was also intensely active writing poems in the dialect of Friuli and short stories that were rural, lyrical and sentimental, as well as joining his mother in offering free schooling to pupils in the wartime circumstances. In the summer of 1943, aged twenty-one, he began to talk explicitly to friends about his homosexuality, and fell in love with one of the pupils.

The move to Rome, a turning point in Pasolini's life, was more a desperate escape than a career choice. In 1945 his brother had been murdered together with several of his comrades by a rival group of partisans aligned with Tito's Yugoslav forces and opposed to working with the Americans and British. "My mother and I were half destroyed by grief," Pasolini remembered. Shortly afterwards, his father returned from the war, paranoid and alcoholic: "He drove us mad, he roared and fretted." Father and son fought: "The battle was ferocious: if a man were to fall ill with cancer, then recover, he would have the same memory of his illness that I have of those years." Pasolini was teaching at a state school now, intensely active in the local Communist Party, and already the published author of four small collections of poems. However, on 29th August 1949, returning from a village fair, he involved three underage boys in some kind of group masturbation. When the story got out, he was pursued by the local anti-Communist authorities and put on trial. He lost his teaching job and was expelled from the Communist Party. In January 1950, he and his mother abandoned his father and set off for Rome.

The impact of Rome, its lively, aggressive dialect, its post-war squalor and violence, thus came simultaneously with an awareness on Pasolini's part that respectability was no longer an option: "Like it or not, I was tarred with the brush of Rimbaud... or even Oscar Wilde." Urgently looking for teaching work, walk-on parts in films, literary journalism, anything to achieve independence and security, he was immensely attracted to the low life around him, who cared nothing for bourgeois values, who lived intensely, carelessly, refusing to be hampered by scruple and convention. As early as 1950 he published the story 'Il Ferrobedò', which, much re-worked, would become the first chapter of *Ragazzi di vita*: during the last lawless days of the German occupation of Rome, a young boy, fresh from his first communion, joins the crowds looting the Ferrobedò, a huge factory producing reinforced concrete.

Ragazzi di vita would be accused of not really being a novel. "It's impossible to summarize the plot decently," Pasolini confessed to its eventual publisher Livio Garzanti, "because there is no plot in the conventional sense of the word." Simply, the narrative would follow a group of boys, principally Riccetto (a nickname that means "Curly"), "from the chaos and hopes of the first days of the Liberation through to the reaction of 1950–51." During this time the protagonists would pass "from infancy to early youth, or rather... from a heroic, amoral age to an age that is already prosaic and immoral".

Pasolini follows this brisk description with a number of reflections on the responsibility of Fascism for having built "those concentration camps that are Rome's outlying housing developments", and again of the post-war government, "which hasn't solved the problem". He even goes on to speak of framing his narrative with two parallel incidents, one in the early pages, where the young Riccetto generously saves a drowning bird, the other towards the end, where he does nothing to rescue a drowning boy, closed as he is in "the selfishness and sordidness of a morality that is no longer his".

Reading the novel itself, one can't help feeling that this reassuring account of its underlying values was little more than an alibi, a false passport that would enable the author to get his writing before the public. The literary and movie scene of the time was dominated by what came to be known as neorealism – bleak, haunting stories of urban and rural deprivation which tended to suggest that suffering was largely a question of political corruption and capitalist greed. The prevailing mood was socialist, and it was important to appear concerned about the underprivileged. Such sentiments never emerge in *Ragazzi di vita*. On the contrary, Pasolini revels in the vitality of the squalid world he so lavishly and energetically evokes. The lyricism and literary allusion of earlier efforts is now bent to conjuring up an urban *Inferno* as vast and hideous as it is colourful and dynamic. One has the impression of a writer who has finally found his subject and style and is rejoicing in it, delighted to throw all caution and respectability to the wind. The only occasion when his characters show any class consciousness comes when the two losers, Begalone and Alduccio, find themselves too broke to pay for a prostitute and see a sports car drive by. "Fucking poverty, what shit!" Begalone declares for the benefit of the neorealists. "You think it's fair, him all spiffed up with that sweet pussy, loaded with cash, and us zilch? Big-shot bastards! But their time is up. The world's changing!" Socialist revolution will mean always having the price of a whore.

If there is no grand plot, nevertheless a clear organizing principle soon emerges: Pasolini's narrative voice moves like a heat-seeking missile, infallibly locking on to situations of great intensity, conflict and comedy. Possessing nothing, his young characters fight to survive and to live. At all costs they must have fun; boredom is death. And if food and fun must be paid for, then money will be found: looting, hustling, scavenging, stealing. Once found, it is immediately squandered on smart clothes and smart shoes, or it is drunk away, gambled away, or simply lost. In everything the characters are both accomplices and antagonists. They need each other, perhaps care for each other, and they compete ferociously. Every boy aspires to be the toughest, the shrewdest, the most unscrupulous punk on the block. Boasting and exhibitionism are the norm. Each must be the best swimmer, have the biggest dog, wear the sharpest clothes. Challenge and mockery abound. Bullying is rife. *Schadenfreude* is a constant consolation. To be cheerful and in the money is also to possess a weapon to have someone else feel down and defeated. As each new episode begins – a warehouse heist, an evening's gambling, a search for sex – the reader can only tremble, waiting for disaster to strike, which perhaps it does, and then again perhaps it doesn't, but in any event never where or when or how you expected. Nothing is predictable.

This is partly because our characters' days and nights are so very long. The novel may unfold over five years, but in these pages it is always summer, as if Pasolini were not interested in his protagonists when they were, so to speak, "hibernating", perhaps at school, or forced by the cold to stay home – only in the interminable scorching emptiness of the Italian summer, when the call to live and to live intensely is most powerful. The weather plays its part, inducing states of extreme irritableness or sun-struck stupor, driving the boys to water, to the crowded beach at Ostia, the filthy banks of the Tiber, the dangerous currents of the Aniene, forcing them to live mainly at night, indeed all night, roaming the city in search of action, any action, hanging on to the platform of a first tram in the grey dawn light so as not to pay. Then the heat explodes in apocalyptic downpours; lightning plays over the tenement blocks, weirdly illuminating the chaos of ruins, shanty towns and building sites. Pasolini is in his element: "his love of summer," he wrote in a poem about himself, "was perhaps the most powerful feeling in his life."

Meantime, any possible drift towards the symbolic or the surreal is held at bay by constant and extremely precise topographical references: streets, districts, schools, hills, factories, parks and apartment blocks are all and always rigorously named. Follow the action on Google Maps, if you will. At the same time, these names often gesture to other ancient narratives: Via Donna Olimpia, Monte di Splendore, Via Nomentana – the contrast between antique glory and contemporary decadence could hardly be starker. The characters' nicknames – when speaking in dialect Italians frequently use nicknames – also bring in other suggestions and ideas: Guaio means "trouble"; Picchio is a "thump", or a "woodpecker"; Caciotta is a type of soft cheese; Lupetto a "young wolf". Songs abound. Borgo Antico is the title of a popular song. When happy, Pasolini's characters cannot resist singing, usually at the top of their voices. There are quotations from Dante and from Giuseppe Gioachino Belli, a much celebrated nineteenth-century Roman-dialect poet. Sometimes it seems Pasolini's text is as busy with literary hints and allusions as his characters are intent on cheating, seducing and doing harm to each other.

Which brings us to the issue of translation. "Mimicking a dialect infiltrated with literary prose is the riskiest, most exhausting and exasperating writing endeavour you could ever take on," Pasolini remarked. On the other hand, when Garzanti worried that some readers might find his text too difficult, he explained that "the dialect words are absolutely essential for me... they give me the fun I need to grasp and capture my characters." For the translator there is the problem that the post-war dialect Pasolini was using is not only near incomprehensible at times, but it locates the characters' speech in place and time. One cannot transfer his characters' dialogues into the demotic of, say, New York's Bronx or London's Whitechapel, since the action is very specifically taking place in Rome, not New York or London, and in the late 1940s, not in our own time. To use a specific British or American idiom would be a distraction. Even the frequently described gesticulation of the characters is a specifically Roman gesticulation. All the translator can do is feel for a mix of the fiercely colloquial and the evocatively literary that is as generic and non place-specific as possible, trusting that Pasolini's insistence on Rome and his lavish descriptions of its districts and street life will do the rest.

There remains a further issue with the status of the Italian text itself. When Pasolini sent his finished manuscript to Garzanti, the publisher lost his nerve and insisted the author remove obscenities and graphic descriptions of sex, and tone down the dialect. "So I'm in the midst of a half-dead text to correct and castrate," Pasolini despaired. Offensive words were reduced to an initial letter followed by suspension points, whole scenes were cut, others were doctored and neutered. In recent years, since the original manuscript still exists, there have been calls to republish the novel in its original form. But Pasolini clearly took advantage of this unwanted edit to refashion and rewrite many aspects of the text that had not proved problematic for Garzanti. It thus becomes hard to say which text might be considered "definitive". On just two occasions, where the cuts Pasolini made were so radical and so poorly hidden that the reader cannot help sensing that something is "missing", I have taken the liberty of translating from the original. These moments are signalled with footnotes which offer the version normally published.

Despite all this self-censorship, *Ragazzi di vita* provoked a scandal, and its author and publisher were put on trial for obscenity, thus guaranteeing the book notoriety and sales. "Perhaps," observes the Italian author Vincenzo Cerami, "what really upset people was not the strong language, but the very idea of... giving a literary dignity to the lowest of the low." Eventually absolved after many celebrated intellectuals had testified on his behalf, Pasolini went on to become one of the foremost intellectuals, cultural critics, novelists and film directors of his time, writing scores of coruscating analyses of Italian public life. Interested readers wishing to savour the milieu conjured up in *Ragazzi di vita* might usefully look up his movie *Accattone* ("Beggar", "Scrounger"), an adaptation of the novel *Una vita violenta*; the extraordinary urban landscape of suburban Rome in this period, the vitality of Pasolini's characters and the urgency and precariousness of their existence is conveyed with an immediacy which one can then fruitfully take back to reading the novels.

Continuing to frequent Rome's low life, Pasolini's own existence was also necessarily precarious. On the night of 2nd November 1975, aged fifty-three, he was murdered on the beach at Ostia, a place he describes in *Ragazzi di vita*, and where he regularly went for sex. The murderer was never identified, and the motive remains obscure. But turning back to his first novel one is bound to notice just how many deaths there are in its pages, how much collateral damage around this thirst for intensity, as if life were hardly life without the risk of death. And then how little pathos accrues to the unlucky victims, how little reward or credit is afforded to anyone who seeks to save another human being. At the end of *Una vita violenta* the wayward delinquent hero, recovering from TB, dives into the turbulent waters of a flooded building site to rescue a drowning girl, and as a result dies himself. At the end of *Ragazzi di vita*, called on to play the hero and save a younger boy, Riccetto reflects that "to dive in the river under the bridge was tantamount to saying you were tired of life: no one could survive". "I love you, you know, Riccetto," the young man assures himself a moment later, in one of the very rare occasions when the author allows his character a moment's introspection.

It is in this sense that Pasolini is indeed a moral writer: the world and experience are presented in such an uncompromising and disturbing way as to force the disoriented reader to re-examine the values underpinning his or her own life.

ITALO CALVINO
(1923–85)

The Illusion of Control

Reviewing Italo Calvino's novel *If on a Winter's Night a Traveller* (1979), the celebrated critic Angelo Guglielmi wondered if Calvino wasn't, "albeit unconsciously", seeking to seduce and flatter "the average reader", who emerges as the hero of the story. Calvino published a nine-page response, which he then inserted as a preface to later editions of the novel: "What I just can't stomach," he writes in a rare moment of animosity, "is that 'albeit unconsciously'... call me a seducer, okay, a flatterer, okay... but to say I'm working unconsciously is offensive."

What emerges from the forty-three articles, interviews and speeches collected in *The Written World and the Unwritten World* is a man anxious to sustain the highest possible level of alertness, always willing to stress and appreciate everything that is lucid and calculated in literature and life. In the title essay Calvino describes the pleasure and relief of moving in "a world made up of horizontal lines where the words follow one another one at a time, where every sentence and every paragraph occupies its set place". His vocation for writing, he confesses, has largely to do with its allowing him to "cultivate the illusion of keeping everything under control". Every move away from the orderly written page into the disorderly "unwritten world" is a "trauma".

A little biography is useful. Calvino was born in Cuba in 1923. His Italian parents were both botanists, on a mission to advise the Cuban government. Two uncles were professors of chemistry. His only brother would become a geologist. "In my family," he remembered, "only scientific studies were respected" (see *Ritratti su misura di scrittori italiani*, edited by Elio Filippo Accrocca, 1960). Calvino was "the black sheep". Looking back to his childhood in

The Road to San Giovanni (1962), he describes a bookish boy, his attention dreamily directed to town and cinema (the family lived in Sanremo, on the Ligurian coast), in contrast and opposition to a father who was entirely focused on his farm holding and the concrete world of nature.

Yet it's evident that Calvino took from his parents, if not the object of his interest, at least some elements of their scientific method. "My father's vocabulary," he wrote, "welled outward into the interminable catalogue of the genuses, species and varieties of the vegetable world – every name was a distinction plucked from the dense compactness of the forest in the belief that one had thus enlarged man's dominion." His father's passion was "to grow everything that could be grown, to offer [himself] as a link in a story that goes on and on". Similarly, describing the task of the artist in these essays, Calvino tells us that the goal of painting is to bring into paint everything that is "paintable", while the writer writes "to make it possible for the unwritten world to express itself", seeking to sense the things "trying to emerge, to signify through language". In short, to write everything that can be written. Like his parents' work, it is a communal endeavour, not a project of self-expression. Rather than inventing or expressing anything, the author "combines and accumulates possibilities" in a process where "the world tends to tell its own story and the writer becomes a tool", producing a "chapter of a super-book made up of all the volumes already written or still to be written by authors known or unknown, in all languages".

If books are thus "made to be many", as we are told in a speech Calvino wrote for an Argentine book fair in 1984, then "a single book has meaning only in that it's next to other books". "We very much feel the lack," Calvino complains, of critics who focus "not on a single book or author, but... [who make] connections between the different works within the general outline of a literary context". Thus, the first of the four sections in this collection, 'Reading, Writing, Translating', amounts to a series of attempts to

apply such an approach to the literary world in which he moved.
'The Failure of the Italian Novel' (1953) traces a succession of
narrative trends back to Alessandro Manzoni's *The Betrothed*, the
flawed fountainhead, as Calvino sees it, of modern Italian fiction.
Categories and literary movements are established and explored,
much as his father explored botanical genera. Inevitably, writing
as he was for Italian newspapers and literary magazines, Calvino
assumes a familiarity with the territory that few anglophone readers will have. All too frequently one finds oneself struggling with
sentences like this:

> But meanwhile more serious national catastrophes were devel-
> oping in the terrain of the novel: Fogazzaro and Fogazzarismo
> (which even now has its successors in a provincial-cosmopolitan
> mode), D'Annunzio and Dannunzianesimo (which, defeated on
> the cultural level, still re-emerges every so often as a "volunteer"
> weed), Pirandello and Pirandellism (this misunderstanding about
> the means of expression, also with its scattered "success").

What the last parenthesis refers to, I have been unable to fathom.
The English edition offers no help, no notes. Nor does it include the
thirty pages of biography provided by the Italian edition (*Mondo
scritto e mondo non scritto*, 2002), which allow readers to check
what Calvino was working on when each article was written, or the
thoughtful afterword by Mario Barenghi. Useful publication details
have been shifted from the main body of the text to endnotes,
where readers are unlikely to consult them. Often the translator,
Ann Goldstein, seems to lack precious context: Giovanni Verga,
we are told, "rediscovered the town as a symbol of Italian reality". "*Paese*" is the word Calvino used, meaning, as the Treccani
dictionary explains, a "*centro abitato di limitate proporzioni*", i.e.
a small settlement. The usual translation would be "village". The
world that "told its story" through Verga's wonderful novellas,
which include 'Cavalleria rusticana', was very much that of the

small peasant community, in which everyone knows and judges everyone else, not the impersonal town, or "*città*".

It's intriguing how often botanical metaphors are deployed. In the sentence quoted above, Calvino's "catastrophes" ripened – "*maturavano*" – "in the terrain of the novel", while D'Annunzio-like publications spring up as "weeds". In 1943 Calvino had enrolled in the faculty of Agrarian and Forestry Sciences in Florence, apparently embracing his family's scientific vocation. However, the German invasion that followed Italy's surrender to the Allies that year made study impossible. Called up to fight for Fascism, Calvino fled, hid for some months, then joined the Communist Party and the partisans. After the war he switched to studying literature in Turin. "Fiction of every type, every era, every country, to me is like a forest of stories," he remarks in one essay. Increasingly active in the Communist Party, he undertook missions to France and Russia. "We were schizophrenic," he later acknowledged. "We wanted to be witnesses of the truth, avengers of injustice... [yet] justified the wrongs done by Stalinism in the name of the cause." Only after the invasion of Hungary in 1956 did he leave the Party and distance himself from political life.

These experiences explain the tone of the early essays, which seem largely intent on withdrawing from polemics and bringing clarity to a turbulence the author is eager to put behind him. Responding to a questionnaire on realism in 1957, Calvino makes his characteristic gesture of establishing the categories involved (the avant-garde and the politically engaged), lists the authors he is thinking of, then considers the many ways in which each category can be thought to have succeeded, or then again to have failed. Delivered with wry irony, it has the effect of cooling down a heated debate. Politically engaged literature, he observes, "has brought up a generation of readers with an alert political conscience... [a] technologically savvy generation" who are, however, "somewhat boring". Elsewhere, having confessed that "what happens in the world... never stops surprising me, frightening me, disorienting me", he imagines being asked why, in that case, he would want to venture into it at all. He answers: "To write. Because I am a writer." And writing, for Calvino, as every page of this book testifies, is a process of bringing order to the world.

But also of entertaining. As early as 1946, Calvino had begun to gravitate around the elite left-wing publishing house Einaudi, where he met Cesare Pavese and Natalia Ginzburg. First he sold books for the company, on hire purchase, then he became part of the editorial team, for which he would work, with few interruptions, until his death in 1985. He understood that books had to amuse and sell. The five pieces in the second section of this collection, 'On Publishing', show how well this side of his career sat with his flair for organization, cataloguing and summarization. 'Notes for a Book Series on Moral Enquiry', the first is called. At once the subject is divided into 'The Morality of Doing', 'The Morality of Research', 'The Morality of Historical Action', 'The Morality of Eros and Love'. Then each section is split up into subsections – 'Fulfilment by Giving Oneself to Others', 'Fulfilment by Giving Oneself to Oneself' – and for each subsection a list of authors is proposed. So a whole area of experience is called into being and given clarity. We see him planning a literary magazine, then a publishing list of short works by major authors and another of fifty novels for young readers, but also analysing the success of the rival publisher Mondadori's celebrated "Biblioteca Romantica" list, launched in 1930, which attempted to create, as Calvino acknowledges, a "corpus... fully representative of world literature". Attentive to all the nuts and bolts of publishing – the typeface, the quality of the paper, the efficacy of the blurbs – Calvino also appreciates Mondadori's stated ambition to put together a package that would not only be "prized by bibliophiles", but also pleasing "to women, the vast majority of the reading public".

It is one of the few mentions women get in this book. At no point is a female author discussed, not even Ginzburg or her close friend Elsa Morante, both of whom published with Einaudi. Asked by an interviewer which novelists he likes, Calvino replies with twenty-four short sentences, each beginning, *I love this or that writer because...* Only three are Italian. Only two are women: "I love Mansfield, because she's intelligent"; "I love Jane Austen because I never read her, but I'm glad she exists".

Is that "read" present tense or past? Has he ever read Austen? "*Non la leggo mai*" is the Italian. Present. "I never read her now" might have cleared up the ambiguity. Translation frequently comes up in this section of *The Written World and the Unwritten World*, since so much of Calvino's work at Einaudi involved the publication of foreign books. In one essay he berates a reviewer for too quickly dismissing a translator's hard work. In another he himself describes a book as having been translated, "alas, very badly", without offering example or explanation. Speaking to a conference of translators in 1982, he confirms that he wasn't averse to flattery, titling his speech 'Translating a Text Is the True Way of Reading It'.

Unfortunately, the assertion is belied by Goldstein's translation of this book. Despite an admirable determination to stay close to the original, there are frequent small misunderstandings. "In Italy there is a rising literary tide," we hear. "*Si sta configurando in Italia una corrente letteraria*," Calvino wrote, meaning a "literary group" is forming (a "*corrente*", in art or politics, is always a group within a larger movement or party). Sometimes the English of the translation is clumsy: "This first period," we are told, "which lasted until after the war, today is obsolete." Can "a period" be "obsolete"? "*Superato*" is the word in the original, indicating something one has gone beyond, in this case simply a period that is over. One can imagine Calvino making a long list of these niggles, carefully classifying them in categories and subcategories. The "incomparable richness" of Italian, he claims in one essay, makes it "essentially untranslatable". This seems an exaggeration on both sides of the equation, but certainly the best readers of Calvino's elegant prose will be native Italian speakers entirely familiar with his context.

Having established that written and unwritten worlds constitute radically separate spheres, Calvino poses the question of how the writer can bring language to the world, or rather how the reality around us can happen on the page. The third section of this collection, 'On the Fantastic', explores one solution that Calvino had made his own. His early fiction in the late 1940s and 1950s oscillated between realism (*The Path to the Spiders' Nests*, 1947; *A Plunge into Real Estate*, 1957; *The Watcher*, 1963) and fantasy (*The Cloven Viscount*, 1952; *The Baron in the Trees*, 1957; *The Non-Existent Knight*, 1959), the former beloved of the Communists as the obvious form for committed literature, the latter offering a line of escape from the minders of left-wing orthodoxy. Introducing an anthology of nineteenth-century *Fantastic Tales* (1983), Calvino talks about the "inner life" and "collective symbology" that this sort of literature maps out, but he is then quick to reassure us that "contrary to what may be believed", the fantastic "requires a clear mind, control of reason over instinctive or unconscious inspiration, stylistic discipline".

Calvino's own adventures in the genre follow a simple pattern: a single fantastical element – the viscount who has been cut into two halves (a good and a bad), or the baron who decides to live his entire life in the trees – allows the world to be evoked with playful virtuosity from an unusual perspective. There are evident analogies with the schematic strategies of the French Oulipo movement, which Calvino joined in 1973. The desire is always to invent a mechanism that, as he says, will "generate stories". "Whenever I think I've grasped a plan, a design, a strategy in an author," he tells us here, "I'm happy" (Calvino's original "*sono tutto contento*" more slyly suggests a man who's really very pleased with himself). Structuralism, the dominant critical movement of the time, is never far away; stories are understood as events "composed into a schema"; "narrative structures" exist independently of any author "like geometric figures". Remembering the anthology of two hundred Italian fables that he had collected in 1956, Calvino describes with evident pleasure how "I rushed into the forest of the folktale… and tried to classify and sort through a thick, tangled vegetation of marvels and enchantments".

The fourth and last section, 'Science, History, Anthropology', sees Calvino reviewing books on Galileo and the last Aztec king, Montezuma, on neuroscience and cannibalism, the history of the sun and the inevitability or otherwise of entropy. It is by far the most entertaining. We hear of his "relief" on discovering that the Aztecs' mass sacrifices of their enemies would conclude with the victims being eaten, this as part of a strategy to complement a protein-poor diet – at least, Calvino reflects, there was something rational behind all that killing, and the meat was enjoyed. In another piece, he is delighted to learn from the book under review that the myth of Parsifal is "symmetrical and inverted" with respect to that of Oedipus. "I had arrived at almost the same conclusion," he enthuses, "trying to tell the greatest number of myths possible with different arrangements of the same cards in a tarot deck." The reference is to his novel *The Castle of the Crossed Destinies* (1969).

A review of an article in *Scientific American* on cosmological models reminds us that Calvino wrote his own history of the universe in the droll, witty stories he called *Cosmicomics* (1965). "The time of molecules and atoms," he is pleased to inform us, "is symmetrical and reversible" – just like the myths of Parsifal and Oedipus. Symmetry is always a source of satisfaction to Calvino, no doubt because it offers an illusion of order and meaning. Comically, he imagines one of his fictional characters, the eponymous hero of *Palomar* (1983) – a man who "collects cosmological models" – reading the same scientific article. Palomar "makes a written summary… then archives it in his collections, where many other universes are lined up next to one another like butterflies pierced by a pin." Expecting "nothing good from the universe… [Palomar] feels the need to keep an eye on it". It is not hard to intuit here the underlying anxieties that fuel Calvino's yearning for pattern and order. Elsewhere, the collapse of Aztec civilization is put down to a crisis of its "warning systems", as a result of which Montezuma, like Palomar, "tries desperately to keep his eyes open, to understand".

Perhaps inevitably, Calvino was drawn to writers for whom he felt a certain affinity. The "unity" of Claude Lévi-Strauss's writing, we are told, "lies in the method of investigation and... in the mental attitude that informs this method, rather than in the subjects dealt with". Calvino must have been aware that the same could have been said of himself. The celebrated ethnologist, he explains, starts from "the reality of the object" and looks for a "perspective" that can "reach the essence of every concept and every problem". This, as it turns out, is one of the strategies listed in the collection's title essay for bringing written and unwritten worlds together: "Fix [your] attention on an ordinary object, the most banal and familiar, and describe it minutely." It is also the strategy of Palomar, who tries to get a grip on the world by offering exasperatingly meticulous accounts of ordinary, if complex, phenomena: waves rolling towards the beach, a deli counter stacked with cheeses, the pale moon in an afternoon sky.

The difference between Calvino and Lévi-Strauss, or again Ortega y Gasset, another writer whom the author reads "not to be convinced by his ideas, but for the pleasure of seeing how the mechanism of his mind works", is that Calvino is not under the illusion that his methodical approach can deliver any ultimate truth. The irony behind all his storytelling, whether it be Marcovaldo's charmingly whimsical metropolitan adventures in the 1960s (see *Marcovaldo, or The Seasons in the City*, 1963), or Palomar's phenomenological obsessions in the 1980s, is that every attempt to master reality, however canny, however elaborately constructed, always falls short of its goal: the unwritten world remains beyond our grasp, and the only possible response is perseverance and playfulness.

Which prompts a last reflection: throughout this collection Calvino insists on a humble stance. His aspiration, he says, was always to be a "minor writer". He does not embark on a book because there is something he knows that he wishes to tell us, but because, like the scientist, there is something he doesn't know that he wishes to explore, or because he has come across a style of writing that he feels is beyond him, and hence, paradoxically, that he must attempt. The ten novel openings that make up *If on a Winter's Night a Traveller* are thus written in ten styles that Calvino felt he wasn't competent to write, and amount to ten explorations of states of mind with which he wasn't familiar. And so on. A writer's biography, he insists, is not important, if for no other reason than because "he has no continuity, he constantly dies and is reborn".

Yet, reading these essays, written between 1952 and 1985, and using them to revisit Calvino's extraordinary lifetime oeuvre, there is an undeniable continuity throughout, both of authorial voice and the position the author assumes with regard to the conflicts and debates of his generation. In 'La Poubelle agréée' (1977), a long essay (not collected here) in which Calvino's daily domestic task of taking out the trash from his Paris apartment becomes the departure point for extended anthropological ruminations, he eventually breaks off to confess: "It's myself I'm talking about, only and always myself – it's my own mental categories I'm applying as I seek to understand the mechanism of which I am (of which we are) a part."

It is for these moments of pathos, irony and honesty, when palaces of dazzling reflection are swept aside and the most adventurous thinking is undone, that one reads Italo Calvino.

ANDREA CAMILLERI

(1925–2019)

The Revolution of the Moon

Fans of the Salvo Montalbano detective stories – hugely popular in Italy as in the UK both in print and on TV – will be familiar with Andrea Camilleri's Sicily. Men in high places are utterly corrupt, avid for wealth and sex, ready to cheat, betray and kill whenever it suits. Parasitic on ordinary folk, grotesquely tasteless and comically hypocritical, they hide behind the island's vocation for baroque bureaucratese.

Fortunately, as the little people suffer and the *cadaveri eccellenti* pile up, there are nevertheless those who, at the opposite extreme, are marvellously upright, self-sacrificing and determined to distribute justice and charity. First and foremost, of course, is our *commissario di polizia*, Salvo Montalbano, but there will usually be a wise and long-suffering woman who sees the world's woes with great clarity and acts with admirable fortitude. These good people are also discriminating about art, literature and food, and though they too have their sexual impulses, they know how to behave with dignity.

As elaborately plotted as the criminal mind is perverse, the Montalbano stories are told in a sly mix of standard Italian and Sicilian dialect, inviting readers to find the island society at once irredeemable and quaint. You're happy the place exists, glad you don't live there and curious to try out one or two of the recipes the novels throw up. Unsurprisingly, the ninety-two-year-old Camilleri, who began his career writing and directing for TV, but has now published more than a hundred books (a good forty of which feature Salvo Montalbano), is Italy's most successful "literary" export.

The Revolution of the Moon, however, published in Italy in 2013, is set in the seventeenth century, some three hundred years before Commissario Montalbano was born. Camilleri began his writing career as a historical novelist, and has kept up with the genre between his detective stories. Nevertheless, the setting is always Sicily, and the corruption remarkably similar whatever era we're in, with the same good folk to offer hope and the same wry style to describe it all.

It is 1677. Sicily is ruled by a Spanish viceroy who governs with the support of a Holy Royal Council. The six councillors are all irretrievably evil, to the point of being hard to distinguish from each other. One runs a refuge for well-to-do orphan girls, which of course is a brothel. The most prominent councillor, the bishop of Palermo, is a paedophile and a murderer. Others merely thieve or embezzle. As the book opens, the well-meaning but sickly viceroy dies during a council meeting, and we discover that, extraordinarily, he has designated his wife, Donna Eleonora, to succeed him. "Holy shit," is the bishop's response. The news spreads round town in "the twinkling of an eye", and dismayed Sicilian men quickly vent their anger at this grotesque inversion of the natural order on their womenfolk. Michiluzzo Digiovanni "laid [his wife] down on the bed and got down to work on her for three hours straight as if she was an animal".

Twenty-five-year-old Eleonora is "so beautiful it was frightening". Unveiling her face, she reveals "a point of light brighter than the sun, so dazzling that it brought tears to one's eyes". Don Serafino, the doctor called to attend on her when she faints, immediately falls hopelessly in love, and will serve her slavishly for the month in which she is allowed to govern, a month when the "ball-busting woman", as the councillors think of her, seeks to put some order in the world, reducing food prices and aiding destitute women, while the evil men, who are also rather stupid, mainly destroy each other, as is the way in Camilleri's books.

In the refuge where the orphan girls are kept in cells and the men view them through spyholes, Don Alterio thrills "at the sight of a twenty-year-old bottom, a pair of white tits as solid as marble and a Mons Veneris whose thicket looked like velvet". But when the girl he chooses falls pregnant, Don Simone has her killed, prompting Don Alterio to take revenge by denouncing his fellow councillor to Donna Eleonora. Don Severino, meantime, who has been deprived of various ill-gotten gains, tries to get rich again by selling information to the bishop about that "slyboots" Donna Eleonora's plan to have him (the bishop) arrested for "practising the foul deed with altar boys". The bishop pays handsomely for this tip-off, and promptly orders another priest to murder Don Severino.

And so on. If the plot is increasingly complex, the psychology couldn't be simpler. The reader sides with the beautiful, virtuous Eleonora and her adoring doctor, and is delighted when she "sticks it straight up [the councillors'] arses", something she can do because, "aside from having all the feminine attributes in the highest degree", she "also possessed a big pair of *huevones*".

Which brings us to the novel's use of language. Mixing archaic Italian and Sicilian with a generous sprinkling of Spanish, the language of Sicily's rulers at the time (and of course of Donna Eleonora herself), Camilleri aims for a witty blend of authenticity and farce. Inevitably, this puts the translator Stephen Sartarelli, much praised for his Montalbano translations, in all kinds of trouble. The register veers wildly from "rogues and greedyguts" who are "tickled pink" one moment and "fucked" the next, "busting [each other's] chops" or "taking it in the arse", while the Spanish is left untranslated and will very likely be incomprehensible to many English readers. In short, what feels endearingly infantile in the Italian seems merely embarrassing in the English.

DARIO FO
(1926–2016)

AND

FRANCA RAME
(1929–2013)

The People's Clowns

A biography of Dario Fo and Franca Rame is inevitably a history of Italy in their lifetimes, and particularly in the decades from 1950 to 1990, when their careers as playwrights, actors and political activists were at their peak. Play by play, show by show, Fo engaged in fierce polemics with more or less every area of Italian society. His work, as Joseph Farrell observes in *Dario Fo and Franca Rame: Theatre, Politics, Life*, contains none of the intimacy, intellectual elucubration or existential angst that one finds in so many artists of the twentieth century. Nor can his biographer find much of it in the life. All Fo's energies were invested in the theatre, or in the clash for which the theatre, or occasionally television, were the chosen instruments.

Once drawn into the influence of this brilliant comet, Franca Rame became one with it, no doubt altering its trajectory and intensifying its light, but not changing its essential nature. For a biography of a couple there is remarkably little that touches on their private world together, perhaps because there was no private world. Their life simply was this bright, festive, cruel light they shone on Italian society. And whatever one thinks about the aesthetic value of this or that play, their endeavours always had the virtue of forcing all sides to come out in the open and declare themselves. As a consequence, Farrell's book is one of the best introductions to post-war Italy I have come across.

Fo was born in 1926 in a village near Lake Maggiore, fifty miles north-west of Milan. His father was a stationmaster, his mother, as they say, of peasant stock. Eldest of three children, he enlisted his younger brother and sister as audience and supporting actors in home theatricals and puppet shows. From the first, Dario was prime mover, energizer and star. At fourteen, his promise was such that his parents sent him to Milan, where he attended the Brera Liceo, a school attached to the city's foremost art college.

At seventeen, this cheerful adolescent received call-up papers to join the army of the Italian Social Republic, or Repubblica di Salò, the northern Italian state that Mussolini had formed with Nazi support after the Allied invasion of Italy from the south. Fo's parents were anti-Fascists. Other young men fled to the mountains to join the partisan resistance. Fo, however, as he later said, "preferred to choose a waiting position and try to dodge the call-up with trickery". Eventually he volunteered for a unit he hoped would not be engaged in fighting. He deserted, re-enlisted and deserted again, hoping "to hide away, to come home with my skin intact". It was a curiously uncertain start to a career that would later be marked by a willingness to assume radically anti-authoritarian positions in the face of aggressive harassment. Perhaps the difference, in 1944, was that Fo hadn't perceived the battle as his own: it wasn't about him – he was merely a pawn. "In the unpromising surroundings of his barracks," Farrell remarks, "Dario managed to perform some comic monologues."

Between 1945 and 1950, studying painting and architecture in Milan, Fo was gradually drawn towards the theatre. On the train back and forth from Lake Maggiore to the city, he would entertain other passengers with comic monologues mocking the status quo. A "Puckish mischief-maker", as Farrell describes him, he invented all kinds of practical jokes, on one occasion selling tickets to a supposed reception for Picasso in Milan, then producing a janitor from Brera who had some resemblance to the artist. When his mother moved the family into Milan, he and his brother and sister sang and acted for friends. He began attending plays directed by the socialist Giorgio Strehler at the newly opened Piccolo Theatre in Milan. He read Gramsci's books, which encouraged the rediscovery and re-evaluation of popular culture as a necessary step on the road to a Marxist revolution. In 1950 he asked Franco Parenti, a successful theatre and radio actor, to listen to his monologues. Parenti was impressed, and later that year Fo signed a contract with RAI (Italy's national public-broadcasting company) to produce twelve comic monologues. At twenty-four, his career had begun.

Despite its uneven quality, there is a remarkable consistency of intent to Fo's work and to the turbulence that invariably develops around it. It begins with an act of appropriation and inversion. A well-known story – Cain and Abel, David and Goliath, *Romeo and Juliet*, *Hamlet*, Christopher Columbus, *Rigoletto* – is taken and turned upside down; we sympathize with Cain, with Goliath, with Juliet's parents; the "official" version of history is perverse and serves a ruling elite. Fo collected his early monologues under the title *Poer nano* – literally "poor dwarf", but with the colloquial meaning "poor sod", "poor loser". The world's injustices are seen from the point of view of the victim, but the sparkling comedy, the energy and sheer fun that Fo injected into his performances, transforms this loser into a winner.

RAI suspected a political agenda and broke off the relationship. It was an outcome Fo would grow used to. In one monologue, based on the *Rigoletto* story, he played a jester who, as Farrell puts it, "faces the dilemma of being either court entertainer, and hence the plaything of authority, or the voice of the people". It was Fo's own quandary. RAI wanted light entertainment. Fo resisted. Very likely his employer's attempts to keep politics out of his work led to his becoming more "the voice of the people" than he originally planned. The tension was fruitful.

Without the radio work, he fell back on cabaret and variety, and in 1951 found himself in the same show as the blonde, glamorous, wonderfully lively Franca Rame. She was three years younger than him and came from a family of travelling actors who could trace back their involvement in popular theatre for hundreds of years. Essentially, the Rames wrote the basic outlines of their stories, often borrowing them from existing plays and novels, then improvised onstage in the Italian tradition of *la commedia dell'arte*. It was theatre without the authorial figures of writer and director, and as such emblematic of the popular culture that Gramsci had sought to champion. Fo was fascinated.

But he did not court Franca. "His grin was toothy," Farrell says, "his nose jutted out like a small promontory, his arms dangled, his legs were seemingly out of proportion to his trunk, and his gait was gangling and tumbling." In short, Fo was no Adonis, and Franca, he later remembered, "was always pursued by hosts of men prepared to go to any lengths. I didn't want to enter the lists." Again events are described in terms of competition: Dario wouldn't get involved if he couldn't win. Eventually, Franca took the initiative and kissed Dario backstage. All too soon the couple had to borrow money for an illegal abortion. Then the "gorgeous bitch", as Dario described her, left him. He had to wait till they were working together in his first show "to win her back". In 1954 the two married "to please her devoutly Catholic mother", and in 1955 Franca gave birth to their only child, Jacopo.

Fo never went to drama school and had no formal training as an actor or director. Nor did he have any ambition to have his plays published as stand-alone literary works. What mattered was the moment of performance, where he was triumphant, and very often triumphantly himself, as storyteller rather than character-actor. The problem throughout his career would be to create a form of theatre that suited his talents and made sense in the rapidly changing socio-political context in which he moved. Crucially, in the two shows he put on with Franco Parenti at the Piccolo in the 1950s, *A Poke in the Eye* and *Madhouse for the Sane*, Fo was able to draw on the stagecraft of Strehler and take lessons with mime expert Jacques Lecoq, who also helped him, as Farrell has it, to "acquire that range of laughs and onomatopoeic vocalizations which were indispensable to his monologues and enabled him to reproduce everything from storms at sea to tigers licking wounds".

In the theatre as on the radio, debunking conventional viewpoints in a carnival atmosphere proved at once popular and controversial.

On tour, his shows met resistance from the Church and local authorities. The script of *Madhouse for the Sane*, Farrell writes, "was massacred by the censors" working under the direct supervision of the future prime minister Giulio Andreotti, then an undersecretary of state. Fo chose to ignore the changes the censors demanded and got away with it.

But along with these invigorating battles with the conservative establishment, there were also disagreements with collaborators. Strehler was a champion of Brecht; Fo found his approach too complacent in positing a savvy middle-class audience; Parenti was an admirer of French absurdism, of Ionesco and Beckett. Fo found these writers too intellectual and abstract. He wanted a more direct, seductive relationship with his audience. He did not want to be trapped in a rigid script.

In 1956 he and Franca went to Rome and made a film, *Lo svitato* ("The Screwball"), reminiscent of Jacques Tati. It flopped, an experience far worse than getting fired for being provocatively popular. "Years later," Farrell observes, "[Fo] could repeat audience figures in various cinemas in Rome, recite box-office takings in an experimental cinema in Milan." He had failed, he felt, because actors were powerless in the cinema. He had lost control of the product. It must never happen again.

He and Franca returned to Milan, set up their own theatre company and produced a string of slapstick farces complete with song and dance that "sat at an awkward angle to the expectations of a middle-class audience in search of a good night out". These were the years of the post-war boom, a general economic optimism coupled with touchy Catholic conservatism, Fo being seen as "a scoffing but jovial bohemian rather than… an enraged iconoclast". This beguiling image was reinforced when the couple agreed to take over *Carosello*, a TV programme consisting of ten minutes of short sketches, each advertising a different product or brand. Still available on YouTube, these hilarious pieces show a charmingly goofy Fo playing dumb beside the voluptuous Franca, the punchline of each two-minute routine producing a well-known brand name like a rabbit from a hat. With only one state-run channel, Italian television was so tediously predictable that *Carosello* became the most popular programme.

In Milan too the couple's complementary charisma was out-selling every other Italian theatre of the time. Titles invited audiences to expect risqué material – *Thieves Mannequins and Naked Women, Bodies in the Post and Women in the Nude*. Light comedy was mixed with political protest, about corruption in the building industry, about the Church's stranglehold on public mores, about bourgeois hypocrisy. Stock figures emerged: the loser who comes out on top, the *faux-naïf* who shows up society's sham, the prostitute with the golden heart, the madman as the only sane person in a crazy world. Fo was always the lead actor, Franca always the leading lady, ever ready to appear in a negligée to keep audiences happy. "Did the plays amount to literature?" asked the theatre magazine *Sipario* when it published the script of *Archangels Don't Play Pinball*. The "best" of the play, it decided, existed only on stage in "the bare-knuckled struggle in which Dario Fo the actor and Dario Fo the author engage... to gain the upper hand". Fo was competing with Fo. He needed stiffer opposition.

And found it in 1962. Invited to take over RAI's hugely successful TV variety *Canzonissima*, Fo injected some sharp political satire into a routine of "high-kicking, scantily clad, sequinned dancing girls". Essentially, he ridiculed the complacency surrounding Italy's economic miracle and the fawning subservience of the white-collar classes. In one sketch, a demented employee caresses and worships the statue of his boss. Typically, the more successful the programme became, the more opposition Fo encountered. Finally, a sketch showing a construction magnate refusing to spend on safety measures, then taking his mistress to buy expensive jewellery, was banned. Fo and Rame walked out. They would not be allowed back on national television for fourteen years. But their name was made, and Fo, who thrived on antagonism, had understood that controversy and celebrity could be one and the same thing.

In the mid 1960s the Italian economy took a dive, while a growing permissiveness drew audiences to plays that were openly provocative. Social conflict took on a new edge. Back in the theatre Fo found ways of dramatizing the kind of tensions he had experienced at RAI and taunting his audiences. One play ends with a chorus of asylum inmates whose brains have been surgically altered to make them acquiescent, singing, "We are happy, we are content with the brain we have, we have the propeller which makes us follow the flow."

But box-office success now made Fo ask if he wasn't actually failing as a political artist. Noticing a fur-coated woman entirely at ease with the performance, he wondered if the pleasures of his clowning and Franca's glamour weren't making it all too anodyne. Again and again, Farrell's biography shows Fo wrestling with the question of how to combine the enjoyment theatre must afford with the arousal of a socially transformative anger that would make his shows relevant and important. He thirsted for bigger battles, more radical victories. He visited communist Eastern Europe, Cuba, declared himself Marxist. He ransacked history for accounts of social conflict that could be dramatized as parallels with contemporary life. Catharsis was condemned as a bourgeois trick that reconciled the spectator to injustice.

Most of all, he began to see himself as a man with a mission, in the tradition of the *giullare*, the jester or court fool who invents stories that speak truth to power and galvanize the populace. Much time would be spent over the coming years researching and to a degree falsifying this historic figure, in an attempt to give dignity to the special position he was creating for himself. When social unrest exploded across Europe in 1968, Fo and Rame abandoned the conventional theatre circuit and set up an actors' cooperative, Nuova Scena, which would play in Communist Party clubs around the country, returning theatre to its popular origins and putting their talents "at the service of revolutionary forces".

Farrell's account of this endeavour points up its fertile contradictions. Fo and the increasingly politicized Rame insisted that Nuova

Scena would be egalitarian: everyone would have a say, everyone would be paid the same. Yet there was an abyss between their talent and that of the young left-wing intellectuals their venture attracted. Resentment against capitalism could quickly morph into resentment against Dario and Franca staying in expensive hotels, hogging the limelight and cashing their royalty cheques, which did not form part of the equal payroll package. On the other hand, audiences wanted Dario and Franca, not the others. Farrell reports long, energy-sapping discussions "conducted in a sub-Marxist jargon which is now as impenetrable as the disputations of medieval monks".

Just as Fo had offended RAI when he worked for them, now he offended the Communist Party, on which he depended for his venues. Seizing on issues of the day and putting them directly to his audience, parallels were drawn between the American presence in Vietnam and the Soviet invasion of Czechoslovakia, while one play showed the Communist mayor of Bologna waltzing with the city's cardinal. The Communist paper *L'Unità* accused Fo of "errors of judgement and perspective". Some venues no longer wanted him. Meantime, Nuova Scena had played to 240,000 people across Italy, ninety per cent of whom had never been to a theatre before. Each performance was followed by a debate with the audience that could go on late into the night. It was exhausting.

In 1969 Fo launched the *Mistero buffo* ("funny" or "buffoonish mystery") – monologues, and at last achieved the leap of quality that would lay the basis for his Nobel Prize in 1997. In his thirst for material to appropriate and his search for popular rather than elite theatre from the past, he had become fascinated by the Middle Ages, and in particular the Christian tradition of mystery plays and apocryphal stories of Christ's life. Many of these had been reworked by Renaissance artists, in particular the actor-playwright Angelo Beolco, better known as Ruzzante, who had become Fo's idol and designated precursor. Appropriating, translating and rewriting, Fo worked these stories up into a cycle of monologues that could go on for many hours.

The performance began with him addressing the audience directly to denounce the scandalous suppression of this more lively version of the Christian story, together with the figure of the *giullare*, the jester. The authorities obstructed popular creativity, he claimed, because it undermines their power. He then gave an outline of the stories, drawing provocative parallels with issues of the day. All this was presented in standard Italian. The audience now primed, Fo transformed himself into the jester figure, launching into the monologue proper in a demotic, onomatopoeic gibberish, or "grammelot", that mixed various northern Italian dialects, Latin and French, archaisms, neologisms and acoustic effects of every kind. For Italians brought up speaking both dialect and standard Italian – the norm in the 1960s – there was at once a powerful feeling of recognition and intimacy, and at the same time the impression of being shifted into some carnival space in a distant past.

Incantatory and often dazzlingly incomprehensible, this torrent of strange language was clarified by the most energetic miming as Fo acted out all the parts in his story in an irresistible tour de force. A gravedigger sells seats to people eager to see Jesus raise Lazarus from the dead. A woman whose baby has been killed by Herod's soldiers believes it has been transformed into a lamb. The boy Jesus tries to make friends by showing off a few miracles then turns a rich bully to terracotta. A drunkard rejoices in the quality of wine at the Marriage at Cana. The execrable Pope Boniface dresses in all his finery, but is shocked when he meets Jesus in rags carrying his cross to Calvary.

Mistero buffo is a rich and flexible package, the perfect vehicle for Fo's exuberant genius. Crucially, while attacking injustice and a corrupt Church, the stories leave respect for the Christian story intact. In this regard they might even be seen as tame and conservative, though that was not how they were perceived at the time, as audiences flocked to watch Fo at the top of his game and in total control of what was now exciting, meticulously prepared material.

Can *Mistero buffo* be performed without Fo's special charisma? Can it be translated? In October 2019, Mario Pirovano performed the monologues in a fiftieth-anniversary production in Milan. Pirovano spent a long time living with Fo and Rame, learnt to imitate him and even to a degree looks like him. He has the mime, the dialect and the grammelot down to a T. But one only needs to see a video of Fo's versions to appreciate how much more dazzling his performances were, how abundant and aggressive the political commentary he worked into his introductions. For all Pirovano's talent, there is the feeling that one is straining for an echo of something lost. English translations of the pieces preserve no trace of the linguistic wealth of the original.

1969 was also the year that left-wing terrorism began in earnest. Advocates of revolution rather than reform, Fo and Rame condemned the violence, but became objects of intense police surveillance, particularly after Franca formed Red Aid, an organization that offered support to imprisoned terrorist suspects. Nuova Scena was wound up, and the company Comune formed, to act out parables of political strife in factories and workers' clubs up and down the country. Typically, Fo insisted that the company bring all the technical paraphernalia of theatre – scenery, costumes and lighting – despite the improvised nature of the venues. It had to be a seductive, professional show. Almost at once Comune was beset by the same internal quarrels that had dogged Nuova Scena, and it disbanded in 1972. However, in 1970 the company did produce *Accidental Death of an Anarchist*, Fo's most successful straight play.

In December 1969 a bomb in a Milan bank killed seventeen people. The police arrested anarchist Giuseppe Pinelli, who died two nights later falling from the window of the police station. It soon emerged that Pinelli had had nothing to do with the bomb. In Fo's play a mad impostor (obviously Fo) convinces the dumb Milan policemen that he is an inspector from Rome come to help create some credible account of Pinelli's death. In scenes as bitter as they are wacky, Pinelli's interrogation is enacted over and over. Since court hearings on the death were proceeding as the play premiered, Fo changed the script almost daily to include material from the trial, much of it as grotesque and surreal as his original imaginings. The play led to forty legal actions against him. In 1972 the police inspector in charge of the interrogation was gunned down by terrorists.

It is with a sense of wonder that one follows Farrell's detailed account of these years – wonder that Fo and Rame survived, wonder that they survived as a couple. Fo was a whirlwind of creativity throwing up turbulence all around. Their house was set on fire. Franca was abducted and raped by right-wing thugs. The couple went on producing plays in which they pretended to spray machine-gun fire on the audience or had actors dressed as police burst into the theatre and tell the terrified audience they were all under arrest. They visited Mao's China and declared it the perfect society. For years they occupied an abandoned building in central Milan, turning it into a theatre and left-wing community. Shown on public television in 1977, *Mistero buffo* provoked fierce national controversy.

Dario had endless affairs with young actresses. Franca announced she was leaving him in a live TV interview. Fo wrote letters of apology and reconciliation that reached her via newspaper publication. It was as if a life were not real if it didn't happen in public. He began to concede her importance and co-authorship of their work. She began to perform monologues of her own on feminist issues. All this while a constant stream of polemical plays was produced, often on controversial questions – Palestine, Chile, drug-dealing – about which Fo knew very little. "Years lived at high speed," Rame later observed. She died in 2013, and Fo in 2016.

What one is invited to consider here is the notion of an artist whose work mattered supremely at the moment and in the place it was produced, and depended largely on the physical presence of Fo and Rame. Directors around the world have produced Fo's work. The British version of *Accidental Death of an Anarchist* is a rare example of successful adaptation. But the sheer electricity and brazen provocation of Fo's original performance is hard to recover, even in Italy. Fo, Farrell claims, "was the least autobiographical of writers." But arguably the plays themselves, his performance of them, were the life, and the marriage. The stage settings were his. He designed and often painted the props. He wrote the songs. He performed himself, directed himself. Rame advised, assisted, edited.

Browsing the scores of videos available online, it's hard not to feel that Fo is happiest with an adoring audience of young people sitting cross-legged on the floor all around while he performs the monstrous Boniface puffing himself up in papal splendour. But however complacent the audience might be about the moral message behind the material, it does not seem that any transformative anger is aroused, or any compassion for the pope's victims, nailed by their tongues to church doors. One is simply agog at the extraordinary virtuosity that is Dario Fo.

UMBERTO ECO
(1932–2016)

Looking forward to the Past

Milan, 1991. A man wakes up after an accident, yet feels he is "still suspended in a milky grey". This greyness is evoked by quoting a dozen or so literary descriptions of fog. Finally aware that he is in a hospital bed, the man is able to answer a number of questions posed to him by a doctor in order to check the proper functioning of his mind. He cites the Pythagorean theorem, mentions Euclid's elements, quotes spontaneously from *Moby Dick* and *The Waste Land*, but cannot remember his name. At some length it is explained that while retaining his "semantic memory", everything, that is, that he ever learnt in the form of publicly available factual knowledge, he has lost his private or personal memory. He doesn't know whether he is married or not, has no recollection of his parents or of the various episodes of his life, no recall of the thousand small personal activities in which one engages every day: cleaning teeth, driving a car, dressing.

Fortunately, the man's legal identity is not at issue. He is Giambattista Bodoni, nicknamed Yambo. At fifty-nine he is a successful dealer in antique books, married to a psychologist, Paola, with two daughters and three grandchildren who soon come to visit him in hospital. He observes them with equanimity, but without interest, and at one point, even as he caresses his grandchildren, his head fills with "a maelstrom of memories that were not mine":

> the marchioness went out at five o'clock in the middle of the journey of our life, Abraham begat Isaac and Isaac begat Jacob and Jacob begat the man of La Mancha, and that was when I saw the pendulum betwixt a smile and tear, on the branch of Lake

Como where late the sweet birds sang, the snows of yesteryear softly falling into the dark mutinous Shannon waves, *messieurs les Anglais je me suis couché de bonne heure*, though words cannot heal the women come and go...

This babble goes on for a full page. Yambo's is no ordinary case of amnesia. He is, as it were, an encyclopedic mind without a self, rather as if the accident had happened to the erudite Eco himself. At once the book becomes a quest: Yambo must rediscover himself. In doing so, we presume that we will be enlightened as to what exactly a self is and how it stands in relation to the collective or public mind represented by Yambo/Eco's erudition.

In the past Eco's novels have involved virtuoso reconstructions of historically distant worlds – the Middle Ages, the seventeenth century – with an authorial voice that hints at the fictional nature of the work and, in the case of *The Island of the Day After*, actually advises us not to take its contents too seriously. The novel was thus a form of playground where a thick web of intrigue and light-hearted intellectual speculation was woven together without our being constrained to suppose that anything particularly important was at stake. Although something of that tendency remains here with the constant resort to literary quotation that necessarily invites the reader into a quiz-show complicity with the author – do you recognize this, do you recognize that? – *The Mysterious Flame of Queen Loana* evidently proposes a more traditional form of identification and seriousness. Yambo is oppressed by his own emptiness and indifference.

...the children were calling me Grandpa, I knew I was supposed to love them more than myself, and yet I couldn't tell which was Giangio, which was Alessandro, which was Luca. I knew all about Alexander the Great, but nothing about Alessandro the tiny, the mine.

The quest to rediscover intimacy in a domestic setting is a problem
of a different order from tracking down a murderer in a monastery
or uncovering the secrets of the Knights Templar.

Yambo returns home, where his affable, reassuring wife fills
him in on the main facts of his life, his childhood in Turin, his
parents' deaths when he was in his late teens. They engage in
further discussion about the nature of memory, this time with
the help of St Augustine and others. Yambo compares himself
to a singer stuck in the middle of a song.

I'm holding a long note, like a stuck record, and since I can't
remember the opening notes, I can't finish the song. I wonder
what it is I'm supposed to finish, and why.

Gianni, a lifelong friend, is also reassuring and affable. He tells
Yambo about school and college years, but this eventually becomes
frustrating, as Yambo fears that his mind is being filled by other
people's memories. To regain a sense of purpose he returns to
work, where he is assisted in his antique-book trade by a beautiful Polish girl, suggestively named Sibila, to whom he is instantly
attracted. Since his wife has already informed him with admirable
equanimity that he has always been a womanizer, Yambo now
wonders whether before his accident he was having an affair
with the girl. If so, how should he behave, how can he find out?
There is scope for comedy here, but little comes of it beyond
some awkward conversation and a further collection of quotations. Instead, Sibila joins the team of helpers who minister to
the author's alter ego, informing him this time about his daily
work habits. Ominously, we discover that for years Yambo has
been collecting literary descriptions of the fog. "Quotations are
my only fog lights," he jokes.

Some seventy pages into the novel, humming an old song about
first love gives Yambo a sensation as "when someone tickles your
pylorus". "A mysterious flame," he calls it. His attentive wife

observes that this song dates back to the 1940s, whereas Yambo normally only sings songs from the Fifties and afterwards. Clearly it is time for our hero to examine his childhood and early adolescence. End of part one.

The true nature of Eco's interest in his novel now becomes apparent. Yambo owns a large country home outside Turin, once the property of his grandparents. During his childhood he spent the summers there. When Turin was under Allied bombardment he was evacuated there for a year and more. Unlived-in now, the home preserves intact all the encyclopedias, books, gramophone records, newspapers, comics and magazines that Yambo's family was reading and listening to in the 1930s and '40s. We thus have the precondition for any Eco novel: a body of texts which can be enthusiastically analysed and a narrative alibi for paying them more attention than one would normally want to.

Yambo leaves his family to go and live in this country house, in a locality called Solara, and sets about reconstructing his childhood through the comics and adventure books he had once read, not forgetting to listen constantly to old 78s from whatever year he is tackling, pretending to himself that they are being played on the valve radio that his grandfather would listen to so assiduously. Although wife, friend and pretty assistant have been left behind in Milan, Yambo is looked after by the housemaid Amalia, who is old enough to be able to fill him in where necessary on his habits as a child. She is as affable and reassuring as our hero's other helpers, but can be distinguished from them because she is uneducated, makes lots of grammatical errors and knows no literary quotations.

The material that Yambo/Eco wades through is fascinating. The many illustrations introduced into the book, showing old comic strips, magazine advertisements, newspaper headlines, etc. are a pleasure, likewise the inventive rhyming translations of so many period Italian songs, though clearly the Italian reader of the original is at an advantage here, as he recognizes things he has already heard and seen. Above all, we see how varied were the messages an educated young boy was exposed to under Fascism. There are religious engravings, pages from encyclopedias showing every possible variety of torture, all sorts of military uniforms. Mickey Mouse in Italian is mixed up with tales of Fascist heroes. Meanwhile, the gramophone sings one moment of romantic love, the next of shedding blood for the Duce.

Most interestingly, Eco shows how the names of the American cartoon figures are gradually eliminated (Buffalo Bill becomes an Italian called Tombolino) as tension between Fascist Italy and the United States grows. He is interesting too when he suggests how alien the morality of Flash Gordon, a hero determined to free people from the slavery of evil dictators, must have seemed to a child used to reading about brave Fascist children battling in the name of Mussolini. As Yambo's researches take him into the 1940s, Eco considers how the newspapers reported on the war, allowing Italians to read between the lines to guess at their army's defeats, while the boys' adventure comics on the contrary remained in a state of denial, having their heroes fighting in Ethiopia long after the country had already fallen.

If there is a problem with all this, it is that the non-fictional interest in the period material works against the fictional treatment of Yambo. "How did I experience this schizophrenic Italy?" Eco has his hero wonder about every three or four pages in an attempt to remind us that the book is supposed to be about his selfhood, "Did I love il Duce?" Or again:

> Did I have some instinctive ability to keep the realm of good domestic feelings separate from those adventure stories that spoke to me of a cruel world modelled on the Grand Guignol?

Unfortunately, these are not questions the author can address, for Yambo simply doesn't remember. The opportunity to consider the formation of the personality in response to the media during Fascism is largely lost. Occasionally some old adventure book or illustration does set off "a mysterious flame" in Yambo's mind. A child's toy may trigger some association, or a phrase ("After looking at the frog... I spontaneously said that Angel Bear must die. Who was Angel Bear?"). But despite melodramatic references to the "desperate struggle" for memory, a mood of complacency and even self-congratulation pervades these pages as Yambo/Eco delves with characteristic energy into all the old boxes of papers that keep appearing in his grandfather's study and attic.

Many of the mysterious flames have to do with women. A profile of a woman in a French magazine is something that must have been "stamped on my heart" in childhood. It is also Sibila's profile, he decides. Ever avid to analyse the self he doesn't have, Yambo fears he has spent his whole life seeking the same magazine-inspired love object. In general, he is haunted by the post-modern anxiety that his life has been entirely foreshadowed in books. Even his nickname, he discovers, is that of a figure in a comic strip. Finally, however, he stumbles on something

that made me feel I was on the cusp of some final revelations. It had a multicoloured cover and was entitled *The Mysterious Flame of Queen Loana*. There lay the explanation for the mysterious flames that had shaken me since my reawakening, and my journey to Solara was finally acquiring a meaning.

Alas, no. This particular comic offers nothing more than a confused story about an African queen who guards a flame that can grant immortality. Yambo is disappointed. However, by this point it is clear that rather than a slow discovery, through action and interaction with other characters, of what it might mean to have a self or to be denied one, Eco has decided that Yambo's past will be discovered like a hidden treasure when some crucial clue is unearthed. Inexorably, and despite the promising opening, the story is beginning to look like Eco's previous novels, which posit vital secrets hidden among dusty pages. No doubt when the truth comes out it will have to do with an incident in the fog and a woman who looks like Sibila, and it will take place in the context created by all that reading from the 1930s and '40s.

A secret chapel is found in the country house. This discovery leads to the story, told in remarkable detail by Amalia, of how Yambo's grandfather protected four partisans there. We also hear how he was forced by a Fascist to drink castor oil and how he saved in a little bottle some of the faeces passed as a result of swallowing the oil, and years later forced the offending Fascist to drink them. Predictably, the old chapel also offers up another generous supply of dusty boxes and papers for Yambo to analyse.

The narrator discovers his school copy books, and finds that in 1942 he wrote an entirely conventional encomium to Fascist militarism. Only nine months later, however, in December of the same year, he wrote a wry little essay about a boy whose mother buys an unbreakable drinking glass, symbol of modern technological achievement, but when the boy tries to show it off to family friends by throwing it on the floor, it breaks. Immediately, Yambo deduces that some crucial change of character must have occurred between the two school essays. "I had become the narrator of a failure whose breakable objective correlative I represented." This sounds rather more like the jargon of Umberto Eco the semiotics professor than the words of Giambattista Bodoni the antique-books dealer.

Yambo discovers some poems written to a first love shortly after the war, when he was sixteen and living in Turin again. A telephone call to Gianni reveals that the girl was called Lila Saba. "Nice name, I let it melt in my mouth like honey." If a few moments before Yambo sounded like a literary academic, now there is nothing to distinguish him from the sentimental sops of the comics he has been reading. Gianni tells Yambo that the relationship was a "A 'Dante and Beatrice' kind of thing." Nothing came of it, however, since Lila's family left for Brazil, but Yambo couldn't get over the girl and "had looked for her the rest of [his] life". After the kind of reluctance that all witnesses must show before disclosing important evidence,

Gianni finally tells Yambo that shortly before the accident that led to his loss of memory the truth had come out that Lila actually died in Brazil, aged eighteen, and hence that Yambo has spent all his life (aside from a long marriage and much womanizing) hankering after a ghost. Gianni also reveals that he has recently found out that Lila was short for Sibila! Yambo is distressed. A poem is quoted:

> I am alone, leaning in the fog
> against an avenue's trunk…
> And nothing in my heart except your memory,
> pallid and colossal.

Many readers will feel sceptical and disappointed. All those dusty pages have been turned in Grandfather's attic to arrive at a piece of information that Gianni could cheerfully have supplied way back, to wit that Yambo, who had seemed such a self-assured, sensible fellow, has spent forty years and more obsessed with an adolescent girl with whom he never exchanged more than two words. It is understandable that at this point Eco hurries the plot on with a little deus ex machina.

Shortly after his arrival at Solara, Sibila had mailed Yambo the proofs of a new catalogue of the books his business is offering for sale. As a joke, she introduced into the list a 1623 First Folio of Shakespeare quoting a very low price, this just to check if Yambo was going through the proofs carefully. He nearly had a heart attack. The reader has thus been made aware of the monumental importance to a book dealer of this rare publication. Now, exactly as Eco's novel seems to have become irretrievably trite, Yambo discovers, in yet another dusty box in this old house… a real 1623 First Folio of Shakespeare:

> Now here I am, in my grandfather's study, touching my treasure with trembling hands… It is not Lila's photo, but it is an invitation to return to Milan, to the present. If Shakespeare's portrait

is here, Lila's portrait will be there. The Bard will guide me towards my Dark Lady.

Thus far we had been given the impression that Yambo's femme fatale was blonde. Never mind. This kind of loose melodramatic rhetoric can be taken as an indication of the trouble Eco is in. Facetiousness comes to his aid. "This is surely the greatest stroke of my life," Yambo announces. Overwhelmed by excitement, he passes out and, reduced by his great stroke to some kind of semi-comatose state... recovers his memory. End of part two.

Unfortunately, though he now repossesses his past, Yambo has no control over the order in which memories play out before his closed eyes, thus delaying various revelations for a further hundred pages and more. We can summarize as follows. In 1944 the thirteen-year-old Yambo was involved in a dramatic war adventure. He and other boys had learnt how to climb the all but unclimbable gorge above Solara to the village of San Martino. One day eight Cossacks fleeing from the Nazis took refuge there. The Germans had blocked the road, but there was a thick fog – the fog we have been patiently waiting for. The partisans convince young Yambo to guide them up the gorge in the night in the fog to retrieve the Cossacks. Arriving at San Martino, they find the Germans have advanced up the road, and they are forced to take two Germans prisoner and bring them along on the return trip down the impossibly steep slope. German dogs sniff them out. They are followed. The pursuers begin to shoot into the fog. To save the situation, Yambo's friend, the anarchist Gragnola, takes the Germans off on another path, kills them and pushes them off the cliff. The dogs won't be able to follow the group now, and the Cossacks are saved. Yambo returns home safely, but Gragnola is captured and slits his own throat to avoid giving information to the Germans. "And I was alive," Yambo remembers. "I could not forgive myself for that." He falls into a deep depression.

Told over fifty or so pages, this is the longest stretch of uninter-rupted realistic narrative in the book. The psychological fall-out for our protagonist, however, seems forced. Yambo has behaved admirably, even heroically, just like the boys in all his adventure comics, but rather than being proud of himself he is oppressed by guilt, irretrievably traumatized, condemned for life to collecting quotations about the fog. A religious crisis with strong echoes of Stephen Dedalus in *A Portrait of the Artist as a Young Man* is followed by sublimated love for Lila, a love extensively compared with Cyrano de Bergerac's love for Roxanne. The promise of the girl can bring him out of his depressed state, but his fear of sin prevents him from touching her.

All is now explained. Yambo, with his regained memory, thinks and reflects in exactly the same way as Yambo without his memory. A self is a trifle. The recovery of his past, however, has not brought with it whatever strategies he must have developed over the years to deal with his unhappy adolescent experiences. We have no sense of how he could have conducted his adult life, or indeed who he really is. No matter. All we need now is a finale. Yambo is distressed that he cannot recall Lila's face. Wryly, comically perhaps, whatever strange mental state he is now in, he calls on Queen Loana (she of the comic strip) to grant him this vision. He is rewarded thus:

And at last, great God, I saw like the apostle, I saw the centre of my Aleph, from which shone forth not the infinite world, but the jumbled notebook of my memories.

Eco now scrambles together all the boy's literature of the previous chapters in a pseudo-religious vision which goes on for a dozen pages and promises to climax in a glimpse of the beloved Lila's face:

Down come the Seven Dwarves, rhythmically reciting the names of the seven kings of Rome, all but one – and then Mickey Mouse and Minnie, arm in arm with Horace Horsecollar and Clarabelle

Cow, bedecked with diadems from her treasure, to the rhythms of 'Pippo Pippo Doesn't Know'.

Et cetera. As the girl is about to appear, we are offered this image:

I… feel on the verge of orgasm, as my brain's corpora cavernosa swell with blood, as something gets ready to explode – or blossom.

But Yambo blacks out and quite likely dies before receiving his revelation. This too – the tease of final revelation denied – is the usual way for an Eco novel to end.

What are one's reflections on having read through the 450 pages of *The Mysterious Flame of Queen Loana* first in Italian, then in English? That life is short; that the translation by Geoff Brock is truly excellent; that when it comes to creating a sense of character no amount of glib quotation and eager textual analysis can substitute for some believable dialogue between characters who are actually engaged in the business of getting through life together; that the supposedly light comic touch of postmodern fantasy can on occasion be no more than the last resort of the inept; and finally that the extent to which celebrity may outlive performance is a marvellous and truly mysterious thing to which Eco, who is a fine essayist, might usefully turn some of his erudite attention.

CLAUDIO MAGRIS
(1939–)

Blameless

Claudio Magris does not write traditional novels. His masterpiece *Danube* (1990) followed a group of friends down the great river from obscure source to diffuse delta, gathering chronicle and anecdote at every meander, placing the lives and reflections of minor provincial figures from Mitteleuropa's near and distant past in relation to the "official" history we know. Always starting with hard facts – a document, a building, a battlefield – Magris nevertheless allows himself the freedom of imagining thoughts and emotions of historical figures. The reader is astonished by his erudition, charmed by the lightness with which he wears it and, in general, encouraged to think of the author as a self-deprecating sage with a wry sense of humour who has the pulse of history and means well.

Microcosms (1997) was a similar project, Magris looking for his material this time in various Italian border territories, from his native Trieste to the South Tyrol, to Piedmont. The aim, again, was to suggest life's immense richness in those nooks and crannies that challenge our penchant for category and stereotype. Any resistance one might feel to this highly accomplished act of seduction arises, ironically, from the growing sense that it is itself a systematic enterprise, another manner of categorizing.

Blindly (2005) adopted the same strategy of accumulation, but marked a decisive departure in terms of tone. Here a dying Communist partisan, Salvatore Cippico, recounts his struggles in Italy and Yugoslavia, his imprisonment in Dachau, his torture at the hands of Tito's thugs and eventual emigration to Australia. However, the speaking voice frequently changes identity, becoming sometimes Jorgen Jorgensen – the Dane who declared himself king of Iceland in the early nineteenth century, only to be imprisoned by the British and eventually deported to Tasmania – and sometimes the mythical Greek hero Jason. English prison ships are superimposed on German concentration camps, Iceland on Tasmania, and the Golden Fleece on the Red Flag, in what amounts to a ferocious denunciation of man's collective cruelty to man, the narrator becoming a universal victim who has lived and died innumerable times, always in horrific circumstances, always falling in love with women whose names begin with M: Maria, Marie, Mariza, Marja, Mangawana.

While *Danube* enjoyed immediate success both inside and outside Italy, the hugely ambitious but humourless and frankly bewildering *Blindly* struggled to find an audience, perhaps because the kind of pathos it strives for would require some credible dramatization of character and event, while all Magris can offer is an interminable insistence on his story's significance.

When they transported us to Dachau, it was always night, in the sealed wagon. In that wagon I was in the world's arctic night, in the blackest black that has ever been. I knew that if life was to be worthy of our living it, we would have to scrape away that blackness from the face of the earth. And, dear God, we have done that, and that counts for more than anything else. Yes, Jason is a thief and liar, and, after his victory, he behaved like a pig. Yes, among other things, I'm a pig too. But I killed the dragon that would have crushed and devoured the world; it said it would last a thousand years, the realm of that dragon, it promised a thousand years of Dachau, but I destroyed it after twelve, I smashed it to bits like a chamber pot.

Closer to *Blindly* than to *Danube*, Magris's new novel, *Blameless*, is again a denunciation – not so much, this time, of man's cruelty, but of the silence that surrounds it, the complacency of those who collaborate with cruelty and escape scot-free: "Evil is a chain of hands that politely shake one another; all you have to do is clasp the last one, cleansed of all traces of blood, to get back to the first one, which still has blood under its fingernails – just as all it takes is an old sock for a trained dog to pick up the scent."

The word "blood" occurs 130 times in the novel, "death" or "dead" 235 times. The man hunting down all this evil is an unnamed obsessive, based, Magris tells us in an author's note, on Diego de Henriquez (1909–74), a Triestine who spent his life collecting weapons of every kind, from swords to submarines, intending to place them in a museum as a pacifist testimony to the awfulness of war. That museum was finally opened in Trieste in the 1990s, but Henriquez, like Magris's hero, died somewhat mysteriously in a fire in one of the buildings housing his collection in 1974. Magris imagines that fire destroying a notebook in which his hero, who sleeps amongst the items of his collection in a coffin, had recorded the names of Triestines who collaborated with the Nazis in the extermination of five thousand Jews and other prisoners in the Risiera, a rice mill transformed into a concentration camp to the south-east of Trieste.

The novel's 340 pages are divided into fifty-three numbered fragments, focusing on the ideas and obsessions of our weapon collector, into which at intervals are inserted eight more substantial sections entitled 'Luisa's Story' and four further titled chapters which recount, in typical Magris style, the stories of intriguing minor figures from the past. So the chapter 'Chamococo' takes its cue from an axe in the collector's possession to tell how, in 1908, the Czech anthropologist and botanist Alberto Vojtěch Frič brought back a Chamococo tribesman from Paraguay to Prague, where, to make a living, the man performed with his axe, demonstrating how his fellow warriors dispatched their enemies. Or again, the chapter 'Private Schimek' gives the history behind a rifle that a Polish soldier may or may not have refused to fire when called on by the Nazis to execute his fellow Poles.

The Luisa Brooks of 'Luisa's Story' is an entirely fictional figure, a government employee who is given the task of planning the collector's museum after his death. Since Luisa's Jewish grandmother on her mother's side died in the Risiera, while her father was a Black American officer who arrived in Trieste with the Allies and whose sister was kicked to death during the war in a racist incident in a London pub, Luisa has a personal interest in the collector's obsessions and seems herself obsessed with her own roots, recovering, in the sections dedicated to her, a long history of persecution on both sides of the family that leads her to wonder if "we blacks... were a lost tribe of Israel". Much space is given to her mother's wartime childhood, and in particular her discovery, after the war, that before being killed in the Risiera her own mother had brought about the deaths of other Jews by informing on them. Plunged into depression, Luisa's mother was saved by the love of Sergeant Joseph Brooks, only to fall back into gloom when he was killed in a banal accident.

Such a summary, however, gives very little idea of how the pages of this book are filled. Though we understand early on that the drift of the narrative is towards two historic moments, the collapse of the Nazi occupation of Trieste in 1945 and the fire thirty years later in which the collector dies and his notebooks are destroyed, Magris does not focus on his core characters, nor dramatize their lives. Rather a process of inflation and conflation, together with a heady rhetoric deployed throughout the book, regardless of who is telling the story, seek to present war as the normal condition not only of human life, but all life, all existence: animals and insects are at war, the plant kingdom is at war, illness is war, cancer is war; our cells do battle, our neurons are at loggerheads.

A true war museum would be a huge CAT scan, many CAT scans and MRIs of a single brain, any brain, randomly chosen. One big brain, the brain of a man, the command centre from which attacks are launched and at the same time a battlefield.

There is a constant fascination for the stench of decay and death, or indeed anything that hints of death.

The Echinocereus pentalophus is a rift in the darkness from which blood gushes, suns light up and collapse, phalanxes of shields pierced by arrows, spears aimed to defend the ship run aground on the shore; stars explode, black holes swallow up corollas, fleecy clouds coil around, and suddenly that nebulous fleece extracts claws that prick deeply.

The vagina dentata turns up twice. A withered cactus flower is "a dry vulva, unwashed for years". But then "History is all a crust of blood." Also, "History is a garbage dump." And, "History is an electroshock." "The train of History has bad breath." The "dazzling joyful reflections" of the sea are "a veil of Maya concealing the blood, the smoke…"

This totalizing phobic nightmare, which monopolizes the book's energy, inevitably undercuts the weapon collector's specific denunciation of Nazis and Nazi collaborationists. In fact, both Luisa and others come to think of the collector as simply "a poor, sometimes embarrassing maniac" – until, that is, the moment in his life, shortly after the war, when he decides to turn his attention to the graffiti on the walls of the Risiera where imprisoned Jews scrawled the names of the collaborators who had informed on them. Recording those names before they can be conveniently plastered over, he becomes "an archangel of justice and revenge".

Why does the collector make this bold and dangerous decision that so transforms his life? Because, we discover in the novel's closing pages, he had run into an old flame, a woman he once desired intensely but had never had the courage to approach. Decades on, she is overweight, but enticing: "Regal shoulders arching above her breasts, pomegranates ready to squirt their seeds in the meadows of asphodel, a deep inlet, a foamy ravine where the sirocco tide of years ebbed." At last sleeping with his dream woman, love allows him to see "the wretchedness of my miserable existence" – after which, he sets about collecting the names of the Nazi collaborators.

It doesn't make much sense. Rather, the specific moral denunciation comes across as an alibi for the expression of a generic and overwhelmingly catastrophist vision. The translator cannot be blamed for the embarrassing prose. Ever reliable and resourceful, Anne Milano Appel has offered a faithful rendering. Yet when one thinks of the power with which Primo Levi tackled the question of collaborationism in *The Drowned and the Saved*, or of the wild genius of Curzio Malaparte in his account of the Nazi regime in the magnificent *Kaput*, it is hard not to feel that this subject has been better handled in the past.

Perhaps the interesting question to ask on putting the book down is why a writer as intelligent as Magris should have chosen to write a book like this. *Blameless* has the feeling of an audacious but unhappily clumsy application for the Nobel Prize.

DOMENICO STARNONE
(1943–)

Via Gemito

The father "always said that he was the best at everything". As a boy, he was the best looker and the best student. Now he is the best lover and the best linguist. The best railwayman. But, above all, the best artist. With the best eye and the best technique. Other painters pale in comparison.

The story is told by the son, who yearns for his father to achieve success and celebrity so that he can stop carping about his menial day job, the miserable conditions in which he has to paint and the envious rivals who stand in his way. At the same time, the son is embarrassed by the father's boasting, irked by his invasiveness, and disturbed by his reduction of every sphere of life to a competition that he must win. Most of all, he is disgusted by his father's treatment of his mother.

The son is the Neapolitan writer Domenico Starnone. His father is, or was, the painter Federico Starnone, whose masterpiece *The Drinkers* graces the cover of the book. Of her autobiographical classic, *Family Sayings*, Natalia Ginzburg commented that it was "all fact. And yet… a novel, because it lacks the objectivity of documentary." Of *The House on Via Gemito* Starnone makes it clear that much of what he writes may not be fact. Nevertheless, it is the story, or stories, his father told, and hence the mental space he grew up in.

Federico claims he was born on 17th January 1917 in one of the poorest areas of Naples, his mother's face illuminated by the glow of bonfires burning in honour of St Anthony. The repetition of the magical number 17, occurring in coincidence with the saint's day, marked him out, he believes, for a "great destiny". But his ID indicates he was born on the 23rd. He claims he learnt to box with

European champion Bruno Frattini, who saw him hitting hard in a street fight. Bruno taught him "to dominate fear by striking first and striking hard". Although the details change suspiciously with every telling, these stories "frightened" the young Domenico: his father, he worries, "seemed to derive enormous pleasure from his ferocity".

Starnone the writer is now eighty. To date just three of his many novels – *Ties*, *Trick* and *Trust* – have appeared in English. All are fairly short, carefully engineered stories where the visceral emotions of difficult love affairs, family struggles and frustrated ambitions are held at ironic distance in measured prose and assured structure. *The House on Via Gemito* is quite different: 450 pages of vivid, fluid, richly detailed drama, tormented and hilarious. Published in 2000, two years after his father's death and more than a decade before the other translated novels, it shows us the crucible in which the author's later style was formed: coolness and control are defence mechanisms learnt in the long struggle with his father.

Via Vincenzo Gemito is a main thoroughfare in a residential district of Naples. You can visit it on Google Street View and see No. 64, where the Starnones lived. But in Italian "gemito" means "moan", or "wail"; the family's second-floor apartment is a place of distress. When the father returns from his railway job "like a warrior home from battle" and sits down to paint, "his presence … erases all notion of play". When he's away, the infant Domenico, or Mimì, as he's called, invents a game where he and his younger brother are overwhelmed by "monstrous powers" in a battle they cannot win. Winning is the prerogative of their father. "I tried to behave meekly," Mimì remembers, "and declined all forms of competition to avoid his boastful ways." Despite this, he can't avoid the fact that his character is forming entirely in relation to his father. "What meaning did I have without him?" he wonders.

Following only the vaguest chronological drift, the novel is divided into three sections. The first, 'The Peacock', opens with the father's claim, later in life, that, in twenty-three years of marriage, he hit his wife only once. Mimì thinks otherwise, and begins a vast exercise in fact-checking. Federico's early working life as railway man and painter is recovered: his wartime marriage to the wry and beautiful Rusinè; his possessiveness and machismo; his supposed service on the Russian front; his endless scams and exploits; his vitality and charisma. "He filled my head with his words," Mimì remembers. "I have none of my mother's."

Naples emerges as a place of perpetual conflict: the Nazi occupation, the Allied occupation, street brawls, feuds, fights with other railwaymen. Federico is relentlessly hostile towards Rusinè's family: all shitheads, opportunists, pilferers. Art too is a struggle: to win a prize, get a place in a show, a mention in the newspaper. An art exhibition "wasn't fun: it was war". And marrying has stymied his career. "You're just not good enough," he tells his wife. Nevertheless, despite Mimì's conviction that Federico regularly beat his mother, he can recall only two occasions with any certainty. Why? And what has any of this to do with peacocks?

His mind settles on an evening when he was five and his father and mother were in the kitchen arguing about money. Violence is in the air. The father orders the boy to fetch his cigarettes. The boy obeys. "I always obeyed my father and never objected," Starnone remembers. But it will take his younger self almost a hundred pages to get down the dark corridor to the bedroom and the cigarettes as the narrative ranges far and wide over Federico's frenetic activities and Rusinè's growing sense of entrapment in one pregnancy after another. At last, entering the bedroom, closing his mind to the yells from the kitchen, the boy beholds, of all things, a majestic peacock, its open fan "reaching to the ceiling… painting the room as many colours as my father left on his palette". But rushing after him, impatient for his cigarettes, Federico sees nothing unusual. Anguished denial has produced a hallucinatory beauty, closely tied to the father's art and looking forward to Starnone's own writerly imagination.

In the second section – 'The Boy Pouring Water' – the mature author intrudes directly into the narrative, describing visits to the places he is writing about: the poor district where Federico was born, the theatre where he painted stage sets during the Allied occupation, Via Gemito itself. We have the first hints of coolness and distance, as if this act of showing how the book is being written made it more possible to control its painful material. The shift meshes well with the main scene evoked in this section: for hours the ten-year-old Mimì sits, or rather kneels, for his father, modelling the figure who holds the water jug in *The Drinkers*.

Again an excruciating experience is spun out over a hundred pages. Federico has been invited to participate in an exhibition of large-scale works. At once he clears the furniture from the sitting room, takes his wife's good hemp bedsheet and stretches it over a huge frame, acting as if he were "in the Royal Alcazar made available to the great painter Velázquez".

Relatives and acquaintances are called to sit for the figures in the painting. Federico rages when they can't stay still. His knee sore from contact with the hard floor, Mimì is "willing to die under his gaze just to help him become the artist he wants". Our feelings for Federico shift. Painting, he tells Mimì about his own childhood: the hostility of his father, who kicked him out of the family as a child and later gambled away his first wages, determined to crush a son who wanted to be "better" than himself.

Meantime, on the canvas, chaos becomes form as heterogeneous household items, old book illustrations and the models themselves are brought together in triumphant composition. Regarding his father with "repugnant admiration", Mimì marvels that, in paint, his uncle and a local street vendor both are and are not themselves. "Is the boy who's pouring water even me?" he wonders. And what is the relation between the painting and the photo of Manet's *Le Déjeuner sur l'herbe* that Federico keeps beside him as he works?

The boy is learning what it is to make art. He realizes it makes his father happy: "Could it be that he was playing the same way that we kids did?" But at the same time the boy's mother is fall-ing chronically ill. Federico doesn't notice, then tries to dismiss her complaints: she just wants to undress for the doctors. All his attention is on his painting. Remembering those months, Starnone is "trying to understand", he tells us, "how life decays when we're overpowered by an obsession for results".

The father-son struggle reaches its climax in the third section, 'The Dancer'. Ever more devout as she declines into illness, Rusinè forces Mimì to take his first communion wearing the brown tunic and sandals of a saint. He will look ridiculous. The embarrassing ordeal convinces the boy God doesn't exist. Afterwards there will be a party and dancing. In his teens now, Mimì is infatuated with the raven-haired Nunzia, overwhelmed by "a tempestuous rush of blood… fantasies of pleasure". She pays him no attention. Her one interest is dancing with her uncle, a dance teacher. Both are present at the communion party, where everyone is smirking at Mimì's absurd tunic. Meantime, the boy's father talks obsessively of sex. His own sexual prowess, that is. His son must live up to the family's reputation for virility: "Mimì, you don't have to ask girls for their permission, you just have to grab them." The boy car-ries a penknife in his pocket ready to stab his father to death. His mother has dressed up for the event, but is not allowed to dance, because men, Federico says, only want one thing from a woman. "If I manage to empty my brain," Mimì thinks, "I won't be his prisoner any more, I won't suffer any more, I'll become invincible."

The novel gains with length. As drama and detail accumulate, we share the boy's difficulty in finding a steady position vis-à-vis his father. Federico is the soul of every party, much loved, much hated, self-obsessed, hugely talented. Finally realizing that his wife is dying, he sketches her with pitiless accuracy, face puffy, gaze empty. For him "dying meant losing". "He knew how to catch the desperation…"

So does Starnone. His prose, ably and fluently translated by Oonagh Stransky, is compelling without being showy. Avoiding

Federico's exhibitionism, he nails down his father in what could seem a tremendous act of revenge, but also a moving celebration of the man's achievement and a profound narrative essay on artistic vocation. The pages where the author seeks out his father's paintings in the dusty meanders of Naples' town hall are a marvellous blend of comedy and pathos; the final anecdote, recalling Federico and Rusinè in a playful tussle when the author was a child, is of such sublime ambiguity we wonder if we have understood anything at all about their marriage.

Outside the text, another mystery contrives to make *The House on Via Gemito* even more intriguing. Published in 1992, six years before Federico Starnone's death, *Troubled Love*, the first novel to appear under the name Elena Ferrante, tells the story of a mother who is treated appallingly by a jealous artist husband with delusions of grandeur. Again the setting is Naples, and although this time the narrator is the mother's daughter, not her son, any number of details anticipate those in Starnone's autobiographical novel, to the point that many in Italy are convinced Starnone must be the writer behind the pseudonym Ferrante. Despite the different emotional tones of the novels, computer analyses of style and syntax appear to confirm the suspicion. Certainly, reading *Via Gemito*, one can imagine how, in ashamed reaction to his father's lewdness, Starnone might have wanted to write from a woman's point of view, or been eager to get this material into print without waiting for his father's death. Or again it could be that like his father he simply wanted "to prove that he could do whatever he put his mind to".

EDOARDO ALBINATI

(1956–)

Crime and Punishment

In a quiet northern suburb of Rome a woman hears noises in the street and sends her son to investigate. Someone is locked in the boot of a Fiat 127. The police arrive and find one girl seriously injured, together with the corpse of a second. Both have been raped, tortured and left for dead. The survivor speaks of three young aggressors and a villa by the sea. Within hours two of the men have been arrested. The other will never be found.

This is not a spoiler. Known as the Circeo Massacre, after the resort area of Circeo seventy miles south of Rome where the violence took place, this atrocity made a huge impact in Italy in 1975; it then came back into public consciousness in 1981, when one of the culprits escaped from prison and fled to Argentina, and again in 2005 when the other condemned man, granted day release to work outside prison, killed a mother and her fourteen-year-old daughter. The dust jacket of the Italian edition of *The Catholic School* tells its readers right away that the book is inspired by this near mythical crime. Particularly shocking, and immediately felt to be an ominous sign of things to come, was that all three rapists came from well-to-do families, while two had recently completed their education at an expensive, highly respectable boys-only Catholic school run by an order of priests dedicated to the Holy Virgin. The author Edoardo Albinati attended the same school in the 1960s and early 1970s.

The logic of the novel, then, is that the school is to be put in relation to the crime, perhaps to serve as an explanation for it. And not just this school, but Catholic schools in general, since the Italian title *La scuola cattolica* could equally well be translated into English with a generic *Catholic School*. The whole idea of a traditional religious education is undermined by the suggestion that, at least in our modern times, what it actually fosters is cruelty and bedlam. It was no doubt this sense that something profound and profoundly evil had been revealed about an institution absolutely central to Italian culture that pushed this mammoth twelve-hundred-page novel into the best-seller lists and won it the country's most prestigious literary prize, the Strega.

But Albinati's book is not so easily pinned down. It's certainly not another *In Cold Blood*, where victims, perpetrators and their respective backgrounds are meticulously researched and the crime analysed in hair-raising detail. Albinati offers no extended dramatization of the events themselves, or the consequent police investigation, or the judicial proceedings. We do not follow the life of the girl who survived, or that of the culprit who escaped. Indeed, one of the charms and irritations of this extraordinary and extraordinarily long piece of storytelling (just a few thousand words shy of *War and Peace*) is how ingeniously it plays with our expectations.

"When I was little... how I loved to go to school!" Albinati tells us. He writes in the first person and uses his own name. "I unquestioningly accepted everything that befalls a kid aged thirteen, fourteen, fifteen..." Until, that is, his brilliant friend Arbus opens his eyes to the absurdity of so much that goes on in school, not least the fact that "ninety-nine per cent of the stuff they teach... won't serve any purpose later on". But then,

> school... isn't exactly a place to study... it's a period of your life when you explore the borders of the known world and what is permitted... And the friendships that you cultivated there were nothing more than a free zone in which to experiment and behave in ways that are otherwise forbidden... You achieved great progress by breaking rules, after which you either suffered cruel but fair punishments, or else you learnt that there was no punishment after all.

Freedom, in short, means freedom to transgress. This is the atmosphere of Albinati's school. There is a total disconnect between the urgencies of adolescence – understanding one's sexuality, getting to grips with the idea of what it means to be a man, meeting girls – and an institution run by poorly paid, second-rate priests-cum-teachers who invent endless rules to stop the boys from growing up. The teachers are no more than "ballast... heavy objects, like so many carved marble animals to be used as bookends".

The situation invites comedy, and Albinati can be very funny. It would be hard to think of a more exuberant, unashamedly intellectual, implacably candid evocation of the preposterousness of male adolescence than is offered in the opening three hundred pages of this book. Deprived of all female contact, the boys are more or less "in prison". "The only woman who wasn't an intruder... was the Virgin Mary." Afflicted by constant, obtuse appeals to behave and engage in "dialogue" rather than conflict, the boys feel compelled to lie, fight and cheat. Fooling the teachers in exams becomes a matter of personal pride. Even when it is easier to pass an exam honestly, the boys prefer to cheat. Anything else is "unthinkable, a shameful alternative". To get by without merit is the only merit that makes sense. "Everyone copied from everyone else... in a maelstrom of total mistrust of themselves." To pass your exams was to be "absolved".

All this would be entertaining and no more than ordinarily disquieting were it not for the terrible crime that hangs over the book. And Albinati lets it hang. Only on page 153 does it get a first brief mention – then, just as the name of the school is reduced throughout the novel to the letters SLM (we are never told what they stand for, but Italian readers might know it was San Leone Magno), so the "Circeo Rape/Murder", the "event that gave rise to this book", becomes "hereinafter the CR/M". From this point on the two acronyms will call to each other over a thousand pages and more, like the values of some fatal equation.

Since Albinati has warned us that he has changed the names of those involved in the crime, every school companion he describes becomes a possible murderer. Of his closest friend Arbus, the kind of genius who never needs to study, we hear that "one of the few things [he] did study, and systematically, were the different ways of killing people". So is he one of the killers? When the young Albinati visits his home, finding a ravishing but quite emotionless sister and a provocative mother who humiliates her acned son by flirting with his friend, it all begins to look extremely ominous. Another boy, Salvatore, first takes Albinati to the local branch of the neo-Fascist party, then invites him to his home to sit on his bed and look through a stack of photos that show nude bodies "in dazzling-white close-up... as if they were dead". "The girls," we hear "were... lying down with their long hair draped along their backs or else bent over, both hands pulling their buttocks wide open." "I don't think Salvatore really liked girls," Albinati comments.

The very intensity with which puberty is evoked becomes sinister – it seems all these boys are potential rapists. Ravaged by an "overwhelming sensuality" but blocked by a "powerful strain of modesty", the author reports feeding on "a guilty innocence... like a termite... in tender wood". The mere thought of, for example, a damp swimming costume has him in a frenzy of excitement. To make matters worse, this explosion of sensuality is cloaked in parental silence. The families who spend heavily to keep their boys in the protected space of the SLM are entirely focused on career and social standing and profoundly unsettled by the swiftly changing mores of the times. Home becomes "the venue of embarrassment". The mothers in particular, disorientated by the dwindling of their maternal role, are casting about for something to do with their sexuality. One mother more or less sticks her tightly skirted butt in Edoardo's face. Another both provokes and then ignores him.

At school, little help can be expected from the priests, whose presumed celibacy both fascinates and horrifies the boys. Are they gay? The question of whether one might oneself be homosexual is on everyone's mind, particularly during gym. One priest and gym teacher, who resembles a "plaster cast of some athlete or boxer found under the ashes of Herculaneum", is obsessed with cultivating the boys' virility. Another, whose priesthood seems "a form of self-mortification in the aftermath of a long-ago crime", is glimpsed late at night on a busy road inviting prostitutes into the school's Fiat 850.

Even the priests break the rules then. It doesn't matter. You confess and are absolved. One boy caresses another's crotch during lessons. Everyone sees, no one does anything. The boy on the receiving end follows the lesson "placidly... like a large grazing ruminant". In line with the rising tide of liberalism outside the school, the priests' apparent severity actually conceals a pathetic weakness: no one is ever punished. When a student has his glasses broken by older bullies, the school simply buys the boy new glasses. Slowly the boys learn the principle that only a sinner is worthy of a priest's or God's consideration. If a little lamb doesn't get lost, it can't be "searched for, found and saved; unless a pilgrim wanders off the straight path... he can just go fuck himself, him with all his rectitude". Since small misdemeanours are barely noticed, the only option for a boy craving attention is to go for bigger ones.

To preserve this perverted state of affairs, a gap between what is said and what is felt must be actively cultivated. "Confession for me was the utmost moment of artificiality," Albinati tells us. The important thing is always to say what is expected, not to feel it. As a result, it becomes hard to know what one is feeling. "With the host in your mouth or your dick in your hand" you simply don't know what's supposed to happen in terms of emotions. When the frustrated Arbus decides to leave school a year early, he spends his last day inking a blasphemy on his desk in letters "fifteen inches high". But since he still has to sit his final exam, the priests have a lever to force him back to school to apologize. Arbus complies, but even as he eats humble pie, everyone understands that this is "a mere formal statement". "There are no sincere phrases," Albinati declares.

We are at page four hundred and still no sign of the CR/M. Expectation is winding up. All the boys' early sexual encounters seem to look forward to the crime. Too shy to ask a girl out alone, Albinati involves his classmate Pik, who seems dangerously autistic. They set up a date with two girls, one of whom takes them to her house, since her parents are away. Pik, who has barely spoken to a girl before, is thrilled with the thought that they are going to "fuck". Albinati can't dissuade him. The girls allow themselves to be taken to separate bedrooms, and the evening ends in tears when, not knowing how to behave, the boys simply jump on them. It's still comedy, just about, but under the looming cloud of the CR/M.

At a spiritual retreat organized by the school, the boys have fun acting out a flagellation depicted in a painting in one of the bedrooms. The chosen victim is a boy suspected of being gay. The others whip his bare back with knotted cords. The game turns nasty. The victim begs them to stop. Only if you "abjure your God", they shout. Albinati is appalled, but doesn't intervene. It goes on and on. As the boy's skin flushes red, his tormentors see blood. At last the boy abjures. He is shocked, bewildered, and his face "split into two bands", a suffering expression above and "a mindless little smile" below. At which Albinati realizes that the boy "had liked it. A lot, really a lot." The flagellation becomes the occasion of his coming out.

Heightened sensuality breeds mental proliferation. As an adolescent, Albinati is always "thinking a great number of different discordant thoughts at the same instant", something that brings happiness, confusion, guilt. The novel itself is an exercise in such proliferation and its accompanying emotions. Just when you thought he couldn't delay the arrival of the CR/M any further, the author launches into a long analysis of the transformation of the Italian bourgeoisie in the 1970s. In this book long means long. The breakdown in the family is discussed. "Relations between the generations, bonds of authority... are now practically null." Yet children are more financially dependent than ever. Parents "disburse more and more money in exchange for being increasingly ignored". Money is at the centre of everything: "We have it, thank Heavens, but we are not to speak of it. *Ever.*" Grand moral statements are made about wealth. "There exists a scrupulous and exacting ethical standard according to which all the things we own are nothing but loans…" From being on the side of boyish transgression, Albinati suddenly seems like the priest in the pulpit. From twelve years at Catholic school, he observes, he developed two contradictory attitudes: "utter hatred for emphasis" and "the involuntary tendency to take on the tone and the pacing of a sermon". When he leaves the SLM to spend his last school year in a state school, he is surprised to find his new companions can all see he's been in "a school run by priests". It's "stamped on your forehead," they tell him. Certainly it's evident in every turn of this novel. "If you're sick of this… just skip," Albinati advises.

Finally, a third of the way into the novel, the crime is suddenly centre stage. It is told in thirteen terse pages. At once we are shocked by the stupidity, clumsiness and randomness of it all, confused because we don't recognize any of the culprits as the boys already described at school, and surprised by their possession of a gun and boasting of previous kidnaps and international criminal connections. In general they don't seem to know what they want from the two girls they've picked up, or why they're taking them to the villa by the coast. They don't understand the consequences of locking other human beings naked in bathrooms and torturing them. "I didn't realize that… would mean the end of any dialogue with them," one killer later reflects, using, Albinati reminds us, "that word so beloved of the priests". They experiment with injecting fluids into their victims. One girl is dragged round the rooms with a leather belt round her neck. The boys are bored. They don't know what to do next.

Fiction "is the exact opposite of chaos", Albinati observes, a desperate attempt to put order in the world. If we want to know, he suggests, what parts of his novel are made up, we should look out for "the ones that don't sound quite as absurd as the others". The crime as told is utterly absurd. Hence very much for real.

What now then, with eight hundred pages still to go? One expects more and more about the CR/M. Intermittently it arrives: some detail about one of the killers' megalomaniac confessions to any number of murders and rapes; some consideration of the likelihood that the killer who escaped joined the Spanish Foreign Legion and died of a heroin overdose in 1994. But the main thrust of the book is now to establish the crime's centrality as emblematic of its era, in Italy in general and in this area of Rome in particular, where quite suddenly there was a spate of violent crime. All the changes taking place in society are found to be reflected in the CR/M. More and more possible underlying causes are discovered and considered. It is as if the crime's very absurdity demanded that a huge amount of explanation be flung at it, none of which quite convinces. Meantime, the CR/M comes to seem "something familiar... in line with the times". One begins to wonder why there aren't more.

Albinati's mind ranges far and wide. We go back to the bourgeoisie, to feminism and the reaction against feminism, the cinema's passion for violence, the television viewers' necrophiliac eye. We discuss the passage from sexual desire to violence, from violence to torture, from torture to murder. Ethical, biological and anthropological approaches are considered, at length. We discover that the sleepy Quartiere Trieste, where Albinati's home and school were located, had become a battleground for opposing gangs of Fascists and Communists. Fascism is described as a state of mind where an action, any action, is justified quite simply because it is action. Everyone had grown used to violence. We hear the tale of a Fascist drug dealer who is lured into a gang rape so as to be murdered when he gets naked. A classmate's sister offered herself as the bait to trap the man. We wonder whether Fascism and gang rape aren't forms of collective homosexuality. This was a "chaotic and violent" time. "No one knew any longer what was right and what was wrong." As the years go by, a surprising number of

Albinati's ex-schoolmates become involved in crime. One dies in an explosion on the roof of an asylum for the criminally insane. Was it an act of terrorism? One is jailed for arson. Another kills himself at the umpteenth attempt after various misdemeanours.

While in the first part of the book all anecdotes looked forward to the crime, now it is the crime that colours everything that comes after. Albinati describes an affair with a German girl met on a student exchange in Spain. She is a virgin. They try to make love, but it's too painful for her. Later they meet by chance in Rome. Egged on by a friend, the German girl now sleeps with him, explaining she has a happy sex life with a boyfriend in Germany. There was never any pain with him, because she loves him. Then she is upset she has betrayed him. She lies lifeless on the sheets as if dead. "In any relationship between male and female... rape is present," Albinati tells us. "We live in a society of rape." "The sex act possesses a dangerous affinity with the act of murder." Rapists can consider themselves "educators", "pedagogues". They are merely getting "to the heart of the matter".

There is an obsessive quality to all this that neither seeks nor requires the reader's assent. Skip if it's too much, we're told again. Many will be tempted to do so. Antony Shugaar's translation, a simply enormous task, comes across well enough with Albinati's engaging narrative style, but less so with the extended op-ed-like sections, where the Italian author blends a driving spoken voice with a sophisticated prose that risks sounding wooden in translation. For pages at a time, the reader longs to get back to the story, any story.

And the main story in this book, we understand now, is Albinati himself. More and more he is present as writer, rather than schoolboy, as a man wrestling with his past and seeking to understand the world that made him what he is. We discover that for most of his working life he has been a teacher in a prison. He is constantly around men who have raped and killed. He started writing this book, he tells us, in 2005, on returning to live in Quartiere Trieste, just a couple of blocks from where that Fiat 127 was abandoned with the girls in the boot. This was the same year that one of the criminals killed again. The apartment where the author used to study with the killer's brother is opposite his new home.

The mad abundance of reflection and anecdote now makes any summary unthinkable – nevertheless, a pattern emerges. Whatever stories he tells of his own life, Albinati puts himself in a bad light. He is driven to sex and feels guilty. After sex his partners seem dead. ("Implicit in the sex act... is the possibility that it will end with a lifeless body"). Writing about his relationship with Arbus's sister, he is "terrified at the idea of contaminating her". He allows a local priest to bless his apartment while he has pornography up on his computer screen. He listens to the super-Catholic Radio Maria in his car and slows down to inspect the bodies of the prostitutes soliciting at the roadside. But "self-accusation" is a "pleasure", hence possibly itself a sin.

Whatever subject is discussed, it is considered in terms of crime and punishment, confession and absolution, contamination and purity. Albinati dreams of being punished for crimes he didn't know he'd committed. He fantasizes about punishing fellow Italians who double-park their cars or don't pick up their dogs' shit from the pavement. He sees woman's physical weakness as "a sin to be expiated". When observing the Italian habit of pruning trees to the bone, he is sure it is a form of punishment for their vitality. The Bible is full of sexual violence, he reminds us, often left scandalously unpunished. Masochism, or self-punishment, he claims, is the characteristic impulse of the middle classes. Inevitably, there are references to De Sade, to Kafka, to Dostoevsky, to Tolstoy, in particular *The Kreutzer Sonata*, whose narrator kills his wife out of disgust for their compulsive sex life.

Albinati's writing itself strives for provocation and transgression. We're told of a man who ejaculates into the mouth of his dead sister in the morgue. We're told that "sex is a singular sort of prison whose bars keep you from getting in, rather than getting out".

Remembering one scene from adolescence, he has to interrupt his writing to masturbate. "The degree of moral involvement in a rape can stretch out to touch the whole of society," he tells us. "You need only open a newspaper to become part of this corrupt community."

A conflicted mindset prevails that we can sum up thus: all violence is wrong, all sex is violent, sex is an imperative that cannot be avoided. Ergo, we are all in the wrong. Especially men. Repression only makes things worse. The truth must be told. Given this predicament and the consequent struggle between longing and disgust, what can one do but seek to annul oneself, to transcend oneself, escape from oneself? How can this be done? Through sex ("I make love to annihilate myself"). Or through religious experience (the endlessly repeated liturgical formulas that lull and enchant the mind). Or perhaps both: "Developing sexual taste is like learning how to pray." Or, finally, through violence: "Only destruction allows transcendence."

Story after fascinating story culminates in moments of transcendence. Confessing to burning down a forest one hot summer day, an old classmate speaks of his euphoria. Recalling an old lover, the author remembers "falling into a deep and wonderful void". A friend explaining how he almost killed his mother tells of a moment of huge mental release. It is the same urge to self-annulment that pushes these characters to sex, to crime, to worship. And indeed to write. "A rampaging narrative... an impetuous flow of words... can lead to a happy state of forgetfulness."

I can think of no author who has prompted in me such frequent shifts from admiration to irritation and back; who has aroused so much pleasure with his stories and reflections, and so much annoyance with his emphatic, exaggerated, paradoxical claims, not to mention the sheer length of this interminable book. Yet it's hard to feel, as the pages roll by, that this is not absolutely willed on the author's part. The book itself becomes the reader's Catholic school, at times a kind of prison where the same concepts are repeated ad infinitum, at times a kind of violence – in any event, not so much a novel about a crime ("I never really did give a damn about it," he tells us on page 1094) as the memoir of a man who cannot help but see every human transaction in terms of crime. Unsurprisingly, we leave him at mass on Christmas Day, eyeing a woman from behind.

ROBERTO SAVIANO

(1979–)

Talking Corpses

"When Lot lived in Sodom and Gomorrah," wrote St Peter in his second epistle, "he was oppressed and tormented day after day by their lawless deeds." Having grown up in Naples, Roberto Saviano is likewise tormented and oppressed. His *Gomorrah* is an account of the lawless deeds of the Camorra, the Neapolitan mafia. Conveniently assonant as the two names may be, the crimes of Naples are not those we associate with the Cities of the Plain, and Saviano is not the righteous man who can simply withdraw when God steps in to incinerate the sinful townsfolk. On the contrary, he seems drawn to what he abhors: he does everything in his power to see the Camorra and its lawlessness close up.

There have been any number of books on organized crime in Italy. What makes Saviano's different is the intensity and complexity of his engagement with the phenomenon. It is not the engagement of a writer like Nando dalla Chiesa, son of a top policeman murdered by the mafia and author of books denouncing the complicity between political parties and criminal organizations. For all his personal investment, Dalla Chiesa's writings remain within the canons of investigative journalism, and his aim is clearly to unmask political involvement at the highest level.

Saviano is more visceral. Under cover of an authentic anthropological interest and an urgent determination to bear witness, he never fails to put himself in the scene. He wants to talk to workers in Camorra-run factories, to child recruits playing with guns, to drug couriers, to the guinea-pig addicts who try out their cocaine for them, to the shadowy figure who takes subsistence money to the wives of the men in jail, to hustlers, murderers. He wants to visit illegal toxic-waste dumps, makeshift warehouses for contraband, the deserted villas of arrested Camorra bosses. He attends the funerals of murder victims and the trials of their killers. He is there in the street when Camorra communities raise barriers against police raids.

But most of all Saviano wants to be at the scene of the crime: to see the shattered windscreens and the corpses riddled with bullets, to hear the moans of the dying, to smell burnt or decaying flesh, and then, when all has been savoured and described, to turn inward and record his own reactions. A chill down the spine, a wrenching in his stomach, a weakening in his legs, an urgent physical need to vomit or to pee or to run: these, more than any statistics, are the measure of the scandal that is the Camorra. Saviano suffers it all, personally, viscerally. And it is this deeply unsettling aspect of *Gomorrah* that gives the book an appeal that goes far beyond a specific interest in Italy or organized crime. We all share a morbid fascination for the crime scene. And we are concerned for Saviano's welfare.

One strategy of the book is to deny the reader a reassuring narrative structure, whether historical or autobiographical. No context or overall trajectory is offered. We plunge straight in. There is the Camorra and there is Saviano. We begin at the port of Naples. Presumably in his early twenties (he was born in 1979), Saviano finds a room to let in return for working at weekends for a Chinese organization that is challenging the local clans. His job is to help convert what is officially residential property into warehouses, so that imported goods can be hidden and import duties avoided. Apartment blocks risk collapse as wall after wall is brought down. It doesn't matter. He describes a 5 a.m. boat trip to a ship out at sea to offload brand-name trainers. They fill the boat so full it seems it must sink. The only thing that matters is profit. Saviano is good at conveying the frenzy of an organization desperate to assert itself in the face of cut-throat globalized competition.

His Chinese employer introduces him to the world of dress-making sweatshops. We learn to distinguish between those who work directly for the clans, handling guns, money and drugs, and the workers who are savagely exploited by them, producing high-quality products for the most miserable black-market wages and with no social security. These men and women are deliberately kept needy and hungry, otherwise they might have the leisure to gain some perspective and leave. Saviano meets a talented local dress-cutter paid a pittance for extremely skilled work. The same man travels in the boot of a car to give well-paid lessons to the Camorra's Chinese rivals, at the risk of his life. A barrage of statistics establishes the role of Neapolitan sweatshops in the world of haute couture. Saviano's style is fragmented, cumulative, insistent, dramatic. The reader must understand how important all this is, and the intensity of its effect on Saviano:

> All the fashion of the parades, all the genius of the most dazzling shows comes from here. From Naples and Salento. The main centres for black-market textiles... Casarano, Tricase, Taviano, Melissano or Capo di Leuca, lower Salento. This is where they're from. From this hole. All manufactured goods come out of the dark. That's the law of capitalism. But to look into that hole, to have it before your eyes, gives you a weird feeling. An anxious heaviness. Like having the truth on your stomach.

At thirteen, walking to school, Saviano saw a car with a man's legs sticking out of the front side window. He had been turned upside down by the force of the machine-gun bullets. When the police pulled the dead man out, an erection was poking through his torn clothes. The young Saviano stared, fascinated. The same fascination was still with him in 2004 when the dominant De Lauro clan faced a schism in the depressed suburb of Secondigliano, two miles north of downtown Naples. "To follow the feud I'd managed to get hold of a radio capable of picking up police frequencies. So riding my Vespa I'd arrive at the [murder] scene pretty much at the same time as the squad cars."

Saviano stays glued to that radio night and day for months as the feud claims a death every twenty-four hours. A girl is found tortured and burnt; a man is beheaded, the head on the back seat of his car; a decaying corpse, atrociously disfigured, has been dumped in a skip. But mostly the killings are hit-and-run executions. A woman answers her door "and someone points the barrel of a pistol in her face and shoots. Blood and cerebral fluid pour from her head as from a broken egg." Men are shot to pieces in cars or supermarkets. Saviano arrives on his Vespa:

Blood everywhere. It's almost as if his soul had drained out of the bullet holes that have scarred his whole body. When you see so much blood on the ground you start touching yourself, to check that you haven't been wounded too, that your blood isn't mixed up with his; you get into a psychotic state, you need to be sure there are no cuts on your body, maybe you've been shot yourself without realizing it. You just can't believe there could be so much blood in one person, you're sure there can't be so much in you. Even when you've checked that none of the blood is yours, you still can't calm down: maybe you haven't haemorrhaged, but you feel empty. You've become a haemorrhage yourself, your legs feel wobbly, your tongue is sticky, your hands have dissolved away into that thick pool of blood, you need someone to look into your eyes to check for anaemia. You need to stop a nurse and demand a transfusion, you need to have your stomach a bit less tight so you can eat a steak, if you could do that without throwing up. You have to close your eyes and take care not to breathe. The smell of congealing blood has saturated the room, saturated even the whitewash, and it has a tang of rusty iron. You've got to get out, go outside, get into the fresh air before they chuck sawdust on the blood, because the mix of blood and sawdust produces a stench that will break down any resistance to vomiting.

It seems that deeper even than the scandal of the Camorra, for Saviano, is the scandal of death itself.

Having seen dozens of murdered men, spattered with blood and dirt, giving off disgusting smells, corpses met by onlookers with curiosity or professional indifference, or kicked aside like toxic waste or wept over in desperation, I have grasped only one thing for sure: an idea so basic it seems dumb: death stinks.

The Neapolitans are renowned, of course, for a cult of death that dates back to the baroque and far beyond, a cult that still outcrops in churches and cemeteries, where skulls are on display. The young initiates into the Camorra, Saviano tells us, are known as "talking corpses", so certain is the end they will meet. Why then do they do it? He quotes a letter written by a jailed adolescent.

Everybody I know is dead or in jail. I want to be a boss. I want to have supermarkets, shops, factories. I want to have women. I want three cars, and when I go into a shop I want people to respect me. I want to own stores all over the world. And then I want to die. But like a real man dies, a man really in command. I want to be murdered.

"The logic of the criminal entrepreneur..." Saviano insists, "coincides with that of the most aggressive neo-liberalism." These men want maximum power for however brief a time. Nothing else interests them. Winning and losing is the only polarity they know, and "morality is the weakness of the loser". "The only thing you learn in this place," says a priest at a fifteen-year-old's funeral, "is how to die."

And why is Saviano doing what he's doing – naming names, describing incidents at first hand, exposing himself to the ire of such a ferocious killing machine? Amid analyses of criminal penetration of the retail business, a trip to Scotland to see

how the Camorra is investing there, reflections on the music
that baby killers listen to while they murder, on the preferred
decor of Camorra bosses, their deviant religiosity, their women,
the supergrasses, Saviano offers few hints of his own background. But they are telling. Of his mother we learn only that
she urgently wishes he would leave Naples and stop visiting
crime scenes. His parents, we understand, are long separated.
His father, he tells us, was once severely beaten when, as an
ambulance doctor, he medicated and saved a man shot by
the Camorra, the usual practice being that when a victim is
found to be still alive, the ambulance waits for the murderers
to come back to finish him off. But Saviano also describes
how his father made it a matter of personal pride that his
son should learn to shoot:

> "Roberto, what's a man with a gun but no degree?"
> "An arsehole with a gun."
> "Right. And what's a man with a degree but no gun?"
> "An arsehole with a degree."
> "Right. What's a man with a gun and a degree?"
> "A man, Daddy!"
> "Right, Robertino!"

Saviano recalls other basic lessons in manhood imparted by his
father:

> "Roberto, a real man mustn't be afraid of anyone – he's got to
> know things, of course, but he's got to instil fear as well. If you
> don't scare people, if people aren't afraid when they look at you,
> then deep down you haven't learnt anything."

Saviano senior is impressed by local bosses and the respect they
command. "Command" is an important word for him.

"There are those who command words and those who command things. You've got to understand who's commanding things, while pretending to believe in the guys commanding words. But you must always know the truth in your flesh and bones. Only the guys commanding things are really in command."

A philosopher is less important than a doctor, Saviano's father tells his son, because a doctor has real power over another's life, whereas a philosopher has no power over anything. Accustomed, Saviano remarks, to being a disappointment to his father, he nevertheless went on to take a degree in philosophy, refusing to accept that things are superior to words. One chapter of *Gomorrah* tells the history of Don Peppino, a priest who spoke out determinedly against the Camorra and was shot dead in his church when the writer was sixteen. Without being a Christian, Saviano feels a strong affinity for Don Peppino, and in particular for the priest's insistence on "the priority of the word", as witness and accusation, the word that "can track down money from its stench", the word that must be "put at the centre of a struggle against the mechanisms of power. Words in the path of cement mixers and rifles. Not metaphorically. Really. Being there to accuse and to testify. The word with its only defence: speaking out."

Of course, Saviano's own huge commercial success demonstrates well enough that words can produce money as well as tracking it down. And to set the word against "the mechanisms of power" is to acknowledge that words are themselves an important source of power and have always been an integral part of the power game. Saviano tells how his father "adored Pope John Paul II" and was hugely impressed by the numbers who listened to him and the power this brought. "All the powerful knelt before him. For my father this was enough to admire a man." Certainly seeing the sales of *Gomorrah* run into millions and its author fêted by Nobel prize winners and politicians of every colour, Saviano's father will have been obliged to revise his position both on his disappointing son and on the power of the word.

Yet, however powerful language and rhetoric may be, we still feel the need... for celluloid. When a book is a big success, the film can't be far behind. In this case, however, there were obvious obstacles. To show Saviano riding his scooter to murder scenes might have seemed like a glorification of the author, or an invitation to worry about his mental health. Even worse would have been a glorification of the criminals with some Hollywood-style plot that engaged us directly in the fates of rival bosses. Faced with a deeply rooted culture of organized crime in Sicily, Naples and Calabria, the Italian film industry has learnt to put aside such entertainments.

Given these restrictions, director Matteo Garrone and screenplay writer Maurizio Braucci opted for the solution of half a dozen intertwining narratives that draw on material scattered throughout Saviano's book to offer a broad picture of the community within which the criminal organization operates. We have the underpaid dress-cutter giving lessons to the Chinese, a handsome young boy who "progresses" from delivering shopping to delivering drugs, the "submarine", or man who takes money to relatives of Camorra men in jail, the entrepreneur buying land to dump toxic waste and, above all, gathering all the strands together, the beginnings of a clan schism and consequent feud with the tremendous anxiety this situation generates as everyone struggles to understand who is on which side and whether they themselves are in the firing line.

The film's strong points are its locations and actors. It was shot in a notorious Secondigliano housing estate made up of three dilapidated apartment blocks full of long open-air walkways and gloomy underground spaces. At every vantage point, Camorra lookouts – often very small boys – shout laconically back and forth to each other whenever an unknown car or stranger enters the area. Close-up camerawork and low or *chiaroscuro* lighting intensifies a sense of entrapment. These people know no other world. There are no views of *la bella Napoli*, no middle-class pleasures, no escape.

Even the occasional landscape scenes are gloomy and untidy, cluttered with relics and abandoned buildings.

To underline the community's suffocating closure and isolation, the film is spoken in a dialect so strong that subtitles are provided even for Italian viewers. For authenticity, Garrone used local people, preferably from Secondigliano, some of them, it has since turned out, themselves involved in the Camorra. There are extraordinary performances from a pair of young men who refuse to join the clans and embark on a life of petty crime, glorying in the thrill and power of the moment, snatching cocaine from a gang of blacks, robbing a billiard hall, running off with arms from the local clan's cache. The film's most striking scene comes when the two splash about on a deserted beach firing off their freshly stolen Kalashnikovs into the sea in a mad frenzy. There is also an extremely powerful moment, shortly after the first feud killings, when one of the men on the losing side bellows, "*Facciamo i nostri morti*" ("Let's do some killing too"). Whoever the victim, killing is always a powerful self-affirmation.

These scenes are persuasive vehicles for Saviano's message, and, in general, throughout the film, the ugliness and poverty of people's homes, the clashing colours of their cheap clothes, the squalor of all public spaces, the absence of any human charm or grace (except in the Chinese sweatshop) amounts to a telling denunciation of Camorra subculture.

Yet in the end the film disappoints. Often it has a perfunctory, box-ticking feel. The toxic-waste dealer and his young sidekick go to Venice to convince a major industrialist to use their services. Message: the rest of Italy cannot escape its responsibility. An elderly peasant woman gives the same waste dealer a basket of fruit which he knows is inedible because of the toxic material they have buried in the area. Message: both land and rural traditions have been polluted and corrupted.

But there is a deeper problem: since the success of the Camorra depends on the suppression of all individuality or independence, and since the only people who rebel in the story – the two young-sters breaking out on their own – are mindless, selfish and them-selves steeped in Camorra culture, the film has no one around whom it can build any pathos. There are any number of killings, but none that touches the viewer.

So one leaves the cinema as one might leave a long and deeply pessimistic lesson, convinced that this world is irretrievably ugly and beyond salvation. To work as a drama that fully engaged its viewers and offered them a shred of optimism that something could still be done, the story would have needed a Don Peppino, or someone, anyone, who spoke out against the Camorra and whose welfare we were able to care about. In short, the film helps us understand that *Gomorrah* the book would not be so interest-ing without Saviano's visceral, obsessive concern, and consequent vulnerability.

Which brings us to the world outside books, films and aesthetics. Saviano lives under a death threat. A Camorra grease has spoken of plans to kill him before Christmas. Having earned himself a considerable amount of money, he now has no ordinary life. Like the Camorra bosses he describes, he must move under armed guard. Inevitably, comparisons have been drawn with the fatwa against Salman Rushdie. But the two cases are only partly analogous. Rushdie was surprised and shocked by the response of fundamen-talists to what were in fact only a few pages in *The Satanic Verses*. The "blasphemy" he supposedly committed and that has made him so vulnerable was hardly central to the thrust of his work.

Saviano on the other hand seems entirely committed to repeating the denunciations that have put him in the firing line. Don Peppino, he writes at the beginning of his chapter on the priest, left the south to study in Rome and "should have stayed there", far away from his home town of Casal di Principe. But "like someone unable to shake off a habit or a smell... or someone who constantly has the intense feeling that he ought to be doing something", he came back. Saviano too comes across as a man who "has the intense feeling he ought to be doing something" – and, what's more, something that no one else can be entrusted to do. One aspect of *Gomorrah* that has attracted criticism is the absence in the book of any enthusiasm for (or indeed much mention of) the magistrates and policemen who are daily at war with the Camorra, risking their lives for modest incomes. At one point, following an impressive analysis of the Camorra's penetration of the cement industry, Saviano suggests that the imprisonment of Camorra bosses actually strengthens the organization, guaranteeing space for the younger members, bringing new blood, new ideas, better business, while elevating arrested bosses to the mythical status that will inspire new generations of criminals.

If one accepts this notion of the limits of repression, the only prospect for change lies in the word, a willingness to speak out, to encourage everyone to speak out, to break the Camorra's control of the collective mind. Such a use of the word must be unerring, "a sentry, a witness, it must never stop pointing to the truth", because to fall silent out of fear would be to hand victory to the Camorra. "The word used like this," Saviano says, "can only be silenced by killing." One must hope that these words will not be prophetic.

Acknowledgements

It is hard for an essayist to work in isolation; one is galvanized by a commission and a deadline. I would like to thank the many editors who accepted my suggestions for these essays, or who proposed titles that fit in with my project: Michael Shae at the *New York Review of Books*, Matt Seaton and Lucy Jakub at the *New York Review Online*, Edwin Frank at NYRB Classics, Mary-Kay Wilmers, Daniel Soar and Joanne O'Leary at the *London Review of Books*, Toby Lichtig at the *Times Literary Supplement*, Christopher Carroll at *Harper's Magazine*, Nigel Warburton at *Aeon* and Jessica Harrison and Josephine Greywoode at Penguin Classics. Most of all, thanks to Alessandro Gallenzi, who commissioned pieces when at Hesperus Books and proposed that these essays be gathered together in the two *Literary Tour of Italy* collections; without him these books would never have been published.

Note on the Texts

The essays contained in this volume are revised versions of those that appeared in the periodicals listed below.

'Between the Guelfs and the Ghibellines' first appeared in the *London Review of Books* in July 2016, as a review of Marco Santagata, *Dante: The Story of His Life*, tr. Richard Dixon (Cambridge, MA: Harvard University Press, 2016).

'Whatever It Takes' first appeared in the *New York Review of Books* in October 2020, as a review of Patrick Boucheron, *Machiavelli: The Art of Teaching People What to Fear*, tr. Willard Wood (New York: Other Press, 2020), and Alexander Lee, *Machiavelli: His Life and Times* (London: Picador, 2020).

'The *Apology*' first appeared as a foreword to Lorenzino de' Medici, *Apology for a Murder*, tr. Andrew Brown (London: Hesperus Press, 2004).